WOMEN, DEVELOPMENT AND LABOR OF REPRODUCTION

WOMEN, DEVELOPMENT AND LABOR OF REPRODUCTION:

STRUGGLES AND MOVEMENTS

EDITED BY

MARIAROSA DALLA COSTA &

GIOVANNA F. DALLA COSTA

Africa World Press, Inc.

P.O. Box 1892
Trenton, NJ 08607

P.O. Box 48
Asmara, ERITREA

Africa World Press, Inc.

P.O. Box 1892
Trenton, NJ 08607

P.O. Box 48
Asmara, ERITREA

Copyright © 1999 Mariarosa Dalla Costa and Giovanna Franca Dalla Costa

First Printing 1999

Book design: Wanjiku Ngugi
Cover design: Jonathan Gullery
Cover art by Yegizaw Michael, *Going to the Market* © 1998 Yegizaw Michael.

Library of Congress Cataloging-in-Publication Data

Donne, sviluppo e lavoro di riproduzione. English
    Women, development, and labor of reproduction : struggles and movements / edited by Mariarosa Dalla Costa & Giovanna F. Dalla Costa.
        p. cm.
    Includes bibliographical references and index.
    ISBN 0-86543-621-5 (hb). -- ISBN 0-86543-622-3 (pbk.)
    1. Women in development--Develooing countries. 2. Human reproduction--Developing countries. 3. Feminism--Developing countries. I. Dalla Costa, Mariarosa. II. Dalla Costa, Giovanna Franca. III. Title.
HQ1240.5.D44D64413 1999
371.2--dc21   99-25029
                                                                         CIP

Dedication

To our grandfather, Giovanni Dalla Costa, who, after seeing his home and harvest burn down, and realizing he would no longer be able to live off his land, emigrated to France. Here he worked in the mines to earn the money necessary to go to America. He arrived in Alaska in 1892, in the place which later was to be called Nome, and here he was renamed Jack Costa. Other members of his family landed in South Brazil; but he would never see them again. Jack Costa, with his brother Frank, dug for years in the icy lands of Klondike searching for gold and, at last, they found it.

Today, again, a new globalization process is sending millions of emigrants around the world. Separated from their land, from their families, in other nations and continents, they still seek some means of survival and a different future for themselves and their children.

CONTENTS

ACKNOWLEDGEMENTS

Our deeply felt thanks go to Dr. Dario De Bortoli, who patiently re-read the whole book and discussed it generously througout, also helping check and finalize some passages; Dr. Giovanna Macchitella, whose accuracy and commitment made a major contribution to getting the book into its final shape; and Mrs. Elisabetta Bressan, who spent many hours at the computer in the critical moments that assail any collective work.

— The Editors

Introduction

Mariarosa Dalla Costa

Today, it is in the mountains of Chiapas, the seas of Mururoa, the delta of the Niger and in cities like Paris that human reproduction most openly stands out as an issue and a terrain of rebellion. This serried sequence of struggles leaped onto the world scene in 1994 to symbolize the great problems which are the object of the debate about reproduction and growth. First among them are the relationships between monetary and non-monetary economics, the new global economy and subsistence economies, formal and informal work, paid and unpaid labor, individuality and community, 'Western' civilization and other forms of civilization. In brief, the relationship between the presumed inevitability of oncoming "higher" levels of development and people's right to elaborate their own future autonomously, asserting above all the right to preserve and defend an economic, social and environmental reality which is in danger of being swallowed up by yet another technological "leap," for no other reason than the quest for profit.

Technology, then, is a myth to be contested. What Marx already denounced as machines for waging war on the workers have increasingly become death machines turned against all humankind and its habitat.

All the essays collected in this volume are concerned with these questions, more or less directly, as they cast light on what is at stake in the struggles and transformations revolving around a further expansion of capitalist relations. This book follows another collection by the same editors *Paying the Price* (Zed Books, 1995), to which it is thematically connected. In *Paying the Price,* the main issue was the significance of the international debt crisis and structural "adjustment" policies for social reproduction and, therefore, women's work and women's struggles. The book argued that these policies, in their systematic, negative approach to reproduction, were designed to break the levels of power expressed by the women's struggles, particularly those concerned with their living conditions. It claimed that the aim of "adjustment" was to impose "debt slavery" on the debtor countries as a function of a further entrenchment of capitalist relations, in the continual attempt to refound class relations and hierarchies within the new global economy.

This new book is intended to continue down the same path by developing a series of hypotheses that were first presented and debated at the Thirteenth World Congress of Sociology (Bielefeld, July 18-23 1994) at the sections on "Women's Development and Housework" and "Development, Democracy and Women's Human Rights" coordinated by myself, Silvia Federici and Giovanna Franca Dalla Costa for Research Committee 02 "Economy and Society". The debt crisis and structural adjustment policies continue to provide the framework for analyzing the relationship between the transformations induced by capitalist development and the demands advanced by the movements which have emerged on the world stage, with attention to the women's, ecological and indigenous peoples movements, all of which aim at a radically different form of development, not based on a capitalist logic.

Today, women are making their voice heard on a broad series of increasingly dramatic problems revolving around the conditions in which life is produced and developed. In this sense, if this book has a protagonist, it is certainly the work of reproduction, an emerging iceberg with a cargo of struggles laden with the rejection of unpaid labor, the pole around which the demand for new living conditions transversally links distant areas. The labor of reproduction which is one of the great issues that reflect the ongoing type of development, for more than twenty years, has formed the focus of a wide and analytical debate, in various countries—a debate that is leaving its mark, with increasing frequency, in the official documents of international organizations, like the United Nations Development Program's, *Human Development Report 1995*. For our part, we feel that, if the condition of women is a significant index of how civilized a society is, the conditions in which the work of reproduction is carried out are a significant index of how humane a given form of development is.

Silvia Federici looks at the changes in the work of reproduction produced by the new international division of labor (NIDL), and their impact on the conditions of women and feminist politics. She criticizes current accounts that reduce the NIDL to the reorganization of commodity production, ignoring the transformations that have occurred in the production and reproduction of labor-power. Arguing that the expansion of capitalist relations is still premised on the separation of the workers from the means of (re)production, she shows how structural adjustment and the politics of economic privatization (the pillars of the global economy) have led to the dismantling, in much of the Third World, of subsistence economies and the formation of a proletariat exclusively dependent on monetary relations, although deprived, in most cases, of access to a monetary income. Federici maintains that these processes have transformed the Third World into an immense reserve of labor-power for the metropolitan areas, and shifted much of the work necessary for the reproduction of the metropolitan work-force on the shoulders of women in and from the Third World. Federici concludes that this situation must be the focus of feminist organizing internationally, insofar as it deepens the power relations among women and undermines women's struggles over reproduction. Thus, the decisive issue for the construction of an international feminist movement is not the struggle against gender discrimination, but rather the subversion of the new international division of labor and of the projects for economic globalization and capitalist accumulation from which it stems.

In Giovanna Franca Dalla Costa's essay, the work of reproduction is read in terms of the problems peculiar to one Latin American country, Venezuela, during the Caldera presidency, which began with a softer approach to structural adjustment policies that had already created an explosive situation and paved the way for a number of coup attempts. One aim of the new administration's project was to re-industrialize the country by relaunching small and medium-sized industry while also introducing methods for bringing Venezuela up to the international standards of flexibility and efficiency. The other was a series of innovative social solutions achieved through the creation of a network of small firms, possibly with the participation of those citizens directly interested in the projects for the development of the *economia solidaria*, under the guidance of a Ministry for Social Development. A network of families was supposed to correspond to this network of small firms, as the ministry's direct talking-partner, in an approach that placed less emphasis than in the past on transforming the family according to the Western nuclear model.

Meanwhile, there may be a rethinking about the role the extended family can play in a resource-hungry country such as Venezuela. New forms of organization of social life—indeed a *network* of social relations—have been devised to integrate and link the new productive and reproductive realities which the *economia solidaria* planned to create. In this socio-economic context, housework, a formidable variable of "adjustment," already subject to various pressures in any phase of development or crisis, has become the object of new means of integration and control. At the level of the "network," a confrontation has been growing between the state response, on the one hand, and the increasingly heavy pressure coming from the women, on the other. Presumably, the state response has taken into account women's strong demand to serve as real partners in the definition of social and economic policies. But it has only allowed women to mobilize "from below," without giving them any real say at the decision-making level. At the same time, on the side of women, there has been an increasing pressure on the government at a grassroots level or "through the network," in a climate of growing conflict and in the face of the parallel growth of feminist organizations, demanding different terms of development. These include life guarantees for everyone coupled with a reassertion of women's autonomy.

Alda Britto da Motta's essay, focuses on the condition and the struggles of female domestic workers in Brazil. It shows the need of domestic workers to free themselves from the space-time continuum of "the masters" house. Domestic workers want space and time that are completely their own. It is clear that there is a convergence between the demands and struggles of Brazilian domestic workers and those of women in the "advanced" countries who, far from being "queens of the home," are deprived of space and time of their own, and since the early 1970s, have made of this demand their first step in the building their autonomy.

While the growth of women's organizations in the "developing countries" is now recognized, not only in Latin America but throughout the world, a country which owes a great deal to their heroic commitment (and that of the journalists who have recorded their voices) is Algeria. Andrée Michel's essay is devoted to them. It analyses the trends that have shaped the country's "maldevelopment," and highlights how women have been made the scapegoats for the policies of previous presidencies, in order to divert the people's attention from the real problems. Michel criticizes the Algerian government for having allowed the growth of Islamic fundamentalism, a movement that has attacked "modernity"

"modernity" as a source of all evil, symbolized by the emancipation of women who exercise a profession and go out without the veil.

Michel maintains that the Algerian fundamentalists have not only violated the most basic human rights, but have opposed any expression of women's autonomy, which had consolidated over the years, by demanding that reproductive labor become women's indisputable and non-contractable destiny. Andrée Michel urges that the strength expressed by the Algerian women form the fulcrum for the growth of ties between citizens on both shores of the Mediterranean, capable of imposing a development founded on social justice, liberty and tolerance. Present in her essay, too, is the crucial role of international debt and its relationship with distorted development models. In this context, Michel reiterates that it is not enough to demand the debt's cancellation; something must also be done to ensure that the debt is not reproduced as would happen if the same model of development were reintroduced, and the same social and sexual inequalities in the First and the Third World were reproduced.

In my own contribution, I have covered some of the themes mentioned at the start of this introduction, crossing the bridge thrown by the Zapatista revolt towards the struggles in "advanced" Europe, a bridge which in real time has linked the "primitive" and continued expropriation of the land with the present expropriation of labor. On that bridge, I have met new protagonists, the indigenous people's movements which, in the last two decades, have achieved ever greater organization and an ever greater hearing, giving new substance to the Western debate on development. Their presence has disclosed how the "primitive" unsustainability of development has simply become broader and more lethal. Their presence has given new substance and a new articulation to the debate on human rights as collective and not only individual rights, as the right to diversity rather than the obligation to homogeneity and the right to reject development. Their presence has brought the word "dignity," which has long been out of use in Western civilization, back to the center of political discourse—the dignity of solitude, the capacity to withdraw, of being able to wait, to conceal one's own heritage. I do not know how many feminists who began their path as activists in the 1970s have identified themselves in the word's various meanings, but this was certainly the path of one part of that feminism. It was the sole salvation in front of the blindness of a female culture that invaded the arenas where knowledge is built with inquiries, questionnaires and useless data, to the detriment of the mental space needed for the growth of thought, creativity and self-determination. This has been the dignity of saving one's own collective history from misleading and hasty historico-sociological reconstructions, so that it may have a future in other places and other times. Now the time for it has come and its place is appearing in outline. The indigenous and ecological movements are feminism's first talking-partners.

It is significant that in the indigenous people's movements, it was the women who immediately asserted themselves as the emergent force, and disposed of the presumed immobility of customs attributed to their community. In this process, they have made people aware of the richness of their activities and their 'charters of rights'. *Their struggle against the unsustainable contradiction they experience in capitalist development—which continually undermines their living and working conditions in economies for the most part not founded on money—is linked to the struggle against the unsustainable contradiction experienced by women in the "advanced" areas.* These are the struggles of the unwaged woman working in a wage economy who, for that very reason is denied the right to survival.

First through the studies of academics, then more directly through the their increasing presence in international forums, indigenous women have sent us a powerful message about their rich heritage, about a different form of knowledge, based on the respect for the most basic ecological equilibriums, as the key for the construction of another type of development. A large part of international feminism has now incorporated their voices. Significantly, various documents at the NGO Forum flanking the

UN Conference on Women in Beijing, on August-September 1995, in addition to denouncing structural adjustment and land expropriation as a major cause of poverty, also raised the issue of the defense of 'traditional' knowledge against its expropriation by scientists and businessmen for commercial ends. Clearly, this different type of knowledge is now the terrain for a confrontation between the logic of capitalism and the logic of a different development. The outcome will depend on the strength of the struggles and the movements.

The labor of reproduction and its crises is the main theme of the essay by George Caffentzis. It examines the theoretical and practical implications of three perspectives that, in recent times, have conceptualized the sphere of social reproduction and the relation between market and non-market activities, with all their accompanying dichotomies: production/reproduction, formal/informal, moral values/market values. After showing the limits of the marxian approach on this question, Caffentzis discusses the alternatives offered in the works of Gary Becker, M. Granovetter, Michel Foucault and contrasts them with the feminist theories that identify the work of reproduction as the pillar of the capitalist creation of surplus value and the accumulation process.

As he shows, neither Becker's approach, that reduced all social relations to market relations, in the context of a triumphant commodity/consumer logic, nor the Foucaultian attempt to interpret the production of life as the working of a new form of 'Power,' can account for the contemporary crises in social reproduction. These are the crises reflected in the human and ecological catastrophes of which capitalist development increasingly is the bearer: war, famines, desertification, the flight of masses of refugees and emigrants. From this vantage-point, Caffentzis concludes that only the feminist theory of reproduction developed in the early 1970s, succeeds in giving a convincing explanation of the present crises, because it takes into account the struggle against reproductive labor and its repercussions on capitalist accumulation.

Reproductive labor, then, returns to close this book as a source of struggles and, thus, a source of crisis in social reproduction. For this very reason, reproductive labor must be seen as something more than a source of capitalist value. For in its antagonism to the process of accumulation, it is now a privileged terrain for those movements that have started exploring new paths for a different development, everywhere on the planet.

DEVELOPMENT AND REPRODUCTION*

Mariarosa Dalla Costa

Zapata and the workers

Zapata's determined gaze and slightly stooped shoulders, in the well loved photograph paraded in the Italian metropolitan workers' demonstrations, was one of the striking journalistic images[1] of 1994, creating a bridge in real time between the Mexican revolt of January and the struggles of Europe's industrial workers and unemployed. A bridge was thrown, through space and historical time, linking the struggles against the continuing "primitive" expropriation of the land to those against the post-Fordist expropriation of labor, which are responsible for the increasing dismantlement of the public system of social rights and guarantees. The "primitive" expropriation of the land, begun five centuries ago with the enclosures in England and still continuing today[2] with the more recent forms of colonization and exploitation of the Third World, is now linked even photographically to the contemporary forms of expropriation and poverty creation in the advanced capitalist countries.

How to build and impose on expropriated men and women the discipline of wage labor (with the unwaged labor it presupposes) was the problem capital posed five centuries ago at the beginning of capitalist accumulation. It is still the problem today for the continuation of the capitalist mode of production and its combined strategies of development and underdevelopment. The creation of mass poverty and scarcity, together with the imposition of terror and violence, as well as the large-scale relaunching of slavery, were the basic instruments used to resolve the problem in the first phase of capitalism.

The expropriation of the free producers from all their means of production, as well as the individual and collective resources and rights that contributed to guaranteeing their survival, was studied by Marx in the section on primitive accumulation in *Capital*, Vol. I, Part 8 (1976). We refer to it for a discussion of the enclosures and all the other measures that accompanied them, notably the bloody legislation against the expropriated, the forcing down of wages by an act of Parliament and the ban on workers' associations. The laws stipulating the compulsory extension of the working day, another fundamental aspect of the period, from the middle of the 14th to the end of the 17th century, are dealt with in *Capital*, Vol. 1, Part Three, Chapter 10, where the subject studied is the working day[3].

Concerning land expropriation, Marx observed that

> The advance made by the 18th century shows itself in
> this, that the law itself now becomes the instrument by

which the people's land is stolen, although the big farmers made use of their little independent methods as well.
The Parliamentary form of the robbery is that of 'Bills
for Inclosure of the Commons', in other words decrees
by which the landowners grant themselves the people's
land as private property, decrees of expropriation of the
people." (Marx, 1976, p. 885)

The "little independent methods" are explained in a footnote to
the same passage, quoting from a report entitled *A Political In-
quiry into the Consequences of Enclosing Waste Lands*:

> The farmers forbid cottagers to keep any living creatures
> besides themselves and children, under the pretence that
> if they keep any beasts or poultry, they will steal from
> the farmers' barns for their support; they also say, keep
> the cottagers poor and you will keep them industrious,
> etc., but the real fact, I believe, is that the farmers may
> have the whole right of common to themselves. (Marx,
> 1976, p. 885, note 15)

This footnote gives a powerful picture of the step-by-step process of expropriation that was used to produce the misery and
poverty essential to establish the discipline of wage labor. But
just as powerful an image is given by the isolation of people from
all living beings, that characterized and still characterizes the human condition in capitalist development. The human being is
isolated not only with respect to his/her own species, but also
with respect to nature—that 'other' is treated increasingly as a
commodity.

Deprivation and isolation are the two great accusations, the
two great terrains of rebellion, symbolised by the poster of Zapata
whose watchword was "Tierra y Libertad." The reappropriation
of land was seen by the Zapatistas in 1911 as a fundamental question, because it opened up the possibility of reappropriating a
collective life free from misery. For even then the reappropriation
of the land was pregnant with a multitude of meanings: the

13

reappropriation of a territory where one could express a different sense of life, of action, of social relations and work; and a place where one could imagine and build a different future. From this viewpoint, Zapata's nine-year revolutionary epic is one of the great suppressed memories of official Mexican history.

Today's explosion of the Zapatista rebellion shows how real the problem of the reappropriation of land remains, but also how much it has been magnified by the complex of issues raised by movements in the North and South over the land question. 'Land,' here, not only refers to a means of subsistence—though this would already be an excellent reason for a reappropriation movement, since many economies based on a non-capitalist relation with the land have guaranteed the possibility of life for millennia to a large number of people to whom capitalist development can only offer hunger and extinction. It also refers to land as the earth: a public space to be enjoyed without frontiers; an ecosystem to be preserved because it is the source of life and, hence, of beauty and continual discovery; and a material reality of which we are part, to be reaffirmed, in contrast to the exaltation (especially by male intellectuals) of virtual reality.

The creation of misery starts and proceeds from *the fixing of a price for the land* as well as land expropriation as Marx pointed out. Pricing the land is the solution used for colonies, where the aspirant capitalist is unable to find a sufficient number of waged workers. When the settlers arrive at their destination, they find a 'free' land where they can settle and work independently.

> We have seen that *the expropriation of the mass of the people from the soil forms the basis of the capitalist mode of production*. The essence of a *free* colony, on the contrary, consists in this, that the bulk of the soil is still public property, every settler on it can therefore turn part of it into his private property and his individual means of production, without preventing later settlers from performing the same operation. This is the secret both of the prosperity of the colonies and of their cancerous afflic-

tion—*their resistance to the establishment of capital.*
(Marx 1976, p. 934)

In this context, we can leave to one side the obvious criticism that the "public" land freely settled by the settlers belonged, in reality, to the indigenous populations.

Marx continues:

> There (in the colonies) the capitalist regime constantly comes up against the obstacle presented by the producer who, as owner of his own conditions of labour, employs that labour to enrich himself instead of the capitalist. *The contradiction between these two diametrically opposed economic systems has its practical manifestation here in the struggle between them.* Where the capitalist has behind him the power of the mother country, he tries to use force to clear out of the way the *modes of production and appropriation which rest on the personal labour of the independent producer.* (Marx 1976, p. 931)

Wakefield, the economist Marx quotes in this context, proclaims aloud the *antagonism between the two modes of production*: "To this end he demonstrates that the development of the social productivity of labour, cooperation, division of labour, application of machinery on a large scale, and so on, are impossible without the expropriation of the workers and the corresponding *transformation of their means of production into capital*" (1976, p. 932).

Wakefield's theory of colonisation tries to solve the problem of ensuring an adequate supply of labor for the capitalist's needs by what he calls "systematic colonisation," which, as Marx notes, England tried to enforce for a time by Act of Parliament. Of Wakefield's theory, Marx adds:

> If men were willing to turn the whole of the land from public into private property at one blow, this would certainly destroy the root of the evil, but it would also destroy—the *colony.* The trick is to kill two birds with one

stone. Let the government set an *artificial price on the virgin soil, a price independent of the law of supply and demand*, a price that compels the immigrant to work for a long time for wages before he can earn enough money to buy land and turn himself into an independent farmer. The *fund* resulting from the sale of land at a price relatively *prohibitory* for the wage-laborers, this *fund of money* extorted from the *wages of labour* by a violation of the sacred law of supply and demand, is to be applied by the government in proportion to its growth, to the importation of paupers from Europe into the colonies, so as to keep the *wage-labour market* full for the capitalists. (1976, p. 938)

Marx also pointed out that the *land price laid down by the state* must be "sufficient," which quoting from Wakefield (1833, vol. II, p. 192) he explains means that "it must be high enough 'to prevent the labourers from becoming independent landowners until others had followed to take their place'."

The reference to the setting of a price on the virgin soil is more than just a reminder of a past problem and its analysis in Marx's *Capital*. Today, putting a price to the land and land expropriation, by illegal, pseudo-legal and violent means, are on the agenda throughout those areas of the Third World where capitalist expansion is trying to destroy economies and societies based on a different relation with the land; economies that have guaranteed people's subsistence from time immemorial and, by the same token, resist the wage-labor discipline and the isolation, hunger and death that accompany its imposition. Silvia Federici (1995) and George Caffentzis (1995) have underlined the destructive role that the commercialization of land has played in 'development' policies in Africa. In their studies of Sub-Saharan Africa and Nigeria in particular, they have stressed the importance of this measure in the strategies of the World Bank, the International Monetary Fund and other investors, also showing, however, how this procedure has become a terrain of struggle and resistance for the African population.

There are many other policies and measures that are creating hunger and poverty, including the lowering of export prices for agricultural products, which ruins the Third World farmers, and the adjustment policies that, internationally, have been implemented in response to the "debt crisis." This topic has been discussed in a recently edited volume (Dalla Costa M. and Dalla Costa G.F., eds., 1995), and has been analysed extensively by the Midnight Notes Collective (1992), among others.

This essay focusses, instead, on the two major operations of land expropriation and the fixing of a price to land. Both are usually ignored by political analysts, but remain as fundamental today for extracting a profit out of the Third World as they were at the dawn of capitalism in Europe. In fact, the present development strategy, based on the 'information revolution,' continues to imply a strategy of underdevelopment, and to require these hunger and poverty-creating operations, in order to constantly refound and re-stratify the global working class.

Obviously, the continuing imposition of the wage-labor discipline worldwide does not imply that all those who are expropriated are destined to become wage-laborers. Today, as five centuries ago, this will be the fate of only a small part of the population; those who can will find employment in the sweat shops of the Third World, or of the countries to which they emigrate. The others will be faced only by the prospect of death by hunger, which may explain the tenacity of resistance and the intensity of the struggles. With reference to the Zapata poster in Milan, it explains the revolt in Chiapas. The *price* of capitalist development understood as a whole, in its combined aspects of development and underdevelopment, is *unsustainable* because it consists of *death*. As I have argued elsewhere (Dalla Costa M., 1995), a central assumption must be that, *from the human viewpoint, capitalist development has always been unsustainable* since it has assumed, from the start, and continues to assume, extermination and hunger for an increasingly large part of humanity. The fact that it is founded on a class relationship, and must continually refound it at a global level, in conflict with the power that

17

waged and unwaged men and women are building through their struggles and resistance, only makes its *original unsustainability* more evident and more lethal in time.

The hunger and poverty producing operations that have accompanied the continuous and progressive expropriation of the land, and its turning into a commodity/capital, have obviously been redefined in ideological and technological terms over time. The "food policies" implemented during this century, officially in order to solve or mitigate the problem of malnutrition, have always been closely linked to "reforms" of the relationship with the land. The outcome has been better nutrition for the few, insufficient nutrition, or hunger, for the many, and above all a powerful tool for social control, used to break those organisations that people, in many areas of the world, had created to obtain a better nutrition and a better standard of living.

The "social reforms" characteristic of these policies have always produced new divisions and a new hierarchy between the waged and the unwaged, as well as within these two groups. Harry Cleaver's essay (1977) remains fundamental for its analysis and the globality of its information, as well as for its reports on numerous struggles and the policies adopted to fight them. We fully agree with his assumption that food crises are basically produced by capitalism's political economy. It is significant, as Cleaver points out, that experiments carried out by the Rockefeller Foundation in China, in the 1920s and 1930s, clearly demonstrated the stabilising effect of better food supplies, coupled with some land reform measures, on peasant unrest. In the 1950s, politicians were still talking about an Asian rice policy as a tool for halting peasant revolt in many parts of that continent. Later, the issue officially became a humanitarian one.

The Green Revolution, on the other hand, was put into effect in the 1960s, in both East and West, on the basis of a technological leap in the mechanical, chemical and biological inputs in agricultural policy. The aim was to apply Keynesian principles to agriculture, linking wage increases to increases in productivity. But, as Cleaver argues, the whole history of this technological breakthrough in agriculture was linked to the de-composition of the class power of the waged and the unwaged, the continual creation of new divisions and hierarchies, and the increasing expulsion of workers having different forms of relationship with agriculture.

Agricultural technology has increasingly been subjected to criticism and analysis by feminist scholars, being closely linked to large scale agriculture, which has caused the expropriation and the expulsion from the land of the unwaged workers, who were making a living from it, and of waged agricultural workers, who were displaced by continual technological change. Important in this connection is the work of Vandana Shiva (1989), whose approach is not a Marxist one, and uses the notion of the "female principle" against a male reductionist science. An outstanding physicist, Vandana Shiva abandoned India's nuclear programme because she realized that the "reaction of nuclear systems with living systems" was being kept secret from the people. In her well-known work, *Staying Alive: Women, Ecology and Development* (1989), she illustrates the ongoing systematic loss of resources for health and subsistence, caused by the reduction of the biodiversity, imposed in India by the agricultural policies of recent decades. Shiva also exposes the dependence and poverty created by the imposition of new laboratory hybrids; the drought and human and environmental disasters created by dams and their irrationality by comparison with earlier forms of water-management. The history of the enclosure, expropriation and commercialisation not only of the land, but also of its plants, animals, and waters is revived in Shiva's analysis, which is centred on the events of these last decades. There are other important works belonging to the ecofeminist current, first of all the works of Maria Mies (1986 and, with Shiva, 1993), to mention only the most famous ones. In contrast Mary Mellor's book (1992), while it has many points of contact with the above cited studies, is more concerned with defining a "feminist green socialism."

I share much of the critique advanced in this blossoming of feminist studies on the relationship between human beings and nature, and on the North-South relationship. I cannot compare more extensively my position to that of ecofeminists scholars here. The only point I can make is that some ecofeminist scholars look primarily at the struggles and forms of resistance that are taking place in the Third World, while they see the First World primarily as an area of excessive consumption, whence the assertion of the need for a reduction of production and consumption. As for myself and the circuit of scholars I have worked with since the early 1970s, we think that while the strategic importance of Third World struggles must be recognized, equal importance should be given to the struggles in the advanced capitalist areas, not only as areas of consumption, but also as areas where labor is expended. Hence our stress on the importance of the struggles of waged and unwaged workers in the advanced capitalist countries and their relationship with struggles in other parts of the world. We also see a need to analyze consumption in a more articulated way; since by definition, consumption by workers, including housewives, has never been high and, today, is falling dramatically. But these are just a few hints in a debate that will develop further.

Let us now return to our discourse. Vandana Shiva (1989) says of water and drought:

> The drying up of India, like that of Africa, is a man-made rather than a natural disaster. The issue of water, and water scarcity has been the most dominant one in the 1980s as far as struggles for survival in the subcontinent are concerned. The manufacture of drought and desertification is an outcome of reductionist knowledge and models of development which violate cycles of life in rivers, in the soil, in mountains. Rivers are drying up because their catchments have been mined, de-forested or over-cultivated to generate revenue and profits. Groundwater is drying up because it has been over-exploited to feed cash crops. Village after village is being robbed of its lifeline, its sources of drinking water, and the number of villages facing water famine is in direct

proportion to the number of "schemes" implemented by government agencies to 'develop' water" (p. 179).

Commercial exploitation of forests, over-exploitation of ground water for commercial agriculture and inappropriate afforestation are the major reasons identified for the water crisis." (p. 181)

Time and again, Vandana Shiva points out, famous British engineers who learned water management from indigenous techniques in India, commented on the "sophisticated engineering sense, built on an ecological sense, that provided the foundation for irrigation in India." Major Arthur Cotton, credited as the "founder" of modern irrigation programmes, wrote in 1874:

> There are multitudes of old native works in various parts of India...These are noble works, and show both boldness and engineering talent. They have stood for hundreds of years...When I first arrived in India, the contempt with which the natives justifiably spoke of us on account of this neglect of material improvements was very striking; they used to say we were a kind of civilised savages, wonderfully expert about fighting, but so inferior to their great men that we would not even keep in repair the works they had constructed, much less even imitate them in extending the system. (p. 187)

The East India Company, as Vandana Shiva adds, took control of the Kaveri Delta in 1799, but was unable to check the rising river bed. Company officials struggled for a quarter century; finally, using indigenous technology. Cotton was able to solve the problem by renovating the Grand Anicut. He wrote later:

> It was from them (the native Indians) we learnt how to secure a foundation in loose sand of unmeasured depth...The Madras river irrigations executed by our engineers have been from the first the greatest financial success of any engineering works in the world, solely

because we learnt from them...With this lesson about foundations, we built bridges, weirs, aqueducts and every kind of hydraulic work...We are thus deeply indebted to the native engineers.

But the lesson has obviously been erased by the full flood of the capitalist science of development and profit, what Vandana Shiva calls "maldevelopment" (4). British engineers in the 1700s and 1800s recognised that indigenous technology and knowledge tended to preserve water resources and make them available for the local people. Today, capitalist water-management projects cause drought and deny survival to entire populations. One woman from Maharashtra State in India sings against the dam that she has to help build so that crops such as sugar cane can be irrigated while women and children die of thirst (Shiva 1989):

> As I build this dam
> I bury my life.
> The dawn breaks
> There is no flour in the grinding stone.
>
> I collect yesterday's husk for today's meal
> The sun rises
> And my spirit sinks.
> Hiding my baby under a basket
> And hiding my tears
> I go to build the dam
>
> The dam is ready
> It feeds their sugar cane fields
> Making the crop lush and juicy.
> But I walk miles through forests
> In search of a drop of drinking water
> I water the vegetation with drops of my sweat
> As dry leaves fall and fill my parched yard.

Responding to this mad "enclosure" of water has increasingly become a key issue on the agenda of the political networks that monitor and struggle against projects of this kind. The immediate future will show the effects of these efforts. An exemplary case is the Bangladesh flood control plan (Del Genio 1994), presented by the World Bank in London in December 1989. Even though it was claimed to differ from previous projects because of its low environmental impact, other estimates of its effects were so dramatic that an international coalition of organizations, opposed to the World Bank's approach to the canalization of rivers, was created in Strasbourg in May 1993.

Considering solely the human impact, the building of the Narmada dam in India was expected to require the evacuation of 500,000 inhabitants and aroused strong opposition from the 'tribals' and the organisations supporting them. The Bangladesh Flood Action Plan (FAP), coordinated by the World Bank on behalf of the Group of Seven, would require the forced transfer of 5-8 million persons in a territory with a population density ten times that of India.

Del Genio's article illustrates the reasons cited to justify the plan—on the one hand, mystifying assumptions and, on the other, the lethal techniques of the Green Revolution. This plan insists on the need to "propagate modern, mechanised agriculture capable of coping with the food crisis," so as to increase the cultivation of modern high-yield varieties of rice which, in turn, requires a large and regular quantity of water and a system of flood control and irrigation to make it available.

The drawbacks of the high-yield varieties include a dependence on the market and laboratories, since they are unable to reproduce, and the reduction of the genetic diversity of local seeds. Awareness of these drawbacks is growing in the world, and rural workers' grass-roots organizations are putting up an increasing resistance against these agricultural improvements, supposedly more appropriate for satisfying their nutritional needs. As for flood control, some of the yearly regular floods bring nutrients that ensure the soil's fertility and top up the water-table as they expand across the plain. Other, purely destructive floods need to be controlled through works different from those being planned, if the aim is to be achieved without destroying the environment, including the humans in it. In this connection, it is worth remembering the level of sophistication achieved in biodiversity, through the long-term cooperation between humans and nature. Among the hundreds of local rice varieties developed in response to the demands of territory and climate, a sub-variety called Aman is capable of growing over 15cm in only 24 hours, if the level of the water rises.

As for transferring 5-8 million persons by coercion, this is in itself inconceivable, since to uproot a population is like cutting a tree's roots, in this case a forest's. The first and obvious question that comes to mind is: where and how are the uprooted peasants supposed to find the money needed to pay the costs of agricultural modernization (machinery, fertilisers, etc.)? The answer is always the same, and has been repeated thousands of times over in the history of the Green Revolution: only the big proprietors and the big enterprises can sustain the costs. And the others? The work for the dam meanwhile has begun...

The peasants and many others working with them in international networks are organizing forms of resistance and opposition. The building of the Asswan dam, and the consequent loss of the soil nutrients, for the peasants who lived off the flooded soil, in addition to the other serious consequences the dam precipitated, inevitably come to mind. First of all, the flooding of part of Nubia and, with it, the burial of major relics of that civilisation, and the abandonment of the land by those who lived there. But this is just one case among the many that could be cited. When I was in Egypt in 1989, there was talk of a project to turn the Red Sea into a lake. I hope that the growth of the ecological movement, the movements of the native populations and others will have relegated this project to the nightmares of a past era.

Returning to Vandana Shiva, the same observations that she and many other scholars are making today about dams and other Western water-management projects in the Third World, can equally be applied to the technologies that are imposed on Third World agriculture, in livestock raising, and in the destruction of forests to cultivate export crops. All these processes involve the destruction of the biodiversity, of the ecological equilibriums, and of the life-cycles that guaranteed subsistence. In short, the production of profit for the big companies involves the denial of survival for the population.

Even though her cultural and theoretical approach is far from Marxist, when Vandana Shiva identifies the logic of the continual enclosure of segments of nature and its effects, she has no difficulty in concluding that the foundations of capitalist accumulation are the science and practice of the culture of death. Her merit is also to have contributed to bringing to international attention struggles and movements otherwise ignored or neglected. Our argument here is that the Chipko movement, in which women organize to stay in the forest even at night, embracing the trees to prevent the logging companies from cutting them down, should be placed on the same level as all the other struggles that are being waged worldwide against various forms of expropriation and the attack against individual and collective rights —both the right to survival, or better, to life, and the right to self-determination.

The economic and life system of the Indian "tribals"[5] who created the Chipko movement—which forms the focus of Vandana Shiva's studies and practical activity—is based on a combination of agriculture, livestock raising and the use/conservation of the forest. The forest has a central and many-sided role in the whole system. The forests bear "soil, water and pure air," sing the Chipko women (Shiva 1989: 77), and they play an important nutritional role. Whatever crisis may hit crops or livestock, say the Chipko women, the children will never suffer hunger, if there is a forest near. Thus embracing the trees to stop them from being felled is like occupying the land to prevent it from being expropriated, or struggling in defence of jobs or a wage, or a guaranteed income, when survival depends solely on money.

This is what we see if we want to spotlight how the different parts of the working social body struggle simultaneously, and in different forms, against the same system that exploits and besieges them in different ways.

This is important for understanding how opposition to capitalist development is growing worldwide, and is refusing to pay its price while seeking other paths for a different future. But the struggles of the Chipko women, and all the other movements for the maintenance and defence of an age-old experience and knowledge in humankind's relationship with nature, are all the more vital for us. This means that the political debate in the 'advanced' areas, empowering the voice of those who refuse to pay the price of this development , must necessarily be an ecological debate as well.

Vandana Shiva (whose work I consider here, even if briefly, because it is representative of an entire school of feminist studies, developed by women in the world's various Souths) also denounces the genetic manipulation of living species. The tampering of the nutritional resources of entire communities is compounded by the genetic manipulation of the species. This topic has attracted extensive attention, in recent years, from the various circuits of women scholars and activists.

> With engineering entering the life sciences, the renewability of life as a self-reproducing system comes to an end. *Life must be engineered now, not reproduced.* A new commodity set is created as inputs, and a new commodity is created as output. Life itself is the new commodity..." (Shiva, 1989, p. 91). "The market and the factory define the 'improvement' sought through the new bio-technologies... Nature's integrity and diversity and people's needs are thus simultaneously violated. (Shiva 1989: p. 92)

This biotechnological trend is matched by the determination to patent and 'bank' the genetic heritage of the living species. This was denounced by a women's meeting in Miami in preparation for the Rio conference (Women's Action Agenda 21, 1991), but such criticism is widely shared. After patenting cotton, the agro-industrial corporations now want to do the same for rice and soy, two of the fundamental foodstuffs for many sectors of the world's population. Increasingly, food, which is already difficult to obtain because of the combination of expropriation of land, technological innovations in farming methods, and the disparity between prices and wages (when there are any), is manipulated, placed beyond reach, privatised, monopolised, patented, 'banked.' A new enclosure. *Food! No Access!*

In this parabola of technological conquest over nature, expropriation reaches its acme: human beings are expropriated, the living species are expropriated, the earth's own reproductive powers are expropriated to be transformed into capital. This mode of production pretends to capitalize the generation and reproduction of life. What a long road capitalism has travelled from the time when, indifferent to life, it was satisfied with nothing more than the appropriation of an excessive number of working hours[6]. That is, when it simply pretended to transform all life into work and, to that end, it drained the life of free workers and also enchained masses of slaves, not caring about the contradiction implicit in the simultaneous exploitation of free and slave labor.

The growth of the various rebellions and struggles worldwide, in rejection of this type of development, is matched by that of massive, lethal and monstrous structures and forms of domination. Considering only the most recent past, from the Gulf War on, the increasingly warlike character of this development has undeniably produced an escalation of war, that removes any residual doubts over whether or not development is founded on the science and practice of death. Mentioning the wars in the Gulf, ex-Yugoslavia, Somalia, and Rwanda-Burundi is only to acknowledge the wars that have received most media coverage in the last three or four years. We certainly do not want to forget the many wars that have been waged worldwide without ever entering the limelight.

If anything, the escalation of war in recent years has confirmed the vacuousness of what the major powers have declared about disarmament. *Rather, war has become increasingly the instrument par excellence for disciplining the working social body at the global level,* through annihilation, terror, division, deportation, and the lowering of living conditions and life expectations. In the end, *humans, when they are not massacred directly, are increasingly 'enclosed'* in refugee camps, and the more or less concealed concentration camps of war situations.

But, at the same time, *the other face of war as a form of development* has been revealed ever more clearly, through the growing monstrosity of the enterprises its macabre laboratory generate. War has always been a great laboratory, but since the greed of capitalist technology has begun to pursue life in the attempt to steal and capitalize its secrets, death has increasingly been discovered as a terrain for profit. In this case, too, there has been a shift from the 'primitive' indifference to the death of masses of individuals, expropriated of their means of production and sustenance, to the usage of death, dead bodies, or bodies destined in a cavalier way to die, in the experimentation of new technologies, or commercialized body parts in the trafficking in organs. Besides the traditional markets of arms, post-war reconstructions, and the techno-industrial experimentation on which our 'peace economy' rests, war today offers, above all, the biggest mass of living/dying guinea-pigs on whom to test, on a mass scale, the new technologies designed to acquire more knowledge of the body and how to operate on it. Here too, it is clear how the part of guinea-pigs has been played above all by the people of the 'non-advanced' nations, even if a similar role has recently been emerging for citizens of the main industrialized countries, those from the most vulnerable sectors of the population, who are being dispatched to war or used, without knowing it, in 'peace-time'.

But war continues to offer new and horrifying terrains on which to reap profits. Trafficking in children,[7] for example. How many for pornography?[8] How many for trafficking in organs?[9] How many for slavery[10] and for the traffic in war cripples?[11] How many for prostitution? How many to be sold for adoption to child- less couples? Trafficking in adult males and females also goes on, for all the reasons mentioned above, apart from the last.

It is strange that, in the discussions about sustainable devel- opment, there is usually no mention of the *unsustainability* for humankind and the environment of the *form* that development has increasingly taken, namely *war*.

The poster with the image of Zapata, from which we set out, comes to us from the Chiapas revolt and the war and truce that resulted from it. Carried as a banner by the workers in Milan, it gave voice to the two great expropriations, that from the land and that from labor. At the same time, it poses, with all the force expressed in the struggles carried on, throughout the world, by those who have been expropriated, the question of what is the contemporary relationship between waged and unwaged labor in this development. In the Third World as in the First, what future is there for unwaged labor?

Zapata and the women.

It may be a provocation, but not an illegitimate one, to think that, in relaunching the increasingly dramatic question of the relation- ship between these two great sectors of labor, the poster of Zapata also relaunches the feminist question that stimulated the women's movement in the early 1970s: that of the unwaged labor expended in the reproduction of labor-power. The woman is, in fact, the unwaged laborer par excellence and she experiences in this de- velopment a *doubly unsustainable contradiction* (Dalla Costa, M., 1995; Dalla Costa, G.F., 1989). On the one hand, her condi- tion, which has been created by capitalist development, is unsustainable, in its typical form in the 'advanced areas,' insofar as she is an *unwaged worker*, who is responsible for reproduc- ing labor-power in a *wage economy* (Dalla Costa, M., James S. 1972). On the other, her situation has become increasingly unsustainable as an unwaged worker in an unwaged *subsistence economy*, where the expansion of capitalist relations increasingly deprives her of the means to fulfil the tasks of reproduction for herself and the community. This contradiction and, with it, the unsustainability of the woman's condition, cannot be solved within capitalism, which is its root. To be solved, it requires a totally different conception and organization of development. By the same token, women's struggles around their condition amplify the demands of other unwaged social subjects, from whose labor this capitalist development continually accumulates value.

Numerous studies of which I mention only some (Michel, Agbessi Dos Santos, Fatoumata Diarra, 1981, Michel 1988; Boserup 1982; Shiva 1989) have shown how the continual realization of capitalist projects in the rural areas of the Third World, beside expropriating the land, makes it more difficult for women to gain access to the basic means for the production of subsistence, from wood for fuel to water for the home and forage for the animals. Now, hours or days have to be spent in fetching things that were previously fairly close. These resources too have been swallowed up by enclosure/ appropriation/ commoditization/ capitalization.

Feminist authors (Mies 1992) have noted the paradox whereby rural women are blamed for harming the environment, precisely because of the activities by which they try to acquire these resources, as well as for having too many children. Supposedly, they destroy the forests, if they go there in search of wood; they pollute and use up the water sources, if they go to fetch water; they use up the earth's resources, if they have too many children. It is a typical case of blaming the victims. At the same time, their working and living conditions, and the entire community's life, are continually undermined by the debt policies imposed on the Third World countries by the major financial agencies, policies of which the expropriation/ privatization of the land is only one, but fundamental aspect (Dalla Costa M. and Dalla Costa G.F., eds., 1993).

When it is not directly the expropriation and expulsion of the rural communities, without anything in exchange, the capitalist 'development alternative' not only removes an assured subsistence and replaces it with an uncertain wage, but deepens the gap between the male and the female conditions. Significant, once more, in this respect, is the example (Shiva, 1989) also quoted by Mies (1992) of the Chipko women, who oppose the felling of trees for commercial purposes, in the Himalayan forests. As often is the case, the men were less determined in their opposition, because they were tempted by the prospect of the jobs they would get in the saw-mills.

But the women wondered how much of that money/wage they would have received and thus they opposed the creation of a hierarchy based on having or not having a wage. Above all, they asked what would happen to all of them once the forest, the basis of their subsistence, would be swallowed by the saw-mills, which would also be closed since there would be no more wood to cut. The women said clearly that they needed no jobs from the government or private businessmen as long as they kept their land and their forests.

In Shiva (1989), there are many other episodes of this kind. After five centuries in which the same scenario has been repeated, the lesson has been learned in the most remote corners of the earth. Thus, there is a great determination not to put one's life in the hands of the planners of development and under-development[12], to stop others from plunging whole populations into a total uncertainty, bound to produce hunger, tomorrow if not today; a determination to avoid being turned into beggars or refugee camp inmates.

Ecofeminist practices and positions, linking nature, women, production and consumption in a single approach, are often criticised for "romanticism" by male scholars. One wonders, just to raise the most simple question, what value do these scholars attribute to the right to survive of those communities—and there are many of them—whose subsistence and life system are guaranteed precisely by the existence of this relationship with nature; while 'development plans' almost always presuppose the sacrifice of the vast majority of the individuals that constitute these communities. Significantly, Mary Mellor (1993) observes in this connection: "I see all this as something that men should prove to be unfounded, rather than as something that the feminists must justify."

As it emerges, with increasing clarity, from the "charters" that various first nation peoples have elaborated, with the growth of their movement, over the last decades, together with the right to land, i.e., the right to survival/life, there is an increasingly strong demand for the right to identity, dignity, to one's own history, to the maintenance of the complex of collective and individual rights belonging to one's own culture, and the right to work out one's own future starting from one's own premises. Obviously, there is no intention here of skating over the contradictions within the existing customs and systems of rules, above all those between men and women. If anything, what needs immediate clarification is that capitalist development, far from offering solutions to these problems, most often aggravates them. Politicians promoting development often try to suppress the women's movements which deal with these questions. Nevertheless these movements have grown and are creating an increasing number of new networks, that struggle, denounce and demonstrate great determination in changing a state of affairs clearly causing women harm.

In this connection, the Chiapas revolt is exemplary since it brought to international attention how the Maya women defined their rights with respect to men and society at large. Work and grass-roots debate in the communities produced a code of rights.[13] Some rights concern the economic/social/civil plane, such as the right to work, to a fair wage, education, basic health care, the necessary food for oneself and one's children, the right to decide autonomously the number of children one wants to have and to rear, to choose one's companion without being required to marry him, to suffer no violence inside or outside the family. Other rights concern the political plane, such as the right to take part in managing the community, to hold office if democratically elected, to hold positions of responsibility in the Zapatista National Liberation Army (ZNLA). The code repeats that women must have all the rights and obligations deriving from revolutionary laws and regulations. And in fact, women participate fully in the highest offices in the ZNLA.

When I was in Chiapas in the winter of 1992-93, and in San Cristobal I was struck by the numerous posters put up by women's right activists alongside the posters in praise of the guerrilla heroes. A year later, the great work achieved by these women took on new substance and became known throughout the world, disclosing how much progress had also been made within the community with regard to the relationship between the sexes. It is significant that an important issue, in the code of women's rights, corresponding to the centrality it has won in the Western world, is violence. I should only add that, during my visit, the year before the revolt, I was told in San Cristobal that the Maya women were no longer willing to go to the hospital to have their children for fear of being raped—evidently not by the members of their communities.

It seems clear that these women's elaboration of their rights was not postponed to a mythical and improbable phase, "after" the movement, that was aiming at a radical change in the state of things, but formed an integral part of it. The same thing happened in the elaboration of their rights by the Eritrean women during the Eritrean liberation war, and it is repeated in an increasing number of situations. These facts show how it is invalid to presume a lack of movement in 'non-advanced' societies because of a supposed observance of tradition.

I would also like to underscore that the relationship with nature[14] is for all of us a fundamental contribution made by the movements of the indigenous, yet there is great resistance to it being recognized as such in the political discourse of urban male intellectuals that try to find a way to change the world.

As the Chipko movement shows—and numerous other examples are available from various parts of the planet—*the leaders are increasingly women in movements that link the maintenance, recovery and reinterpretation of a relationship with nature with a defence of economic subsistence and the conservation of the identity and historical-cultural dignity of the communities/ civilizations to which they belong.*

Insofar as their primary task is the reproduction of individuals in waged and non-waged economies, insofar *as they are unwaged subjects par excellence in both types of economy*, and their possibilities of autonomous subsistence are progressively undermined in the proceeding of capitalist development, *women* emerge as the *privileged interpreters* for the unwaged of the earth's future. Today, their critique and their theoretical contribution form a necessary moment in the formulation of a different development, or in any case in reasserting the right not to be developed against their will and interest.

On the other hand, international networking between feminist scholars, women active in various organizations concerned with women's condition, development and the condition of indigenous peoples, have created a greater awareness of these experiences of resistance and struggle, also among Italian women researchers. Several among these internationally known initiatives are cited by Cicolella (1993). One is the *Green Belt Movement* founded in 1977 by Wangari Maathai, from Kenya, who starting from the idea of 'afforestation for life,' has created green belts around cities in 12 African countries, where forests had been replaced by open spaces. The *Gabriela* group, in the Philippines, began its activities by safeguarding a mountain precious for its natural equilibrium and fragile ecosystem. The *Third World Network* , founded by a Chinese jurist Yoke Ling Chee, aims at forms of development that respond to people's real needs and, above all, are independent of aid from the industrial nations. The *Mapuche* movement in Chile, led by Alicia Nahelcheo, who was already active against the Pinochet dictatorship, is today struggling against development projects, the expropriation of land to build power stations, and the cropping for commercial purposes of the araucaria tree, whose fruit is a basic foodstuff.

But these are only a few examples. The ways in which many men and women try to guarantee their survival, and fight against this type of development, can be expected to multiply. Meanwhile, broad initiatives are growing at the international level[15] designed to challenge the legitimacy of the World Bank and the IMF, and to block their directives. At the economic and social level, these are the key centers in the management of contemporary development, as well as the main factors in the poverty and degradation of the 'developing' countries.

Strong critiques and resistance against this form of development have produced a vast and articulated debate, in the course of which various interpretations of what a different development should be have emerged. Recent summaries (Gisfredi 1993) of the major positions stress the central role of the environment and the cultural context for the elaboration of any autochthonous project.[**] They also stress the significance of typologies that, in identifying the fundamental goals of development, list as basic needs, not only those concerning purely physical survival, but those concerning security, welfare, identity and liberty, against violence, material poverty, alienation and repression, which typify government rule in many "developing" countries.

A central element in these types of approaches remains self-reliance,which is guaranteed by mobilising all the human and material resources available locally and by using technologies compatible with the cultural and natural environment. Other approaches could be mentioned. To the list of basic needs, self reliance, and eco-development, presented by the Dag Hammerskjold Foundation (1975), others have been added, as the debate has since significantly developed. The most questioned idea is 'sustainable development,' which emerged from the famous world commission for the environment and development chaired by Gro Harlem Brundtland. The main criticism moved to it is that it confuses development with economic growth and confuses "everyone's future" with the future of the First World.

In any case, it is clear that any new approach concerning development makes sense only in so far as it expresses the demands of those men and women who have so far paid the heaviest price for development, while gaining the least from it; and in so far as it recognises *the right to reject development,* in all situations where people refuse it, as it often happens in many different parts of the world. As Gustavo Esteva said, as early as 1985, in his comments on a conference of the Society for International Development: "My people are tired of development, they just want to live." (quoted in Shiva 1989: p13)

Granted the perspective described above, a look at the contribution made by movements wanting to approach the question of development from a feminist viewpoint shows, in my view, that the most interesting approaches include eco-feminism, because its starting-point is respect for human life and the life of living beings in general. Since it appreciates, rather than devaluing, the knowledge and experience of women in indigenous communities, eco-feminism relaunches a perspective that valorizes the relationship with nature as the source of life and subsistence, the right to self-determination, and rejects the capitalist model of development.

I think that a cross between this feminism and the more radically anti-capitalist feminism, that has analysed the condition and struggles of women and the unwaged in this model of development, may make a very interesting contribution. In this context, I would like to recall, if only briefly, Vandana Shiva's conception of nature which forms the foundation of her discourse.

Shiva uses a reading of Indian cosmogony in which Nature (*Prakrti*) is an expression of Sakti, the female principle, dynamic primordial energy, the source of abundance. Joining up with the male principle (*Purusa*), *Prakrti* creates the world. Women, like any other natural being, have in themselves the female principle and, therefore, this capacity for creation and the maintenance of life. According to Vandana Shiva, the reductionist vision typical of Western science continually expels the female principle from the management of life, by the same token interrupting the life cycles and therefore the regeneration of life itself, creating destruction in its place. The reductionist vision with respect to nature and women ensures that they are reduced to means for the production of commodities and labor-power.

Patriarchal categories which understand destruction as "production" and regeneration of life as 'passivity' have generated a crisis for survival. Passivity, an assumed category of the 'nature' of nature and women, denies the activity of nature and life. Fragmentation and uniformity as assumed categories of progress and development destroy the living forces which arise from relationships within the 'web of life' and the diversity in the elements and patterns of these relationships. (Shiva 1989: p 3)

Feminism as ecology, and ecology as the revival of Prakrti, the source of all life, become the decentred powers of political and economic transformation and restructuring. (Shiva 1989: p 7)

Contemporary women's ecological struggles are new attempts to establish that steadiness and stability are not stagnation, and balance with nature's essential ecological processes is not technological backwardness but technological sophistication. (Shiva 1989: p 36)

The discourse on land, on water, on nature return to us, brought by the indigenous peoples' movements and the knowledge of indigenous women, the most precious of the riches that ancient civilizations hid and the secrets that they kept.

But with the land, there also returns to us the immense potential of a human diversity that has been able to resist and preserve its cultural heritage. And now it gives forceful expression to the will to work its own future autonomously. The need for a relationship with the earth, for liberty, time, for an escape from the constraints of labor and the relations that the capitalist model of development wants to continue to impose on us, also represents something the expropriated Western humanity is thirsting for. Perhaps, the fact that the Chiapas revolt was heard so widely across the world, is because it gave many people their first perception of the real possibility of a different life project, which they had resignedly relegated to an impossible dream world—a world in which life would not be all work, nor nature an enclosed park, in which relationships are prepackaged, pre-codified and atomized. It is evidently because these deep and painful chords were struck in the psyche of the expropriated Western humanity that the whole social body vibrated with the Chiapas rebels, beating a thousand keys, transmitting, declaring, sustaining. A thousand arms and a thousand legs were moved, and a thousand voices heard.

A hinterland of communication and liaison has been constructed with the growth of the indigenous, "first nation" movements across the Americas and in the world, during the last twenty years. Relations, analyses and information have been more closely and more strongly interwoven, especially in opposition to the North America Free Trade Agreement. And all of this has become the primary tissue for communication between, and action by, different sectors in the working social body. Workers and non-indigenous people, ecological movement militants, women's groups, and human rights activists have been attracted into a complex support action, helping and monitoring from various parts of the world. But it is clear that, in the last analysis, what has moved all these individuals, groups and associations is the fact of having recognised their own demands in the demands of the indigenous peoples' movements; of having seen their own liberation in the indigenous peoples' movement's chances of liberation.

The indigenous people have brought the keys, and they are on the table. They can open other doors to enter the Third Millennium. Outside, the full flood has arrived, breaking the concrete banks and drowning the latest high-yield variety of rice...The peasants take out their hundreds of seed varieties, while Aman pushes its stems out above the water.

Notes

1. See *Il Manifesto*, February 8 1994, but many other newspapers have used the same image.
2. This is the subject of the third part of Midnight Notes Collective (1992).

3. In lectures on *Capital* that I used to give each year, I devoted some comments in 1970 to the fundamental question of the two opposite tendencies characterising the history of the working day. They were published later (Dalla Costa M., 1978). In my university courses, I continue illustrating fundamental parts of *Capital*, especially those concerning primitive accumulation. The social processes in this period that were neglected by Marx in *Capital*, e.g., the great witch-hunt, have been analysed by the feminist scholars I worked with (Fortunati 1981; Federici and Fortunati 1984), with the aim of clarifying the capitalist sexual division of labor and the construction of proletarian women's individuality in capitalism. It is no co-incidence that this period is considered as crucial by various currents of feminist thought.

4. The term *maldevelopment* and its French equivalent *maldeveloppement* were originally coined with a biological meaning in mind, rather than a political one. The reference to the idea that the wrong type of development is male-related is clear.

5. India has about 50 million members of tribes, recognised as such by the Indian constitution because of their particularly disadvantaged situation. They are found most extensively in the states of Orissa, Andhra Pradesh and Maryana, and are at most marginally integrated into the market economy. Their specific social organization tends to be non-masculinist and generally speaking egalitarian, with a particularly 'sustainable' approach to natural resources. But they are considered as without caste, and are despised and exploited as cheap or unpaid labor when they are forced to join agricultural or industrial units. Consequently, 'tribals' referring to India, has not only a social-anthropological meaning but a juridical one as well.

6. "Capital asks no questions about the length of life of labour-power"... "What experience generally shows to the capitalist is a constant excess of population"... "*Après moi le déluge*! is the watchword of every capitalist and every capitalist nation" (Marx, 1976, Vol. 1, p. 376, 380, 381).

7. In *La Repubblica*, May 17, 1994, an article entitled, "Where have the Sarajevo children disappeared to?" Wondering where the children evacuated from the Bosnian war have ended up, the article quoted

spine-chilling figures from the humanitarian organizations on trafficking in children, and reported the case of one 14-year-old girl
who ended up with Italian go-betweens and managed to escape. Also
mentioned is an article in the weekly, *Focus*.

8. The large number of children used in the pornography market was
re-ferred to with increasing frequency in the Italian media in 1993-94.

9. International criminal networks and international crime organizations with legal terminals are growing around the clandestine traffic in organs. The Italian public television broadcasted a series of
programs on this issue. One of the most interesting, on March 5,
1994, on the second state channel, provided evidence of a relationship between these organizations and legal terminals in France.

10. It seems worthwhile putting this question given the incredible figures on slavery published recently: 200 million in the world, according to the *Economist* of January 6, 1990. 100 million are reportedly
children, according to *Il Manifesto*, 8.06.1994, which quotes a
UNICEF report published on the previous day.

11. *Il Mattino di Padova*, 4.06.1994, published an article on the discovery and denunciation of an organization that was exploiting women
and war cripples from ex-Yugoslavia. In Mestre (Venice), the former
were sent to work as prostitutes, the latter as beggars.

12. An effective description of the creation of under-development through
development, in the Port Harcourt area in Nigeria, is provided by
Silvia Federici (1992).

13. Since January 1, 1994, the day when the revolt broke out, there has
been a continual flow of information in the press. In Italy, *Il Manifesto* and other newspapers have reported the main demands of the
rebels and, with them, those of the women of Chiapas as they were
being put forward. Two articles, with precise information on the
Zapatistas' demands and mobilisation, are Gomez (1994) and Cleaver
(1994). A brief synthesis of the women's rights, as stipulated in the
Women's Revolutionary Law, is to be found in Coppo and Pisani
(eds. 1994). I must add that a book not to be missed for learning
about the condition of the Maya women, this time in Guatemala, is
Burgos (1991), *My name is Rigoberta Menchù*.

14. It must be recognized that, in recent years, there has been a growth, internationally, of attempts to link different theoretical perspectives with approaches whose focus is the relationship with nature, particularly Marxism and ecology. The magazine best-known for publishing this type of debate is *Capitalism. Nature, Socialism,* which is explicitly located in an eco-Marxist perspective. In this magazine, a particularly broad discussion has developed around the O'Connor (1992) theses on the "second contradiction of capitalism." On the relationship between the left and ecological issues, see, among others, Ricoveri (1994).

15. Just to mention two initiatives: the Circle of the Peoples coordinated a wide range of associations in a counter-summit against the Naples Summit of the Group of Seven on July 8-10, 1994, and, in the first ten days of October of the same year, a large number of associations took part in a counter-summit in Madrid for the annual assemblies of the World Bank and the IMF, that year marking the fiftieth anniversary of Bretton Woods and the international financial organisations created there. For the same event, the League for the Rights of the Peoples worked at the Lelio Basso Foundation in Rome to produce a statement on the Bretton Woods institutions to be published when the summit was on in Madrid, just as it was done for the IMF general assembly in Berlin in 1988.

---

*   This article was first published in English in *Common Sense* n. 17, 1995. Some of its main thesis have been since then further developed in "Some Notes on Neoliberalism, on Land and on the Food Question" (Dalla Costa M. 1997) and in "The Native in Us, The Land We Belong To." (Dalla Costa M. 1998)

** Autochthon, from the Greek [ott pl.] are of the earliest known inhabitants of any country and/or an animal or plant that is native to a region, Greek meaning "from the earth itself." [Editor]

Bibliography

Barry, K. (1995), *The Prostitution of Sexuality. The Global Exploitation of Women.* New York: New York University Press.

Boserup, E. (1982), *Il lavoro delle donne. La divisione sessuale del lavoro nello sviluppo economico.* Torino: Rosenberg & Sellier.

Burgos, E. (1991), *Mi chiamo Rigoberta Menchù,* Firenze:Giunti.

Caffentzis, G. (1993), "The Fundamental Implications of the Debt Crisis for Social Reproduction in Africa," in Dalla Costa M. & Dalla Costa G.F.(eds.) (1995).

Cleaver, H. (1977), "Food, Famine and the International Crisis" in *Zerowork, Political Materials 2, Fall.*

Cleaver, H. (1989), "Close the IMF, abolish debt and end development: a class analisys of the international debt crisis" in *Capital and Class,* n. 39, Winter.

Cleaver, H. (1994), "The Chiapas Uprising and the Future of Class Struggle", in *Common Sense,* No. 15, Edinburg, Scotland, Great Britain.

Coppo, P. e Pisani, L. (eds.) (1994), *Armi indiane. Rivoluzione e profezie maya nel Chiapas messicano,* Milano: Edizioni Colibrì, Milano.

Cicolella, O. (1993), "Le donne tra crisi ambientale e sviluppo insostenibile", in *Res,* No. 7, gennaio-marzo.

Dalla Costa, G.F. (1989) 1991 2 ed., *La riproduzione nel sottosviluppo. Lavoro delle donne, famiglia e Stato nel Venezuela degli anni '70,* Milano: Franco Angeli.

Dalla Costa, M. and James S. (1972), *The Power of Women and the Subversion of the Community.* Bristol: Falling Wall Press.

_____. (1978), *Note sulla giornata lavorativa in Marx. Appunti da un lettorato del Capitale.* Padova: Cleup.

_____. e Dalla Costa, G.F. (eds.) (1993), 1995 2nd ed. *Donne e politiche del debito. Condizione e lavoro femminile nella crisi del debito internazionale,* Milano: FrancoAngeli. (English translation: *Paying the Price: Women and the Politics of International Economic Strategy,* London: Zed Books 1995).

_____. (1995), "Capitalism and Reproduction," in Bonefeld W. et al. (eds.) (1995), *Open Marxism,* Vol. III, London: Pluto Press.

———. (1997), "Some Notes on Neoliberalism, on Land and on the Food Question", in *Canadian Women Studies, Les Cahiers de la Femme*, Vol. 17, No. 2, Spring.

———. (1998) "The Native in Us, The Land We Belong To", in: *Common Sense* No. 23, July, Herlington, York, Great Britain.

Dag Hammarskjold Foundation (1975), *What now? Another Development*, Uppsala.

Del Genio, G. (1994), "La Banca inonda il Bangladesh", in *Capitalismo Natura Socialismo*, No. 1, Jan.-April.

Duràn de Huerta, M. (a cura di) (1995), *Io, Marcos,* Feltrinelli, Milano. *The Economist,* 6.01.1990.

Federici, S. Fortunati, L. (1984), *Il Grande Calibano. Storia del corpo sociale ribelle nella prima fase del capitale,* Milano: FrancoAngeli.

Federici, S. (1992), "Development and Underdevelopment in Nigeria," in Midnight Notes Collective (1992).

Federici, S. (1993), *Crisi economica e politica demografica nell'Africa sub-sahariana. Il caso della Nigeria,* in Dalla Costa M. and Dalla Costa G.F. (eds.)

Fisher, J. (1993), *Out of the Shadows. Women, Resistance and Politics in South America,* London: Latin America Bureau.

Fortunati, L. (1981), *L'arcano della riproduzione. Casalinghe, prostitute, operai e capitale,* Padova: Marsilio (English translation: *The Arcane of Reproduction,* New York: Autonomedia,1995).

George, S (1988), *A Fate Worse than Debt,* Harmondsworth: Penguin Group, England.

George, S. (1992), *Il boomerang del debito,* Roma: Edizioni Lavoro. (original title *The Debt Boomerang*).

George, S. e Sabelli, F. (1994), *Crediti senza frontiere,* Torino: Edizioni Gruppo Abele. (original title *Faith and Credit. The World Bank's Secular Empire*).

Gisfredi, P. (1993), "Teorie dello sviluppo ed egemonia del Nord", in *Res,* No. 7, January-March.

Kuppers, G. (1992), *Compañeras. Voices from the Latin American Women's Movement,* London: Latin American Bureau.

Gomez, Luis E. (1994), "La nuova cavalcata di Emiliano Zapata" in *Riff Raff,* March.

Il Manifesto, 8.02.1994.

Il Manifesto, 8.06.1994.

Marx, K. (1976), *Capital. A Critique of Political Economy*, Volume One, London, Penguin.

Matsui, Y. (1989), *Women's Asia*, Zed Books, London.

Il Mattino di Padova, 4.06.1994.

Mellor, M. (1992), *Breaking the Boundaries. Towards a Feminist Green Socialism*, Virago Press, London.

Mellor, M. (1993), "Ecofemminismo e ecosocialismo. Dilemmi di essenzialismo e materialismo", in *Capitalismo Natura Socialismo*, March.

Michel, A., Fatoumata Diarra A., Agbessi Dos Santos H., (1981), *Femmes et multinationales*, Karthala, Paris.

Michel, A. (1988), "Femmes et development en Amerique Latine et aux Caraibes", in *Recherches feministes*, vol. 1, No. 2.

Michel, A. (1993), "Donne africane, sviluppo e rapporto Nord-Sud," in Dalla Costa M. and Dalla Costa G.F.(eds.)

Midnight Notes Collective (ed.) (1992), *Midnight Oil. Work, Energy, War 1973-1992*, Autonomedia, New York, N.Y.

Mies, M. (1986), *Patriarchy and Accumulation on a World Scale. Women in the International Division of Labor*, Zed Books, London.

Mies, M. (1992), "Global is in the Local," report at the Mount Saint Vincent University, Halifax, Canada, 25.02.

Mies, M., Bennholdt-Thomsen, V., von Werlhof, C., (1988), *Women: the Last Colony*, Zed Books, London.

Mies, M. and Shiva V. (1993), *Ecofeminism*, Zed Books, London.

O'Connor J., (1992), "La seconda contraddizione del capitalismo: cause e conseguenze", in *Capitalismo Natura Socialismo*, No. 6, December.

Potts, L. (1990), *The World Labor Market. A History of Migration*, Zed Books, London.

Raymond, J. (1989), "The International Traffic in Women: Women Used in Systems of Surrogacy and Reproduction" in *Reproductive and Genetic Engineering*, vol. 2, n. 1.

Raymond, J. (1989), "At Issue. Children for Organ Export?" in *Reproductive and Genetic Engineering*, vol. 2, n. 3.

La Repubblica, 17.05.1994.

Rich, B. (1994), *Mortgaging the Earth. The World Bank, Environmental Impoverishment and the Crisis of Development,* Boston:Beacon Press.

Ricoveri, G. (1994), "La sinistra fa fatica ad ambientarsi", in *Capitalismo Natura Socialismo*, No. 1, January-April.

Shiva, V. (1989), *Staying Alive: Women, Ecology and Survival in India,* London: Zed Books.

Shiva, V. (1993), *Monocultures of the Mind: Perpectives on Biodiversity and Biotechnology*, London: Zed Books.

Sawyer, R. (1988), *Children Enslaved*, London: Routledge, New York.

Smith, J., Wallerstein, I., Evers, I., (eds.), (1984), *Households and the World Economy,* Sage, Beverly Hills (CA).

Sparr, P. (ed.) (1994), *Mortgaging Women's Lives: Feminist Critiques of Structural Adjustment,* London: Zed Books.

Wakefield, E. Gibbon, (1833), *England and America. A Comparison of the Social and Political State of both Nations*, London.

Wallerstein, I. (1974), *The Modern World System,* New York: Academic Press.

Women's Action Agenda 21 (1991), in *World Women's Congress for a Healthy Planet*, Official Report, 8-12 November, Miami, Florida, USA, United Nations, New York.

Zapatistas! Documents of the New Mexican Revolution, (1994), New York: Autonomedia.

Reproduction and Feminist Struggle in the New International Division of Labor

Silvia Federici

Introduction

Starting with the recognition that patriarchy and accumulation on a world scale constitute the structural and ideological framework within which women's reality today has to be understood, the feminist movement worldwide cannot but challenge this framework, along with the sexual and the international division of labour which are bound up with it. (Mies 1986)

.....capitalist development has always been *unsustainable* because of its *human impact*. To understand this point, all we need to do is to take the viewpoint of those who have been and continue to be killed by it. A presupposition of capitalism's birth was the sacrifice of a large part of humanity—mass extermination, the production of hunger and misery, slavery, violence and terror. Its continuation requires the same presuppositions. (M. Dalla Costa, 1995)

It is generally recognized that over the last two decades the women's liberation movement has acquired an international dimension, as feminist groups and movements have formed in every part of the world and, in the wake of the United Nations sponsored global conferences on women, feminist networks and initiatives have also grown worldwide. Thus, there seems to be today a broader understanding of the problems that women are facing in different countries than at any other time in the past.

However, if we examine the perspectives that inspire feminist politics in the United States and Europe, we must conclude that most feminists have not yet reckoned with the changes that the new global economy[1] has produced in the conditions of women, or have recognized their implications for feminist organizing. In particular, many feminists fail to acknowledge that the restructuring of the world economy is responsible not only for the global spread of poverty, but also for the emergence of a new colonial order, that deepens the divisions among women, and that this new colonialism must be a main target for feminist struggles if women's liberation is to be possible. Presently, despite the fact that most feminists, in the United States and Europe, are concerned with global issues, such an awareness is missing. Thus, even those who are critical of the global economy and of the policies pursued by international agencies like the World Bank and the International Monetary Fund (I.M.F.), often settle for reformist positions that condemn gender discrimination, but leave the structural problems connected with the global hegemony of capitalist relations intact. Many feminists, for instance, deplore the "unequal burden" that structural adjustment and other austerity programs place on women (Beneria and Feldman eds.1992; Elson 1992; Bakker 1994),[2] and recommend that development agencies pay more attention to women's needs, or incentivize women's "participation in development planning." More rarely they take an open stand against the programs themselves, or the agencies that impose them, or acknowledge that poverty and economic exploitation are across the world a male destiny as well.[3] There is also a tendency to think of the problems that women internationally are facing through the category of 'human rights,' and therefore to privilege legal reform as the primary arena for governmental intervention,[4] an approach that again fails to challenge the international economic order and the economic exploitation upon which it is based. Also the discourse on violence against women, has generally centered on rape and domestic violence along the lines set by the United Nations[5], while it has often ignored the structural violence inherent in the logic of capitalist accumulation: the violence of economic policies that condemn millions of women, men and children to starve, the violence that accompanies the land expropriations demanded by the World Bank for its "development projects" and, not last, the violence of the wars and counter-insurgency programs that, through the 1980s and 1990s, have bloodied almost every corner of the world and represent the other side of development.

As I have suggested, one of the main limits of contemporary feminist politics is that they are not strategically rooted in an analysis of the changes that have taken place, since the late 1970s, in the material conditions of women's lives, as a consequence of the restructuring of the world economy and the international division of labor. We do have many case studies detailing the impoverishment that women across the world have experienced, and the new forms of exploitation to which they are being subjected. What is often missing, however, is an overall analysis of the ways in which women's work, and particularly the work of reproduction, has been restructured internationally, and the implications of this restructuring for the possibility of a feminist international movement. These are the questions that I address in this essay.

My first objective is to demonstrate that the global economy, and the new international division of labor, are rooted in the crisis of social reproduction provoked, in the Third World, by the policies adopted by international capital since the late 1970s. For millions of people in Africa, Asia, Latin America would not have become dependent on the world economy for their survival except for the fact that they lost every means of subsistence, as a result of war and economic "adjustment." Second, on the pauperization of the Third World an international reorganization of reproduction has been built that transfers from the "North" to the "South" a significant part of the work required for the reproduction of the metropolitan work-force, which means that third world women are being "integrated" in the world economy as producers of labor-power to be used and "consumed" in the industrialized regions of the world, as well as producers of commodities for export. Last, I argue that these processes have opened up a crisis in feminist politics, as they have introduced new divisions and hierarchies among women, that consolidate the mechanisms of female exploitation. This, I argue, is a crisis that must be addressed as a matter of political priority, if international feminism in the "metropoles" is to be a women's liberation project and not simply a vehicle for the further "rationalization" of the world economic order.

The New International Division of Labor (NIDL)

In order to evaluate the consequences of the new international division of labor (NIDL) for the conditions of women it is necessary, however, to reconsider what we mean by this concept; for the conventional theory provides a partial vision of the changes that have occurred on this terrain. As is well-known, the NIDL is usually identified with the restructuring of commodity production that has taken place internationally since the mid 1970s when, in response to intensifying labor conflict, the multinational corporations began to relocate in the "developing countries" part of their industrial outfits, above all in the labor-intensive sectors, like textile and electronics. The new international division of labor is thus equated with the formation of Free Trade Zones (FTZ)-

-industrial zones free from any regulation and organized for export-oriented production—and with the capacity acquired by the transnational corporations (TNCs) to restructure their productive activities on the basis of a true "global assembly line" (Michalet 1976; Nash and Fernandez-Kelly eds. 1983; Grunwald and Flamm 1985; Alger 1988; Ward 1990; Carnoy et al 1993).[6]

It is on the basis of this theory that both the media and economic planners have relaunched the myth of capitalism as the great equalizer, and the promoter of "interconnectedness," this time presumably achieved on a planetary scale. As the argument goes, we are witnessing the industrialization of the third world. This process (we are told) will both eliminate the hierarchies that historically have characterized the international division of labor, and have a positive impact also on the sexual division of labor. For the women who form the bulk of the work-force in the Free Trade Zones presumably benefit from their engagement in industrial labor, by gaining a new independence and the skills necessary to compete on the international labor market (Lim 1983 : 81).

Although accepted by neo-liberal economists,[7] this theory has not been exempt from criticism.[8] Already in *The New Helots* (1987), Robin Cohen observed that the movement of capital from the "North" to the "South" was not quantitatively sufficient to justify the hypothesis of a "New" International Division of Labor. By the end of the 1980s, in fact, only 14% of the world manufacturing activities was taking place in "developing countries," and the industrial "boom" was concentrated in a few areas: South Korea, Honk Kong, Taiwan, Mexico (Cohen 1987: 242-243; Guelfi 1985: 142). It has also become evident that the introduction of Free Trade Zones, by its nature, does not develop the industrial basis of the host countries, nor does it have a positively effect on their employment levels, while it is a drain on the local resources (Nash and Fernandez-Kelly eds., 1983). As for the women employed in the Free Trade Zones, their organizations have often denounced that this work is a form of "underdevelopment," if not a hidden form of slavery, both from the viewpoint of income levels and of the technological know-how. (McAfee 1991: 87-89; Sistren 1986).[9] As is well-known, wages in the Free Trade Zones are kept below subsistence and are many times lower than the minimum wages in the industrialized countries; [10] in addition, women there are forced to work long hours in very unsafe conditions, they are persecuted when they try to organize and are subjected to constant abuses, like daily body searches, to check if they take anything out of the plants, compulsory forms of birth control, to ensure that they do not get pregnant and disrupt production (National Labor Committee 1995), and cruel prohibitions concerning their movements. In these "free" zones, women are often locked up, to make sure that they fill their 'quotas,' so that, for hours and hours, they cannot take a break from a job that, at times, continues even into the night. As a result, both in Mexico and China, hundreds have died, because they could not flee from buildings shaken by an earthquake or burning up in flames.[11]

These, however, are not the only, or the main reasons why the conventional theory about the new international division of labor should be revised. Most important is the fact that the only area of work and economic activity which the conventional theory recognizes is the production of commodities, while it gives no attention to *reproduction*, despite two decades of feminist writings and debates showing the crucial role of this process for the accumulation of capital. Thus, the conventional theory of the NIDL has practically nothing to say about the macroscopic changes that the expansion of capitalist relations has introduced in the reproduction of labor-power and the conditions of social reproduction in the third world. It is significant that the only aspect of reproduction mentioned by theorists of the NIDL is the impact of work in the Free Trade Zones on women's family life and housework management. [12] This, however, is only part of a much wider process that has devastated people's lives throughout the third world, and without which the introduction of the Free Trade Zones, and the restructuring of the international division of labor, would not have been possible.

If we look at the globalization of the economy and the NIDL from the viewpoint of both production and reproduction, we arrive at a very different conception of what both these developments represent, and the mechanisms and policies that sustain them. We can recognize, first, that the expansion of capitalist relations is premised today as well (no less than at the times of the English Enclosures, the *conquista* of the Americas, and the Atlantic slave-trade) on the separation of the producers from the means of their (re)production. This means that the global economy is built upon a major restructuring of social reproduction and class relations worldwide, designed to destroy any economic activity that is not market-oriented, beginning with subsistence farming, and that it has been leading to the formation, in every part of the third world, of a proletariat deprived of any means of reproduction, and thus forced to depend on monetary relations for its survival, even though it is most often deprived of any access to a monetary income.

This is the situation that has been created in much of Africa, Asia, South America by the World Bank and the International Monetary Fund (I.M.F.) through the "debt crisis," the enforcement of Structural Adjustment Programs and the politics of economic liberalization which, combined, are the pillars of the new world economic order, precisely because they have separated millions of people from any income and means of reproduction, and have forced them to depend upon, and compete on the international labor market.

If we look at the NIDL from the viewpoint of these economic policies we also draw a picture far different from that projected by the advocates for the New World Order.[13] The devastating consequences of these policies for the populations affected are by now so abundantly and unequivocally documented (Altvater et al 1987; Gai 1991; McAfee 199; Rau 1991) that even the World Bank has had to concede to possible mistakes. What needs to be stressed, however, is that these policies have undermined the conditions of social reproduction in much of the third world, and erased the most important achievement of the anti-colonial struggle, i.e. the commitment by the new independent states to invest in the reproduction of the national proletariat. They have also led to a state of generalized poverty that has no precedents in the post colonial period.

The crisis of social reproduction in the third world has directly resulted from the massive cuts in government spending for social services, the continuous currency devaluations, the wage freezes, the liberalization and privatization policies that constitute the core of 'structural adjustment' and "neo-liberalism." As part of these policies, we must also mention the ongoing land expropriations that are being carried on in many third world regions, in homage to the commercialization of agriculture and the privatization of land property relations,[14] and because of the increasing institution of a state of endemic warfare. Endless wars, massacres, entire populations in flight from their lands and turned into refugees or exposed to famines: these are not just the consequences of a dramatic impoverishment that intensifies the contrasts due to ethnic, political or religious differences, as the media encourage us to believe. Rather, they are the necessary complements of the privatization process (Hanlon 1991; Macrae and Zwi 1994; de Waal 1997), and of the attempt to create a world where nothing escapes the logic of profit, the ultimate means to expropriate populations who, until recently, had access to some land and natural resources (forests, rivers) which now are being appropriated by multinational corporations.

Structural Adjustment and economic liberalization have also dismantled the local industry in much of the third world, and marked the end of the development plans pursued in the 1960s on the basis of 'import-substitution,' that were supposed to guarantee third world nations a certain degree of industrial autonomy. For opening the domestic markets to foreign imports has allowed the transnational corporations to flood them with their products, with which the local industries could never compete.[15] The introduction of Free Trade Zones, wherever it has taken place, has not remedied this situation, but has only exploited it, as the impoverishment of the population in so many third world countries has enabled foreign companies to impose wages below subsistence levels. This is the reason why the Free Trade Zones function today primarily as a springboard for emigration (Sassen 1990: 99-114).[16]

That the industrialization of the third world is a myth is also proven by the fact that, throughout the 1980s and 1990s, the transfer of capital and industries from the first to the third world has been superseded by the transfer of capital and labor from the third to the first world. The scale of this phenomenon can be measured by the fact that the remittances of the emigrants represent the second largest international monetary flow after the revenues of the oil companies, and in some parts of the third world (e.g. in Mexico) entire villages are dependent upon them. According to World Bank statistics, from $24 billion in the 1970s, remittances have grown in the 1980s to $65 billion, and these figures refer only to the remittances that pass through the banks and do not include those "in kind," like the furniture, TV sets and other goods that emigrants bring back with them in their visits home (Stalker 1994: 122-123).

The first consequence of the impoverishment to which economic liberalization has condemned the third world proletariat has been, in fact, the take off of a vast migratory movement from the "South" to the "North," that has followed the transfer of capital caused by the payment of the external debt. This migratory movement of biblical proportions,[17] structurally connected to the new economic order and bound to globalize the labor-market, is a telling evidence of the ways in which the international division of labor has being restructured (Colatrella 1999).

It demonstrates that the debt crisis and the politics of "structural adjustment" have determined a situation of *global apartheid*, as they have transformed the Third World into an immense pool of labor, that functions with respect to the metropolitan economies in the same way as the "homelands" functioned with respect to the white areas in South Africa. Not accidentally, it is regulated by a similar system of passes and restrictions,[18] which guarantees that in the countries of arrival immigrants are twice devalued, both as immigrants and (increasingly) as undocumented workers. (Contrary to what is commonly assumed, it is by introducing restrictions that force immigrant workers to be undocumented that the state can use immigration to cut the cost of labor. For only if foreign immigrants are socially and politically vulnerable, can immigration be used to contain the demands of the local working class) (Sassen-Koob 1983:184).

For those who cannot emigrate, or do not have access to remittances sent by emigrants, the alternative is a life of hardships and a burden of work hardly imaginable by people who live in the 'advanced' capitalist countries. Lack of food, medicines, potable water, electricity, schools, viable roads, mass unemployment, are now the daily reality in most of the third world. It is a reality that is reflected in the constant outbreak of epidemics, in the disintegration of family life,[19] in the phenomenon of children who live in the streets or work in near slavery conditions (Sawyer 1988). This reality is also reflected in the intense struggles, often taking the form of riots, by which every day, in the 'adjusted' countries, the population resists the closing of the local industries, the hike in the prices of basic goods and transports, and the financial squeeze to which they are subjected in the name of paying the debt (Walton and Seddon 1994).

Just on the basis of this situation, it should be possible to agree that any feminist project that is concerned exclusively with sexual discrimination, and fails to place the feminization of poverty in the context of the advance of capitalist relations, is condemned to irrelevance and/or co-optation. In addition, if we examine the restructuring that the new international division of labor has introduced in the work of reproduction, we clearly see that either the feminist movement opposes this process, or it becomes the accomplice of a deeply anti-feminist politics. For an essential aspect of the NIDL is an international redistribution of reproduction work (as well as a redistribution of production) that not only creates deeper divisions among women, but also strengthens the hierarchies inherent to the sexual division of labor.

Emigration, Reproduction and International Feminism

If it is true that the remittances sent by emigrants constitute the main international monetary flow, after the revenues of the oil companies, then we must conclude that the most important commodity that the third world exports to the first world today is labor. In other words, also in the present phase of capitalism, capitalist accumulation is above all the accumulation of workers, and today this process occurs primarily in the third world. This means, however, that a significant part of the reproduction work necessary to produce the metropolitan work-force is performed by third world women. Behind emigration, in fact, an immense "gift" of domestic labor is hidden.[20] It is labor that is never taken into account in the computation of the third world's external debt and yet is essential for the accumulation process in the industrialized countries, where emigration serves to offset demographic decline, to keep wages down, and to transfer surplus from the colonies to the "metropoles" (Nash and Fernandez-Kelly eds.1983: 178-179). Thus, *through emigration, third world women directly contribute to the accumulation of wealth in the 'advanced' capitalist countries,* not only as producers of goods but also as (re)producers of workers, for the factories, the hospitals, agriculture and commerce. This is a fact that the international feminist movement must acknowledge, both in order to unmask what "integration in the global economy" actually involves, and to demystify the ideology of "aid to the third world," that hides an immense theft of unpaid work at the expense of third world women.

In the course of the 1980s and 1990s, other phenomena have developed that demonstrate the attempt to redistribute the work of reproduction of the metropolitan work-force on the shoulders of third world women. Among the most significant we must include :

(a) the employment, on a large scale, of emigrant women coming from Asia, Africa, the Caribbean Islands, South America, as domestics in the industrialized countries, as well as in the oil producing countries of the Middle East[21]. As Cynthia Enloe has observed, the economic politics of the International Monetary Fund have enabled the governments in Europe, the United States and Canada to resolve the housework crisis that was at the origin of the feminist movement, and to "free" thousand of women for extra-domestic work. The employment of Filipino or Mexican women who, for a modest sum, clean houses, raise children, prepare meals, take care of the elderly, has allowed many middle class women to avoid a burden of work that they did not want, or could no longer perform, without, at the same time, reducing their standard of living (Enloe 1990: 178-179). Enloe adds that many European and North American women have justified this choice, with the illusion that, by hiring a domestic worker, they are contributing to resolve the problem of poverty in the world. However, this solution represents a set back for the feminist struggle; for solidarity among women enters into crisis when what brings women together is a "maids and madams" relation, which is all the more problematic as it is tainted by all the social biases that still surround housework—for instance, that it is not real work and, therefore, should be paid as little as possible, that it must be accompanied by an emotional involvement in the lives of the people it reproduces, that it does not have well defined boundaries (Romero 1992: 97-112). The employment of a domestic worker, moreover, once again makes women (rather than the state) responsible for reproduction, and weakens the struggle against the sexual division of labor in the family, since it spares women the task of confronting their male partners concerning the sharing of the housework (ibid.: 102). As for immigrant women, taking jobs as domestics is a painful choice, since the work is low paid, and demands that they care for other people's families while they often had to leave their own behind, and face many years of loneliness, and the dangers connected to a position that socially and legally is very vulnerable. Not accidentally, the destiny of Flor Contemplacion, the Filipino domestic worker who was hung in Singapore in March 1995, upon the false charges of her employer, has become a symbol of their condition for the women who from the third world go abroad to work as domestic workers.

(b) the development of a vast international *baby-market*, organized through the mechanism of adoptions. Already, by the end of the 1980s, it was calculated that an adopted child entered the United States every 48 minutes (Raymond 1994: 145) and, at the beginning of the 1990s, from South Korea alone, 5,700 children were being exported yearly to the United States (Chira 1988). Today, what feminists have described as the international "traffic of children" has spread also in the former socialist countries, above all in Poland and Russia, where the discovery of agencies that sell children (in 1994 more than 1,500 were exported just to the United States) has fueled a national scandal (Stanley 1994, 1995). We have also seen the development of *baby farms*, where children are produced specifically for export (Raymond 1994:141-142), and the increasing employment of third world women as surrogate mothers (Raymond 1989a: 51-52). Surrogacy, as well as adoption, allow women from the 'advanced' capitalist countries to avoid the risk of interrupting their career, or jeopardizing their health, to have a child. In turn, third world governments benefit from the fact that the sale of every child brings foreign currency to their coffers; and the World Bank and the International Monetary Fund tacitly approve this practice, because the sale of children serves to correct "demographic excesses," and is in harmony with the principle that debtor nations must export all the resources they have (Raymond 1989b, 1995).

(c) the massification, in some countries of Asia (Thailand, South Korea, Philippines), of the *sex-industry* and *sex-tourism*, that serve an international clientele ranging from tourists to the employees of Japanese companies to whom, in recent years, "pleasure trips" have been offered as a bonus, to the U.S. Army which, since the Vietnam War, has used these countries as Rest and Recreation areas (Thorbeck 1987; Enloe 1990, 1993; Truong 1990; Raymond 1989, 1994; Barry 1984, 1995). By the end of the 1980s, it was calculated that, in Thailand alone, out of a population of 52 million people, one million women worked in the sex-industry.

To this we must add the enormous increase in the number of women from the third world, or the former socialist countries, who work as prostitutes in Europe, the United States and Japan, often in conditions of slavery (Sawyer 1988; Barry 1995), as in the case of the Thai women recently found in a New York brothel, where they were kept prisoners by the organization that had paid their trips to this country, and convinced them to come to the United States with the promise of a job (Goldberg 1995) (22).

(d) the "traffic" of "mail-order brides" that, in the 1980s, has developed on an international scale (Villapando 1989; Raymond 1994; Narayan 1995; Barry 1995). In the U.S. alone, about 3,500 men every year marry women chosen by mail-order. In the great majority of cases, the brides are young women coming from the poorest regions of South East Asia, or from South America, although, more recently, also women from Russia and other former socialist countries have chosen this means of emigration. In 1979, 7,759 Filipino women have left their country by this means (Barry 1995 : 154). The traffic in 'mail-order brides' exploits, on one side, the desperate poverty of women and, on the other, the sexism and racism of European and American men, who want a wife over whom they can exert a total control, and count on the vulnerability of women who are forced to make this choice.

(e) the massification of the tourist industry that relies primarily on the labor of women as hotel maids, laundry workers, cooks, artisans (80% of the work-force in the great tourist hotels is made of women) (Enloe 1990: 34-35; 1993: 113-115).

Taken as a whole, these phenomena demonstrate that the new international division of labor is the vehicle of a fiercely anti-feminist political project and that, far from being a means of female emancipation, the expansion of capitalist relations intensifies the exploitation of women. First, the new international division of labor brings back, at the center of the organization of work, forms of slavery that we would have imagined extinct with the demise of the colonial empires. Further, it reproposes the image of woman as a sexual object and breeder; and it deepens the divisions among women, through a specialization and fixation of tasks that reduce our life possibilities, and introduce among us new hierarchies and stratifications, objectively jeopardizing the possibility of a common struggle.

The new international division of labor means that many third world women must work as domestics or prostitutes, at home or abroad, because no other options are available to them; meanwhile many first world women, particularly among the middle class, are liberated from housework, but at the price of becoming like men, that is, at the price of not having time for a family and children, not to mention time for friendships, community relations and political activity. Thus, the NIDL strengthens the sexual division of labor; it strengthens the separation of production from reproduction, and separates not only women from men, but women from women, instituting among women a relation similar to that which existed between white and black women, under the *apartheid* regime in South Africa.[23]

The anti-feminist character of the new international division of labor is so evident that we can ask to what extent it has been the work of the "invisible hand" of the market, or it has been a consciously planned response to the struggles that women have waged, both in the third world and in the metropoles, against discrimination, unpaid labor and "underdevelopment" in all their forms. Be it as it may, it is obvious that in Europe and the United States as well, feminists must organize against the alternatives which the new international division of labor forces upon women, and the recolonization attempt on which it is based, which includes 'structural adjustment,' the politics of military intervention, the global take over by the transnational corporations.

In addition, feminists must reopen their struggle with the state on the terrain of reproduction.

It is not enough, in fact, to condemn any particular practice or form of behavior, if we want to put an end to the divisions that are being created among women internationally. It is not enough, for instance, to criticize the women who employ domestic workers, as it is often done among feminists, as if these women were

especially insensitive to their "sisters" needs. For as long as reproduction remains an individual or family responsibility, many
women may not have much of a choice but to hire a domestic, in
a context where more than 50% of women, both in Europe and
the United States, have an extra-domestic job, and work-condi-
tions that do not allow for much "flexibility." This is one reason
why many women who have young children are on welfare; but
even this alternative is no longer available, at least in the United
States, as welfare is on the way to extinction, the object of a reform that is practically abolishing it (Firestone 1995). There is
also the danger that condemning the employment of domestic
workers, without proposing and struggling for a real alternative,
may reinforce the illusion that housework is reducible at will, and
can be easily combined with another job, that is, the illusion that
housework is not necessary work. This is an illusion that has
plagued feminist politics in the 1970s, and we now know that we
have paid a high price for it, since it has meant that at present
most women do not even have access to child care. There is no
doubt, infact, that if in Europe and the U.S. the feminist movement had concentrated on making the state recognize the work of
reproduction as work and take financial responsibility for it, we
would not have witnessed the dismantling of even the few services available in this field and a colonial solution to the "housework problem."[24] Today as well, a feminist mobilization forcing
the state to pay for the reproduction of labor, would be more
effective than any moral condemnation to put an end to the employment of domestics, or to change and improve the conditions
of this employment and open the way to a new international solidarity among women.

Similar considerations apply to the efforts that feminists have
made to convince governments to criminalize domestic violence,
the "traffic" in women, and penalize any form of sexual discrimination. As crucially important as these initiatives have
been, they appear limited in their capacity to liberate women, as
they do not go to the roots of the abuses being perpetrated against

them, nor do they reckon with the plans of international capital and the agencies by which its globalization is promoted.

Will more severe punishments, for instance, remedy the abject poverty that leads parents, in some countries, to sell their children into prostitution? And how can third world governments commit themselves to upgrade the conditions of women when they are required by the World Bank and the International Monetary Fund to cut all social spending, and to adopt the strictest austerity programs? How, for instance, can third world governments give women equal access to education, or better health care, when they are required by structural adjustment, to cut all subsidies to public education (CAFA n. 2, 1991; n. 4, 1993; n. 5, 1993), healthcare, and, in many cases, to introduce fees even in elementary schools? (Z.M. Roy-Campbell: 220). And, again, how can parents be convinced to send their daughters to schools when even their sons who obtain a diploma remain unemployed? (Federici 1995). What meaning can the passing of a law, or even a United Nations declaration against all forms of sexual discrimination, have in this context?

If international feminism and "global sisterhood" are to be possible, it is indispensable that women in the first world make their own the struggle that third world women are carrying on against structural adjustment, the payment of the external debt, the introduction of intellectual property laws, which are the means by which the new international division of labor is being organized, and the strongest evidence that capitalism is unsustainable for the majority of the world population (Mies 1986, 1988a; Dalla Costa 1995). It must also be stressed again, as third world feminists have already so often done (Jonson-Odim 1991), that the inequalities that exist between women at the international level also pollute the politics of the feminist movement. For access to greater resources (travel, grants, publications and rapid means of communications) has allowed European and North American feminists to impose their agendas on the occasion of global conferences, and to play a hegemonic role in the definition of what feminism and feminist struggles must be (ibid.: 323-324).

The power relations generated by the new international division of labor are also reflected in the role that women play in the metropolitan Non Governmental Organizations (NGOs) that finance projects for women in the third world. Beside mobilizing third world women's unpaid labor, to compensate for the loss of social services and collective entitlements produced by structural adjustment, it is obvious that these projects create a patron-client power relation among women, not unlike that existing between "madams and maids." For it is the prerogative of the metropolitan NGO members to decide which projects to finance, how to evaluate them, which women in the community to take as points of reference, all of this with practically no accountability to the women whose labor they organize. It should be noticed that the function that the metropolitan non-governmental organizations play with regard to third world women is in part a neo-liberal response to the weakening of the role of the husband and the state in the third world as supervisors of women's work (through wage cuts and cuts in the budget devoted to social reproduction). As many men have left their homes to emigrate, or do not have the money to support a family, and as the state, in most of the third world, has been advised to defund social reproduction, *a new patriarchal regime is being enforced that aims to place women in the third world under the control of the World Bank, the International Monetary Fund and the numerous organizations that manage "income generating projects" and "aid" programs.* This new patriarchy relies on the collaboration of European and North American women who, like new missionaries, are being recruited to train women in the 'colonies' to develop the attitudes necessary to become integrated in the global economy.[25]

Conclusion

An analysis of the new international division of labor shows the limits of a feminist political strategy that accepts the worldwide expansion of capitalist relations, and does not place the struggle against gender-based discrimination in an anti-capitalist framework. It shows that not only does capitalist development continue to be the production of poverty, disease, war and death, but it can survive only by creating new divisions within the proletariat internationally—divisions that, to this day, are the main obstacle to the realization of a society free from exploitation.

It is in this sense that feminist politics must subvert the new international division of labor (Mies 1986) and the project of economic globalization from which it originates. These are the politics that inspire the struggles of "grassroots feminists" and the indigenous peoples' movements across the planet—struggles that demand the return of the expropriated lands, the non-payment of the external debt and the abolition of 'adjustment' and privatization. These are also the politics of the third world feminists who, for years, have been reminding us that the discourse on equality cannot be separated from a critique of the role of international capital in the plunder and recolonization of their countries, and that the struggles that women are carrying on, on a daily basis, in order to survive, are political struggles and feminist struggles (Fisher 1933; Kuppers 1992; Caipora Women's Group 1993).

Notes

1. We speak of the "new" global economy because, as "world system theorists" (I. Wallerstein 1974) and feminists theorists (M. Mies 1986) have often underlined, capitalism was born and in each phase has consolidated as a "world economic system."
2. Consider what Diane Elson writes in *Unequal Burden* (Elson is a British economist who has worked with the Food and Agriculture Organization (FAO) and the Swedish International Development Agency (SIDA), and is the editor of *Male Bias in the Development Process* (1990):

   Restructuring opens up new opportunities as well as closing old opportunities. Oppressed and disadvantaged groups find that change creates the conditions for new forms of struggle. Trying to resist the tide of change... rarely works. A more creative approach that tries to influence the terms of the restructuring... may have more chance of success.

It would be overoptimistic to expect such an approach to fully protect oppressed and disadvantaged groups from the adverse effects of a crisis. But out of the crisis may come some progressive transformation of the conditions of struggle of oppressed and disadvantaged groups and the forging of new links between them... The very poorest people, on the barest margins of survival, may be unable to do more than desperately seek to adapt to the adverse conditions through existing strategies; and even in this they may fail... But for those able to survive there may be the possibility of strategies going beyond survival to transformation of existing social relations of oppression and disadvantage. (pp. 29-30)

In order to mitigate the effects of structural adjustment on the conditions of women, Elson recommends that male privileges be reduced and suggests that new taxes be introduced on cigarettes and alcohol, because this type of consumption drains the family's resources available to women (pp. 41-42).

3. Exemplary are the recommendations made by Pamela Sparr at the end of *Mortgaging Women's Lives, Feminist Critiques of Structural Adjustment* (1994), one of the first books to document the impact of structural adjustment on the conditions of women. Sparr proposes that the World Bank and the IMF:

(a) "Include gender and distribution by household as criteria in social impact assessment for project and policy lending."

(b) "En-gage in broad consultations about proposed policy and project loans" and "[m]ake the consultations politically and culturally safe for women" (p.196).

(c) "Develop an ongoing monitoring and feed-back loop concerning the impact of loans. Include women and households as factors to be monitored."

(d) "Make gender sensitivity and encouragement of local participation in the lending process (especially among women) features of all staff's jobs and major criteria for staff career enhancement and upward mobility".

(e) "Ensure that, at all times, at least one of the three members of the World Bank's independent inspection panel is a woman."

(f) "Inform women's groups that they have the right to bring a complaint to the inspection panel. Educate panel members and NGOs about how changes in women's conditions are ground to bring a complaint."

(g) Engage in gender training among all staff, including the I.M.F. and World Bank.

(h) "Raise gender concerns to the level of a vice president at the World Bank." (197) Five other similar recommendations follow. In order to reform structural adjustment, Sparr proposes that a "more creative" (but not better specified) solution" be adopted with regard to the unpaid work done by women in the home, in the community, in the fields; and in addition that public spending be geared to eliminating "gender" differences; that taxes be used to create day-care centers, so as to alleviate women's double burden—all measures, Sparr assures us, that are compatible with a neo-classic model of economics. Similar recommendations are offered in an appendix to J. Kerr ed., *Ours By Right* (1993).

4. A significant document with respect to this strategy is the collection of essays contained in *Ours By Right. Women's Rights are Human Rights* (Kerr ed. 1993), where programmatically all the problems that women face—including poverty and economic exploitation—are treated as "human rights violations" and attributed to the unequal treatment to which women are subject (pp. 4-5). The proposed remedy, then, is a better implementation of the Universal Declaration of Human Rights adopted by the United Nations in 1948 and the ratification by every country of the United Nations Convention on the Elimination of all Forms of Discrimination against Women (CEDAW) that the United Nations have adopted in 1979 (ibid.).

According to Kerr, this last Convention "provides a comprehensive framework for challenging the various forces that have created and maintained discrimination based on sex" (p.5). As the essays contained in the book demonstrate, on a practical level, adopting the methodology of human rights means to document the abuses against women, to publicize them with the international agencies, to monitor the activities of the United Nations and the agencies presiding over "aid" and cooperation with the third world.

5. See the essay by Dorothy Q. Thomas "Holding Governments Accountable by Public Pressure". In J. Kerr ed., (1993): p.82-88.

6. See *The Global Assembly Line* (1986), a documentary that examines the internationalization of commodity production and the condition of work in the Free Trade Zones, with particular reference to Mexico and the Philippines.

7. For a recent version of this theory see the report prepared by the participants in the World Economic Forum, on the occasion of their annual meeting held in Davos (Switzerland) in the summer of 1994. In this report, however, the prevailing attitude is one of alarm, in front of the alleged industrialization of the third world, which is seen as the cause of the economic decline of the 'advanced' industrialized countries. According to the report, the spread of modern technologies to the "developing countries" is de-industrializing high-income, high wage nations; capital is being transferred to the third world where low-cost producers are flooding the world markets with manufactured goods. The report concludes that, in the future, this tendency will accelerate, producing more unemployment and wage losses in high-income countries (Paul Krugman, "Fantasy Economics." *New York Times* 9.26.94). In criticizing this thesis, which he considers dangerous for the expansion of the "free market," Krugman (who is professor of economics at Stanford University) points out that exports from the third world absorb only 1% of the first world income, and in 1993 the total capital transferred from the first to the third world amounted only to $60 billions, "pocket change," in his view, "in a world economy that invests more than $4 trillion a year" (ibid.). Krugman too, however, believes in the growing prosperity of the third world, claiming that the growth of exports, in recent years has allowed "hundreds of millions of people in the Third World to get their first taste of prosperity" (ibid.).

8. A different type of criticism of the conventional theory is presented by Manuel Castells (1993) who argues that what distinguishes the new international division of labor is not only the restructuring of world production, but the use of information. Castells reproposes the stereotype theory according to which industrial competitiveness does not depend on cheap labor, but on access to technology and information. From this viewpoint, the third world no longer exists, having been replaced by the countries of East Asia that have industrially developed and by the emergence of a "fourth world" distinguished by its inability to access the "information economy" and its consequent marginalization (pp. 22-39). It turns out, from Castells' analysis, that almost all of Africa and South America, as well as a good part of Asia, fall into this "fourth world" (pp. 35-39). However, this does not prevent him from maintaining that the work done by the populations of these regions is irrelevant for the objectives of the world economy and for capitalist accumulation.

9. This does not mean that workers in the Free Trade Zones have been passive victims of the penetration of capitalist relations in their communities (Wolf 1990, pp. 27). For many young women, factory work can be a choice, when the alternative is work in the fields under the tutelage of their parents. It is also true that, from Mexico to the Philippines and the Caribbean Islands, women workers in the Free Trade Zones have built support networks and organized struggles that have often put company managers, and the governments who had given the green light to the Free Trade Zones on the defensive side. (Enloe 1990: p.168-174; Walton and Seddon 1994: p.75-80; *The Global Assembly Line*). But these mobilizations have occurred precisely in response to the abject conditions in which the women were forced to work.

10. In Indonesia, factories in the Free Trade Zones pay so little that the families of the workers must supplement their incomes (Wolf 1990: p.26).

11. We refer to the female workers who died in the earthquake of Mexico City in September 1985. The earthquake demolished about 800 industrial plants where women were locked up (Enloe 1990, p. 169). The greed of the employers can be measured by the fact that they

rushed to extract the machinery from the debris (Enloe 1990, p. 170), and only because of the protests of the workers, who at the, moment of the earthquake were outside the plants waiting for a new shift, finally helped the wounded.

12. Among the most significant works on this topic is the volume edited by Kathryn Ward, *Women Workers and Global Restructuring* (1990). It includes the essay by D. L. Wolf on the families of female factory workers in the rural areas of Giava, and that by Susan Tiano on women employed in the *maquilas* at the border between Mexico and the United States. See also *Households and the World Economy* edited by Smith, Wallerstein and Evers (1984).

13. The concept of a "New Economic Order" is used here with a different, in some respects opposite meaning from the one the term had when it was coined, in the second half of the 1970s, by the third world elites. In its original meaning, the idea of a "New Economic Order" expressed the demand by the third world bourgeoisie for a different relation with the industrialized countries, a different distribution of wealth at the international level, and the possibility of a national road to development. Therefore, the concept of a "New World Economic Order" prospected the end of the disparities between the first and the third world (Guelfi 1985). In this text, instead, the term is used to refer to the political and economic set up that has emerged with the imposition, at the world level, of economic neo-liberalism. It is in this sense that the term is now generally used.

14. For an analysis of the responsibility of the World Bank in this respect see *Mortgaging the Earth* (1994) where Bruce Rich documents the social and ecological catastrophes caused by the projects financed by this organization in the third world.

15. As in the former socialist countries, the programs of the World Bank and the I.M.F. have led to the closing down of the national industries: the tin mines in Bolivia, the copper mines in Zambia, the jute industry in Bangladesh, the textile industry in Tanzania, and the state-supported industries in Mexico.

16. As Saskia Sassen has observed (1990, p. 99), the countries receiving the highest quota of foreign investment destined to export-oriented

production are those that send the highest number of emigrants abroad. They are also those where emigration is on the rise.

17. According to estimates of the International Labor Organization (ILO), by the mid 1980s, there were about 30 million people who had left their countries to seek work abroad. If, as Lydia Potts suggests, to these figures we add the families of the immigrants, non-documented immigrants, and refugees, we reach a figure beyond sixty millions (Potts 1990: p.159). Among these, in the United States., more than two thirds come from third world countries; in the oil producing countries of the Middle East the figures reaches nine tenths. In the European Economic Area there are today 15 million documented immigrants, including political refugees, and approximately 8 million undocumented immigrants (*World of Work* n. 3, April 1993). However, their numbers are destined to increase because, with mathematical precision, the politics of adjustment and liberalization continue to create new poverty and, with as much persistence, the World Bank and the other international agencies continue to repropose them, so that everything leads us to believe that the Diaspora from the third world will continue into the next century. This fact demonstrates that we are not facing a contingent situation, but rather a macroscopic, worldwide restructuring of work relations. On this issue see also the path breaking work of Steven Colatrella, "Structural Adjustment and the African Diaspora in Italy."(1999)

18. A. Makhijani (1993) writes on this topic:

"The global reality of capitalism, as opposed to its mythology, is that, as an economic system, it is approximately like South Africa in its dynamic and divisions, and in its violence and inequalities (p. 108)... The South African system of pass laws is reproduced on an international scale by the system of passports and visas by which mobility is easy for a minority and difficult for a majority (p. 108)... Even the statistics match—the same divisions of White and non-White; similar differences of income; similar differences in infant mortality, similar expropriation of land and resources; similar rules giving mobility to the minority and denying it to the majority (p.109)."

19. Even when one of the two partners does not emigrate, rarely do families remain united in front of male unemployment and the need to

find some form of sustenance. The politics of structural adjustment, thus, has put into crisis the attempt to impose the nuclear family in the third world (Dalla Costa G. F., 1989; 1995).

20. Two pioneering essays by Mariarosa Dalla Costa (1974, 1981) have analyzed the relation between emigration and reproduction. The first (1974) studies the dynamics of emigration in relation to the countries of departure and arrival, and its role in the formation of a multinational working class in Europe; the second (1981) looks at the role of emigration from the third world in the stratification of work, in particular reproduction work, in Italy.

21. Contrary to what Diane Elson claims (p. 41), emigration is not only a "male survival strategy." According to statistics provided by the ILO, more than 50% of the emigrants from the third world are women (Heyzer et al 1994; Stalker 1994). Among them, the majority find work as domestics (maids, nannies, aids for the elderly), or in the service sectors specializing in reproductive labor: tourism, health care, entertainment, prostitution.

22. The "traffick" in women, that feeds the sex industry and sex-tourism, has been over the years the target of many feminist protests, both in Thailand and the Philippines (Barry 1984). Moreover, by the initiative of Kathleen Barry, an American feminist, a Coalition Against the Trafficking in Women has been formed. This is an NGO that opposes the commercial exploitation of women in prostitution and whose aim is to make the United Nations ban it as a violation of human rights.

23. See, for a comparison, the article by Jacklyn Cock (1988) "Trapped Workers: The Case of Domestic Servants in South Africa." In Stichter and Parpart (eds.). *Patriarchy and Class. African Women in the Home and in the Workforce* (1988).

24. As Romero has observed (1992), the feminist movement in the United States has not succeeded in imposing a collective solution to the problem of domestic work; it has not even managed to obtain provisions that, in other countries, have for a long time been taken for granted, such as paid maternity leave.

25. These projects usually consist of either credit unions—that is cooperatives that make loans to their members, who then take on collec-

tively the responsibility for the payment, on the model of the Grameen Bank—or programs that teach women to develop "income generating activities." As Jutta Berninghausen and Birgit Kerstan (1992) have written, in their study of the activities of the Javanese NGOs, they have a stabilizing/defensive function rather than an emancipatory one (p. 253) and, in the best of cases, they try to recuperate at the micro-level of individual or community relations what has been destroyed at the macro-level of economic politics.

References

Alger, C. F. (1988). "Perceiving, Analyzing and Coping with the Local-Global Nexus." *International Social Science Journal,* n. 117, 1988.

Alexander, M. (1990). "ERP (Economic Recovery Program) hits women hardest." *NSAMANKOW. Voice of Patriotic and Democratic Forces in Ghana.* (8.2).

Altvater, E. *et al.* (1991). First edition 1987. *The Poverty of Nations. A Guide to the Debt Crisis from Argentina to Zaire* . (Translated from the German by Terry Bond). London : Zed Books.

Asian Women United of California (ed.) (1989). *Making Waves, An Anthology of Writings By and About Asian American Women.* Boston: Beacon Press.

Bakker, I. (1994). "Engendering Macro-economic Policy Reform in the Era of Global Restructuring and Adjustment". In I. Bakker (ed.) *The Strategic Silence. Gender and Economic Policy* (1994), pp. 1-29.

Bakker, I. (ed.) (1994). *The Strategic Silence. Gender and Economic Policy*. London: Zed Books.

Barry, K., C. Bunch, S. Castley. (1984). *International Feminism: Networking Against Female Sexual Slavery*. New York : International Women Tribune Center.

Barry, K. *The Coalition Against Trafficking in Women. History and Statement of Purpose*, 1991-1992, (non-dated printed document of the organization).

Barry, K. (1995). *The Prostitution of Sexuality. The Global Exploitation of Women*. New York: New York University Press.

Beneria, L. and Feldman, Sh. (eds.) (1992). *Unequal Burden, Economic Crisis, Persistent Poverty, and Women's Work*. Boulder (Colorado) Westview Press.

Bennis, P. and Mushabeck, M. (eds.) (1993). *Altered States. A Reader in the New World Order*. Brooklyn (NY): Olive Branch Press.

Berninghausen, J. Kerstan, B. (1992). First edition 1991. *Forging New Paths. Feminist Social Methodology and Rural Women in Java*. London: Zed Books.

Blot, D. (1990). "Demographics of Migration." *OECD Observer* 163 (April-May).

Bolles, A. L. (1983). "Kitchens Hit by Priorities: Employed Working-Class Jamaican Women Confront the IMF." In Nash and Fernandez-Kelly (eds.) (1983).

Bonefeld, W. et al. (eds.) (1995) *Open Marxism* 3. *Emancipating Marx*. London: Pluto Press.

Campbell, H. and Stein H. (eds.) (1991). *The IMF and Tanzania*, Harare (Zimbabwe): Natprint.

Caffentzis, G. (1995). "The Fundamental Implications of the Debt Crisis for Social Reproduction in Africa." In Dalla Costa, M. and Dalla Costa G.F., eds., (1995).

———. (1998). *From Capitalist Crisis to Proletarian Slavery: An Introduction to the U.S. Class Struggle. 1973-1998*." Toledo (Ohio): Midnight Notes.

CAFA (Committee For Academic Freedom in Africa). (1991). *Newsletter*, n. 2, New York (Fall).

CAFA. *Newsletter* n. 4, New York (1993).

CAFA. (1993) *Newsletter*, n. 5, New York (Fall)

Caipora Women's Group (ed.) (1993). *Women in Brazil*. London: Latin American Bureau.

Carnoy, M. *et al*. (1993). *The New Global Economy In the Information Age*. University Park (PA): Pennsylvania University Press.

Castells, M. (1993). "The Informational Economy and the New International Division of Labor." In Carnoy *et al*., (1993).

Chioma, Filomina, (ed.) (1993). *Women and Children First. Environ-*

ment, Poverty and Sustainable Development. Inc., Rochester (VA): Schenkman Books.

Chira, S. (1988). "Babies for Export: And Now the Painful Question." *New York Times* (4.21.1988).

The Coalition Against Trafficking in Women, *Coalition Report.* (Summer 1993).

Cock, Jacklyn (1988). "Trapped Workers: The Case of Domestic Servantsin South Africa." In Stichter S. B. and Parpart J. L.(eds.). (1988).

Cohen, R. (1987). *The New Helots. Migrants in the International Division of Labor.* Aldershot (England): Gower Publishing Co.

Commonwealth Secretariat. (1990). *Engendering Adjustment for the 1990s.* London: Commonwealth Secretariat.

Colatrella, S. (1999). "Structural Adjustment and the African Diaspora in Italy" In: Mwaria C. ed., *African Visions.* Westport (CT): Greenwood Publishers. Forthcoming.

Dalla Costa, G. F. (1989). 2nd 1991 *La riproduzione nel sottosviluppo. Lavoro delle donne, famiglia e Stato nel Venezuela degli anni '70.* Milano: FrancoAngeli. (First edition. 1980. Padova: Cleup).

_____. (1995). "Development and Economic Crisis: Women's Labour and Social Policies in Venezuela in the Context of International Indebtedness." In Dalla Costa and Dalla Costa (eds.). (1995). (orig. ed. 1990. Padova: Upsel).

Dalla Costa, M.. (1974). "Riproduzione e emigrazione." In Alessandro Scrafini (ed.).

_____. (1981) "Emigrazione, immigrazione e composizione di classse in Italia negli anni 70," in: *Economia e lavoro,* No. 4 ott-dic.

_____. (1995). "Capitalism and Reproduction." In Bonefeld W., et. al. (eds.) 1995.

_____. and Dalla Costa, G. F. (eds.) (1995). *Paying the Price. Women and the Politics of International Economic Strategy.* London: Zed Books.

Elson, D. (ed.) (1990). *Male Bias in the Development Process.* Manchester: Manchester University Press.

Elson, D. (1992). "From Survival Strategies to Transformation Strategies: Women's Needs and Structural Adjustment." In L. Beneria L. and S. Feldman (eds.). (1992).

Enloe, C. (1990). First edition 1989. *Bananas Beaches and Bases. Making International Sense of Feminist Politics.* Berkeley and Los Angeles: University of California Press.

Enloe, C. (1993).*The Morning After. Sexual Politics at the End of the Cold War.* Berkeley : University of California.

Federici, S. (1992). "The Debt Crisis, Africa and the New Enclosures." In Midnight Notes Collective (ed.), *Midnight Oil: Work, Energy, War, 1973-1992.* (1992).

Federici, S. (1995). "Economic Crisis and Demographic Policy in Sub-Saharan Africa. The Case of Nigeria." In Dalla Costa, M. and Dalla Costa, G.F. (eds.). *Paying the Price. Women and the Politics of International Economic Strategy.* (1995).

Fisher, J. (1993). *Out of the Shadows. Women, Resistance and Politics in South America.* London: Latin American Bureau.

Firestone, D. (1995), "Gloom and Despair Among Advocates of the Poor". *New York Times* 09.21.1995.

Gabriela (1988). (Documentary video). Trix Betlam (ed.), Betlam Film Production/ Novib, Netherlands.

Gai, Dharam. (ed.) (1991). *The IMF and the South. The Social Impact of Crisis and Adjustment.* London: Zed Books.

The Global Assembly Line. (1986) (Documentary video). Directed by Lorraine Gray, New Day Films, Wayne (N.J.).

Goldberg, C. (1995). "Sex Slavery, Thailand to New York. Thousands of Indentured Asian Prostitutes May Be in U.S." *New York Times* 9.11.1995

Goldschmidt-Clermont, L. (1987). *Economic evaluations of unpaid household work : Africa, Asia, Latin America, Oceania.* Geneva: ILO Publications, Women, Work and Development, 14.

Grunwald, J. and Flamm, K., (1985). *The Global Factory. Foreign Assembly in International Trade.* Washington D.C.: The Brookings Institution.

Guelfi, C., (1985). "Il Dialogo Nord-Sud e i Suoi Problemi." In Rainero (ed.) (1985).

Hanlon, J. (1991). *Mozambique: who calls the shots?* London: James Currey.

Hell to Pay. (1988) (Documentary video). Directed by A. Anderson and

A. Cottringer. Produced by A. Hamilton. Published by Women Make Movies, New York.

Heyzer N. et al. (1994). *The Trade in Domestic Workers. Causes, Mechanisms and Consequences of International Migration*. Published by the Asian and Pacific Development Centre, Kuala Lumpur, Malaysia, in association with ZED Books, London.

Johnson-Odim, Ch. (1991)."Common Themes, Different Contexts, Third World Women and Feminism". In Mohanti, Russo, Torres (eds.), (1991).

Kelly, D. M. (1987). *Hard Work Hard Choices: A Survey of Women in St. Lucia's Export-Oriented Electronic Factories*. University of the West Indies, Institute of Social and Economic Research. Occasional paper n. 20. Cave Hill (Barbados).

Kerr, J. (ed.) (1993). *Ours By Right. Women's Rights as Human Rights*. Zed Books in association with the North-South Institute, London.

Krugman, P. (1994). "Fantasy Economics."*New York Times* (26.9).

Kuppers, G. (1992). *Compañeras. Voices from the Latin American Women's Movement*. London: Latin American Bureau.

ILO (1993). "Migrants from Constraint to Free Choice". *World of Work* n.3, (April). Geneva: ILO Publications.

Lim, L. (1983). "Capitalism, Imperialism and Patriarchy." In Nash and Fernandez Kelly (eds.) (1983).

Macrae, J. and A. Zwi. (1994). *War & Hunger*. London : Zed Books with Save the Children.

Makhijani, A. (1993). "Economic Apartheid in the New World Order." In P. Bennis and M. Mushabeck (eds.). (1993).

Maids and Madams (1985) (Documentary video). Written and directed by Mira Hamermesh. Produced by C. Wrangler, Associated Film Production. Channel 4 Television Co., London.

McAfee, K. (1991). *Storm Signals. Structural Adjustment and Development Alternatives in the Caribbean*. Boston: South End Press in association with Oxfam America.

Meisenheimer II, Joseph R. (1992). "How do immigrants fare in the U.S. labor market?" *Monthly Labor Review*. (December).

Melotti, U. (1992). *L'immigrazione una sfida per l'Europa*. Capodarco di Fermo (AP): Edizioni Associate.

Michalet, C. A. (1976). *The Multinationals Companies and the New International Division of Labour*. Geneva: ILO, World Employment Programme Research. Working Papers.

Midnight Notes Collective. (ed.) (1992). *Midnight Oil: Work, Energy, War, 1973-1992*. New York: Autonomedia.

Mies, M. (1986). *Patriarchy and Accumulation on a World Scale*. London: Zed Books.

Mies, M. (1988). "From the Individual to the Individual: In the Supermarket of 'Reproductive Alternatives.'" *Genetic Engineering*, Vol. 1, n. 3, pp. 225-237.

Mies, M., Bennholdt-Thomsen, V., von Werlhof, C. (1988). *Women: The Last Colony*. London: Zed Books.

Mies, M. and Shiva, V. (1993). *Ecofeminism*. London: Zed Books.

Mohanti, C.T., Russo, A.,Torres, L. (eds.) (1991). *Third World Women and the Politics of Feminism*. Bloomington and Indianapolis: Indiana University Press.

Morgan, R. (ed.) (1984). *Sisterhood is Global. The International Women's Movement Anthology*. New York: Doubleday.

Morokvasic, M. (1984). "Birds of passage are also women." In *International Migration Review* (IMR). Volume XIII, n. 4, pp. 886-907.

Mwaria, Cheryl. ed. (with S. Federici and J. McLaren). *African Visions*. Westport, (CT) : Greenwood Publishers. Fortcoming

Narayan, U. (1995). Mail-Order' Brides. in: *Hypatia,* vol. 10, n. 1. (Winter 1995).

Nash, J. (1983). "The Impact of the Changing International Division of Labor on Different Sectors of the Labor Force." In J. Nash and P. Fernandez-Kelly (eds.) (1983).

Nash, J. and Fernandez-Kelley, M. P. (eds.) (1983). *Women, Men and the International Division of Labor*. Albany (NY): SUNY University Press.

National Labor Committee. (1995). *Zoned For Slavery. The Child Behind the Label*. New York: Crowing Rooster Arts.

New York Times (1993). 2. 5.

Ode, J. (1990)."Women Under SAP." (Nigerian) *Newswatch*, (7.9).

Ogundipe-Leslie, M. (1994). *Re-Creating Ourselves. African Women and Critical Transformations*. Trenton (N.J.): Africa World Press.

Pietila, H. and Vickers, J. (1994). First edition. 1990. *Making Women Matter. The Role of the United Nations.* London: Zed Books.

Pitelis, Ch. N. and Sugden, R. (1991). *The Nature of the Transnational Firm.* New York : Routledge.

Potts, L. (1990). *The World Labor Market. A History of Migration.* (Translated from the German by Terry Bond). London: Zed Books.

Rainero, R. H. (ed.) (1985). *Nuove Questioni di Storia Contemporanea.* Vol III, Milano: Marzorati.

Rau, Bill. (1991). *From Feast to Famine.* London : Zed Books.

Raymond, J. (1989a). "The International Traffic In Women: Women Used in Systems of Surrogacy and Reproduction." *Reproductive and Genetic Engineering.* Vol. 2, n. 1, pp. 51-57.

Raymond, J. (1989b). "At Issue. Children For Organ Export?" *Reproductive and Genetic Engineering,* Vol. 2, n. 3.

Raymond, J. (1994). *Women as Wombs. The New Reproductive Technologies and the Struggle for Women's Freedom.* San Francisco: Harpers and Co.

Rich, B. (1994). *Mortgaging the Earth. The World Bank, Environmental Impoverishment and the Crisis of Development.* Boston: Beacon Press.

Romero, M. (1992). *Maid in the U.S.A.* New York and London: Routledge.

Roy-Campbell, Z.M. (1991). "The Politics of Education in Tanzania: From Colonialism to Liberalization." In Campbell and Stein (eds.). (1991).

Sassen-Koob, Saskia. (1983). "Labor Migrations and the New Industrial Division of Labor". In J. Nash and M. P. Fernandez-Kelly (eds.). (1983). pp. 175-204.

Sassen, S. (1990). First ed. 1988. *The Mobility of Labor and Capital. A Study In International Investment And Labor Flow.* Cambridge: Cambridge University Press.

Sawyer, R. (1988). *Children Enslaved.* London, New York: Routledge.

Serafini, A. (ed.) (1974). *L'Operaio multinazionale in Europa.* Milano: Feltrinelli.

Sistren. (1986). Published by the Sistren Theatre Collective, Kingston (Jamaica), (August-September).

Smith, J., Wallerstein, I. and Evers, I. (eds.) (1984). *Households and the World Economy*. Beverly Hills (CA): Sage.

Sparr, P. (ed.) (1994). *Mortgaging Women's Lives: Feminist Critiques of Structural Adjustment*. London: Zed Books.

Stanley, A. (1994). "Nationalism Slows Foreign Adoption in Russia." *New York Times*. (12.8).

Stanely, A. (1995). "Adoption of Russian Children Tied Up in Red Tape." *New York Times*. (8.17).

Stalker, P. (1994). *The Work of Strangers: A Survey of International Labour Migration*. Geneva: International Labour Office.

Stichter, Sh. B. and Parpart, J. L. (eds.) (1988). *Patriarchy and Class. African Women in the Home and in the Workforce*. Boulder and London: Westview Press.

Stichter, Sh. B. and Parpart, J. L. (eds.) (1990). *Women, Employment and the Family in the International Division of Labour*. Philadelphia (PA): Temple University Press.

Thomas, D. Q. (1993). "Holding Governments Accountable by Public Pressure". In J. Kerr (ed.), *Ours by Right*. (1993), pp. 82-88.

Tiano, S. (1990). Maquiladora Women: A New Category of Workers? In K. Ward (ed.). (1990).

Thorbeck, S. (1987). *Voices From the City. Women of Bangkok*. London: Zed Books.

Truong, T. (1990). *Sex Money and Morality. Prostitution and Tourism in South-east Asia*. London: Zed Books.

Turshen, M. ed. (1991). Women and Health in Africa. Trenton (N.J.): Africa World Press.

Villapando, V. (1989). "The Business of Selling Mail-Order Brides." In Asian Women United of California (ed.), *Making Waves*. (1989), de Waal, Alex. (1997). *Famine Crimes. Politics and the Disaster Relief Industry in Africa*. London : Zed Books.

Wallerstein, I. (1974). *The Modern World System*. New York: Academic Press.

Walton, J. and Seddon, D. (1994). *Free Markets and Food Riots. The Politics of Global Adjustment*. Oxford: Basil Blackwell.

Ward, K. (ed.) (1990). *Women Workers and Global Restructuring*. Ithaca (NY): Cornell University, (School of) Industrial Labor Relations Press.

Wolf, D L. (1990). "Linking Women's Labor With the Global Economy: Factory Workers and their Families in Rural Java." In K. Ward (ed.) *Women Workers and Global Restructuring* (1990), pp. 25-47.

World Investment Report 1993. Transnational Corporations and Integrated International Production. (1993) New York: United Nations.

World of Work (1993). n. 3 (April). Geneva: ILO Publications.

Venezuela in the 1990s:

Social Implications of Structural Adjustment and Caldera's New Economic Policies

Giovanna Franca Dalla Costa

General Uncertainty

The political and institutional situation in Venezuela is so unstable that any predictions based upon statistical data and forecasts is bound to fail. Indeed, all hypotheses concerning the country's future social and economic development are problematic. Not surprisingly, when the 1994 edition of Venezuela's Annual Forum on the state of the nation was held, after Rafael Caldera's election, the researchers of the Instituto de Estudios Superiores de Administracion (IESA) refrained from making their traditional forecast, because of the unstability of the nation (Fuentes 1994a:10).

More than ten years have passed since the time in 1986 when, in inaugurating a seminar on Venezuela's future, *Venezuela hacia el 2000,* the late economist J. A. Michelena commented that the political situation in the country raised serious doubts about the utility of planning, since few dared to think six months ahead, knowing that a solution to the economic crisis could only come in the long run (Michelena, 1987: 23-24). Despite the continuing political uncertainty, however, some observations can be made about the recent political developments and this is the objective of this essay.

First some facts. On June 27, 1994, the newly elected president Rafael Caldera took the following steps to spur the country's economic recovery.

He banned the trade in foreign currencies and introduced a fixed, government backed exchange rate. In response to the banking crisis he placed stronger controls over the banking system, in addition to those adopted to deal with the Latin American crash. He set price controls over a broad number of goods and services, threatening tough punishments for those violating the new rules.

He suspended six constitutional guarantees. Three were of a political nature: the right not to be arrested and detained without a warrant; the right to the inviolability of one's home and the prohibition of searches without a warrant; the right to free circulation in the country, entering it as well as leaving it. The other three were of an economic nature: the right to pursue legal commercial activities; the abolition of restrictions upon property holding and acquisition; and the right not to be expropriated without due process. Caldera also agreed to the payment of a special bonus of about 6,300 Bolivares (or about $35 at the time) to public and private sector workers earning less than 45.000 Bs.

These measures were taken after months of clashes among the different political factions, in the context of a banking crisis that was causing an unprecedented chain of bank failures (Perry 1994:4; Brooke 1995). Businessmen were on the war path because of the bank crisis' impact on industrial and commercial activities, and so were the political observers and the public. Re-elected president after 25 years, Caldera inherited a conflictual political and social situation that placed strict limits on the country's economic and financial possibilities and institutional manoeuvering.

The Legacy of Carlos Andres Perez

When Caldera was proclaimed president in December 1993, during President Perez' second mandate (1989-1993), the latter had already opted for a very different economic policy from that which he had adopted during his first term in office (1974-79). The new policy was strongly oriented towards the privitization of all economic sectors, including the most strategic ones (Velasquez 1993). In the 1970s, to promote the industrial take off, the leading industrial sectors had been nationalized. But with *El Gran Viraje* ("the great turn-around") in the Perez VIII Plan for 1989-1993, the place of the state in the economy was radically changed, its function as the regulator of 'import substitution' was undermined by the hegemonic role assigned to the market, that was to be the main regulatory mechanism (Iranzo 1994). The change was promoted by the *Comision Presidencial Para la Reforma del Estado* (COPRE), a body set up in 1990 to "reform the state," and working from the start under the auspices of the UNDP (United Nations Development Program) (Velasquez 1992).

The context in which this reform took place was Venezuela's agreement to implement a tough structural adjustment program that (like in other Latin American countries) called for privitization, economic deregulation, the reduction of public spending for social services, and the opening of markets to foreign goods and services (Iranzo 1994: 66).

Although adopted later than in other countries of the region, the *adjuste* (officially started in 1989) was applied, under Perez, with such intransigence that it tore apart the social fabric. A new industrial policy was introduced to make companies more productive and efficient enough to compete under free market conditions. An attempt was made to redefine business management and administration, again, to boost productivity and flexibility (Iranzo 1994:67-68; Lucena 1994:117). In key situations (for instance, the Guayana industrial area) and, more extensively, in the country's central and southern regions and the ports, policies were applied that weakened collective bargaining, radically undermining workers' benefits and worsening their living conditions.

A cornerstone of the reconversion demanded by the "adjustment" was a policy of blanket firing. In the ports, all the workers were fired, with the consent of the unions that accepted as compensation an inequitable severance pay applied with a blatant cronyism (Iranzo 1994: 75). In the Guayana steel zone and at the Sidor complex, the reconversion caused the closure of 13 plants and an enormous loss of jobs (Lucena 1994: 123). Unemployment rose to such levels that each month 70,000 new jobless people were showing up at the offices of the *Seguro de paro forzoso* (Iranzo 1994: 71). The situation was all the more worrisome because it occurred in the presence of a collapse in the real wage that, after two years of steady depreciation, was worth less in 1990 than in 1950.

Among workers, the conditions created by the economic reconversion led to the creation of new forms of collective representation, more deeply rooted in the rank and file, and ready to challenge the traditional trade unions for their weak bargaining posture in the '80s, and their subordination to political parties no longer trusted by workers and the rest of the population (Lucena 1994).

In political terms, Caldera's presidency began at an advanced stage of an institutional reform designed to carry further the "modernization" of the state, in conformity with the programs of international organizations like UNDP, and under the supervision of COPRE. The reform included a change in the electoral process for the election of governors, mayors and councillors, and a bill promoting decentralization. Both measures had matured under the previous government (Colomine 1994:8), but their impact on national politics was felt during Caldera's presidency, generating new social, political and territorial contradictions. Decentralization, in fact, turned out to be an obstacle to the application of the new economic course, even though it had been urged on Venezuela by the international organizations precisely to accelerate it. UNDP, for instance, in its fifth planning cycle (1992-1996) for Venezuela, had made the "modernization" of the state, including its decentralization, one of the top conditions for technical and financial assistance. UNDP had also set up a world fund to support the development of the state's managerial capacity, a project of which COPRE had been part since 1990 (Blanco coord. 1993).

Against the intention of international organizations, decentralization strengthened the resistance of local governments against free-market reforms, provoking deep political splits that made Venezuela unique in Latin America. Indeed, as Bailey wrote in 1994, the "eyes of the hemisphere" are all on Venezuela as the main Latin America country that has managed to slow down the course of free-market reform (Bailey 1994:14).

In political and social terms, Caldera faced widepsread opposition and lack of confidence. This is not surprising. During his second term, his predecessor had experienced a year (1989) of violent popular uprisings known as the "bread riots," and repeated coup attempts, before being impeached in 1992 on corruption charges and forced to resign before the end of his mandate (he was replaced by Velasquez as interim president). The country's instability in that period led the Moody's credit rating agency, to classify Venezuela as a BA-1 risk in 1991, and in April 1993 Standard & Poor's classified it as a BB risk (M.L.C. 1994). At the end of November 1993, direct foreign investment had dropped by 56.3%, compared with the same month the year before (Guanipa 1993: 8). Even the entrenched two-party system, whereby *Accion Democratica* and *Copei* had alternated in power for decades, broke down under the strain. Amidst the fragmentation of traditional alliances, Caldera had to seek a new coalition, where the basis of his support ranged from the left to the center-right. The outcome was the formation of *Convergencia Nacional*, an *ad hoc* political formation that could only have restored political stability if the president had taken some concrete initiatives. Effective measures were needed also to consolidate people's confidence in the president. It is symptomatic, in this respect, that the first initiative that Caldera took, after his election, was the liberation of 22 coup plotters, which signalled a policy of social reconciliation with the groups that had taken part in the coup attempts of 1992 (*El Nacional* 1994).

Rafael Caldera's Economic Choices

Caldera did not continue the policy of complete economic liberalization that had characterized Perez' second term in office. He did not abolished all controls over prices and exchange rates, and did not insist on a free-market development strategy, achieved at the cost of further destabilization and de-industrialization (Iranzo 1994; Tovar 1994). Responding to the strong opposition to "adjustment," he proposed to revise the program.

Political Industrial, the document drawn by *Convergencia'* experts, was openly critical of the policy pursued during the previous five years. The document saw industrialization as the pole for a reconversion of production and suggested urgent measures for economic areas capable of medium term revitalization (Tovar 1994). The objective of the *IX Plan* was sustained economic growth, with a projected increase ranging from 2% for 1995, up to 6% for 1998 (Cordiplan 1995: 88).

The plan followed three guidelines. (a) The adoption of a more dynamic export policy coupled with import controls, so that imports would grow only as fast as industry and agriculture (Cordiplan 1995: 87). (b) An increase in productivity, but a "sustained and sustainable" increase (Cordiplan 1995:60). (c) An increase in the number of small, medium size and large firms, aimed at expanding the country's productive apparatus (ibid: 159). More specifically, the plan had the following objectives .

Reversing the de-industrialization process, through (i) the creation of a new industrial framework, and (ii) a quick reconversion of the existing industries, redefining domestic production and market shares, generating new economic initiatives and establishing new cooperative links between productive units.

Relaunching small and medium size firms that, in Venezuela, account for 53% of the total (Garcia 1994b: 24). A plan to implement this strategy was drafted by *Pequegna y Mediana Industria* (PYMI), the sectorial business association (Fica and Tova 1994). It made provisions for the salvaging of firms, by making space for them in major projects, including the Orinoco Park (Garcia 1994b: 24); for the renegotiation of the sectorial debt with the banks, and for the activation of an already allotted international credit of $100 million (Fica & Tovar 1994; Garcia 1994b). Through this program, 15,000 new firms were to be added to the existing 10, 000 (Fica and Tovar 1994:12).

Being labor intensive, small and medium size firms were given a key role in the revitalization of employment in areas like tourism and construction, especially of housing. They were also to interact with the *economia solidaria*, by creating associative style micro-firms capable of generating "stable employment" and "alternative income sources." The plan was supposed to develop 500 associative firms linked to the *equipamiento* (plant) *de los barrios*, *abastecimiento solidario*, and other activities related to the popular economy creating, directly or indirectly, 50, 000 jobs (Cordiplan 1995:86). Training and qualification programs were also to be developed in the context of the *economia solidaria*, (ibid. 41: 85).

Giving preferential treatment to productive areas identified as leading sectors—such as petrochemical, alluminum, steel, tropical wood cultivation—that could revitalize industry and the tertiary sector.

Promoting commerce and creating a system for channelling resources into industrial investment. For this policy to succeed a reform of the agencies funding the sector was needed, and a return to traditional protectionist measures was considered. This move was opposed by businessmen and political organizations, that favored the free-market approach of the previous period (Tovar 1994); but it was strengthened by the measures Caldera adopted in June 1994—a government backed exchange rate, limits on the buying of foreign currency, price controls on many goods and services, import controls.

Reducing the cost of electricity for business, shifting some of the benefits of the public monopoly over electricity to the advantage of industry (Tovar 1994).

Setting up a special program to boost the demand for domestic industrial production , above all by revitalizing the construction industry and, through it, manufacturing, and directing public procurement towards domestic productcs. Thus, a "preference decree" was proposed as a short-term measure, being criticized as a return to the old *compre venezolano* campaign (Tovar 1994).

Caldera also decided that the wage increases for state employees (public administrators, technicians, white collars workers), and the increase of the minimum wage for public sector blue collar workers, decreed by Velasquez's interim government in 1993, would have to be subordinated to the approval of new tax revenues. Thus, wage increases for a total of 60,000 million Bs were frozen until new taxes would be approved (Fuentes 1994: 10).

The decision to create a visible link between wages in the public sector and taxation was meant to build support among all social sectors in the increasingly difficult search for more tax revenues. It was also to make more transparent the taxation process, which is the main mechanism in the *adjuste* program, and the barometer for the relationship betwen wages and the servicing of the external debt. In an oil producing country like Venezuela, the fiscal mechanism makes the impact of both the fall in the oil price and debt servicing on wages immediately visible.

For years, the objective of the "new fiscal logic" (Cordiplan 1995: 64) had been to make the budget less dependent on oil revenues and more closely linked to domestic taxation. Even though the Venezuelan economy continued to be based on oil, the role of oil in tax revenues, already significantly lower that in the past, was expected to fall even lower. The contribution made by oil was 18.3% of the GDP in 1991; 11.7% in 1992 and 9.7% in 1993 (Hernandez 1994). According to estimates from IESA, (Fuentes 1994a:10), *Petroleos de Venezuela* produced revenues of $17,000 million in 1981, but was producing no more than $4,300 million by 1994 . The price of oil was expected to rise again in the future, as it happened at the time of the Gulf War (Garcia 1994a), but the international price of $11.50 a barrel that it fetched in 1994 meant a reduction of national revenues of over $3, 000 million in one single year.

Among the many fiscal estimates that have been made about the Venezuelan economy, that of *Convergencia's* top economic expert Asdrubal Baptista, who was a strong candidate for the direction of Cordiplan, has to be mentioned. According to Baptista, Venezuela needed a titanic effort if it was to reconcile its different business interests. Baptista also warned that shelving the IVA tax (*Impuesto valor agregado*), originally approved but later suspended by Caldera, and postponing the increase in the price of gasoline (that Caldera was supposed to have introduced) could push the fiscal deficit as high as 8% of the GDP, since inflation was running at 55% a year.

Introduced during the Velasquez interim government, the IVA generated so much conflict that it became the fiscal emblem of the Venezuelan opposition to the International Monetary Fund's fiscal dictates. Caldera first revised it; he suspended it for retailers, shifted it on to various kinds of luxury products, then eliminated it altogether.[1] Meanwhile, the IVA question not only filled the pages of the business press and catalysed public debate; it also became a test of political stability. The taxpayer's refusal to pay it escalated into a *civil disobedience movement* led by two state governors (Fuentes 1994a: 10), elected by direct suffrage under the recent electoral reform. Decentralization, in fact, has had an immediate impact on tax collection and resource management at the local level (Cordiplan 1995: 65).

Conflicts immediately broke out, around the IVA question, between the central government and the local authorities. These conflicts were all the more intense as the local governments do not reflect the same political equilibriums on which the power of the national government is based, but answer instead to regional constituencies. The conflict between center and periphery, moreover, was compounded by splits within the central government itself (some parts of Pérez's government, for instance, disowned his political choices), and was of crucial importance since it was rooted in the country's most productive regions, starting with Ciudad Guyana, the main center for the prduction and processing of iron.

The main concern for the ordinary Venezuelan, after IVA, was a possible increase in the price of gasoline, which many economists were urging to boost tax revenues and reduce the deficit. But for workers who depend on mass transit, this measure was unacceptable, since it inevitably would have led to an increase in transport prices.

The debate surrounding the increase in the price of gasoline demonstrated the crucial place that taxation has in governmental policy, given its ability to directly affect living conditions, from wages to subsidies and benefits of various kinds, to the cost of social services health, education, transport. Kept under close watch by "adjustment experts," it can shift the main areas of support, or opposition, in favor or against both government policy and the President itself.

More than once Caldera was warned that if his government insisted on eliminating the IVA and did not raise the price of gasoline, the revenue crisis caused by the fall of the oil price would become unmanageable, and the country would experience a "fiscal storm" (*tormenta fiscal*) (Fuentes 1994a:10), whereas , if correctives were introduced by the end of 1995, Venezuela would be on the path of recovery.

Social Policy in the Five Years of Drastic Adjustment

Caldera inherited a difficult situation also with respect to social assistance. The period between 1989 and 1993, the years of Perez's "adjustment" program, have shown the inadequacy of the country's social security and welfare systems in front of the dramatically worsening economic conditions. To provide a buffer against the "shock" of adjustment, a new assistance policy was adopted with a shift from indirect to direct subsidies, that supposedly were more accessible to the recipients, more easily applied and controlled, more innovative, efficient and focussed in their goals. The plan was to disburse 200,000 million Bolivares over a period of five years (Dagher 1994:10) and the initiative was publicized as a social megaproject (*megaproyecto social*). But its implementation did not reduce the exasperation of the poorest Venezuelan and was criticized even by the IMF.

The plan was to be innovative in three ways. It was to *target the most vulnerable groups* (children under five, pregnant and breast-feeding women); it was to promote social integration and *greater participation by grassroots communities and non- governmental organizations* (NGOs); it was to define the appropriate conditions for obtaining loans from the World Bank and the *Banco Interamericano de Desarollo*, the two bodies providing the technical and financial assistance to operate the transition from indirect to direct subsidies. One wonders, however, how truly innovative these measures actually were in their objectives, compared with the system of direct subsidies (subsidies given directly to the citizens), that had characterized the country's traditional welfare policy.

One novelty with respect to the past was the new positive attitude that was adopted towards international financial organizations, now seen as sources of economic resources and management techniques. This was in sharp contrast to previous development phases, like the 1970s, when the goal was to achieve economic and managerial independence from the international organisms. In those years, for instance, family planning ceased to depend from the Ford Foundation and became a ministerial service.

A quick comparison with the social policies adopted during Pérez's first term in office shows a great homogeneity, as far as content and style, between what was disbursed in the early 1990s to compensate for the damages caused by structural adjustment and what was disbursed during Pérez's first presidency, which was a period of economic prosperity and industrial take off, when employment was growing and incomes were rising (Conasseps 1994). However, it is obvious that initiatives that had been considered adequate to check a phenomenon of "persistent marginalization," in a context of economic recovery, could not apply, at the dawn of the 1990s, to a situation that over a decade had dramatically deteriorated, and in a context of increasing deindustrialization. An altogether different type of social policy was needed, based on immediate and effective interventions, and conceived as the country's development's pole. It is enough here to remember that the real value of wages had fallen to that of forty years before—wages in 1990 being the equivalent, as far as purchasing power, to wages in the 1950s; and, moreover, that the same dramatic collapse was visible in all the crucial factors of reproduction, beginning with nutrition, health and education (Cordiplan 1995).

Nevertheless, while on the economic level drastic measures were taken—measures that were to have deep consequences for the population and by official admission, called for immediate subsidies catering to social needs—no effective social policy was introduced. As far as subsidies were concerned, the initiatives adopted were "business as usual," and they were again applied with all the usual delays and disfunctionalities typical of public administration. Even the positive sides of the welfare policies of the previous period, were lost in the new approach. The population was deprived of its means of subsistence and, even in the official circles, it was recognized that the "megaproject" had not succeeded in putting an end to the deterioration of economic conditions.

The direct subsidy programs were in large part implemented by the traditional organs of the state, above all the ministries of family, education and healthcare. The ministry of education took care of the implementation of food and school subsidies (*Bono lacteo*, *utiles y uniformes escolares*). The minister of health and social welfare was put in charge of the food programs for both mothers and children (*Programa alimentar materno-infantil*), of the food program for school students (*Merienda escolar*), and of the center of nutritional recovery (*Centro de recuperacion nutricional*). To the minister of the family was assigned the Fund for the Cooperation and Financing of Associative Enterprises (*Fondo de Cooperacion y Financiamiento de Empresas Asociativas*), the Socio-pedagogical and Cultural Subsidy Program (*Programa compensatorio socio-pedagogico y cultural*) and the expansion of the *Hogares de cuidado diario* (day-care families).

Almost all these programs were already in place, and were implemented in an almost identical manner, in the 1970s (G. F. Dalla Costa 1980), when the objective was to speed up the development of *La gran Venezuela*. At that time too, during Pérez's first presidency, social participation in the management of welfare programs—for example in the planning of the *modulos* (centralized neighborhood services) was encouraged under Decree 332.

The untimely application of the direct subsidies created further problems (Pujol 1993). The food subsidy (*beca alimentaria*), announced in April 1989, became effective only in November of the same year; the *bono lacteo* and the *utiles y uniformes escolares* got started almost a year later, in September 1990. They became effective with a delay of about eighteen months, when the drastic adjustment measures had already done their harm. The plan also failed to address the most needy groups. Some sources reckon that the food programs for mothers and children reached only 60% of the targeted recipients, and mistakes were also made in favor of better off families. As in the 1970s, part of the problem was the use of the school system as the distribution network (G.F.

Dalla Costa 1980). This excluded the poorest sections of the population whose children do not go to school or drop out (Cordiplan 1995: 14-15). As a result, the subsidy program failed to attack people's nutritional and health problems at their roots, and the most vulnerable groups received only one fifth of the subsidies allocated (Cordiplan: 15).

Social Conditions in Venezuela After Drastic Adjustment

While there is little agreement between official and non-official sources, all the studies conducted immediately after the 1989-1993 period, on which the *IX Plan de la Nacion* (published in 1995) relied for its analysis of the social situation in the country, give a dramatic picture of the deterioration provoked by the 'adjustment' program (Cordiplan 1995).

According to official sources, critical poverty levels extended to include 42% of the population, and in 1993 the real wage dropped to 60% of what it was in 1988 (ibid: 11). Thus, while in 1987, 37% of the Venezuelan families had an income below the subsistence level, five years later this figure had reached 66% (ibid.: 13). The degree to which health and nutrition have deteriorated can be seen from the drastic slowdown in the fall of infant and maternal mortality rates and the increase in the number of undernourished children and children born underweight (ibid.: 14). There has also been a significant increase in the number of people dying of diarrhea, parasitic and respiratory deseases and, in the case of children under five, malnutrition (Cordiplan: 14; *Republica de Venezuela, Consejo de economia nacional 1994*:35). In epidemiological terms, the situation became very serious, as pathologies typical of poor countries coexisted with others (like cancer and cardio-vascular deseases) that affected both the poor and the better-off, and with others again, like AIDS, that have started to spread more recently but are propagating very quickly (Cordiplan 1995: 14).

A crucial factor in the deterioration of health conditions has been the reduction of public spending for healthcare. Especially severe cuts have been made over the last ten years, in the funds for the control of endemic diseases, for vaccination, immunization, maternal and infant health programs (ibid.: 16) The ministry of health and social welfare has also reversed its budget priorities with 71% of its resources being earmarked for hospitals, 12.6% for first aid and out-patient services, 5.6% for environmental services, 10% for epidemiological programs and 0.3% for social policy promotion (ibid.: 16). The lack of coordination between public and private measures has also taken its toll (ibid.: 15). The result has been a total lack of confidence in the health ministry's planning and management capacity, making it the target of severe social and political attacks (ibid.: 15).

There has also been a reversal with respect to the quality and quantity of education provided. Aside from the continuing existence of high illiteracy rates that affect 10% of the adult population, compulsory preschool education has deteriorated to such an extent that it covers only 50% of the children in the relevant age group. Primary education is now of a very low quality, with many children leaving school before the age of nine, so that many people are not able to read or write, although they have received a certain amount of elementary education (Cordiplan: 16-17). As for secondary education, the services provided are totally inadequate to the new needs of the labor market. Through the ups and downs of the recent decades, it has virtually shown no expansion, covering 33% of the relevant age grop in 1970 and 35% today, while in other Latin American countries access to secondary education has substantially increased over the same period. Mexico, for instance, has moved from 22% to 53%, and Chile from 39% to 74% (ibid.: 17).

'Adjustment' has also worsened housing conditions. The problem is certainly not new in Venezuela (Martinez Olavarria 1991), but it has been exacerbated by the new economic course. Shortages are concentrated primarily in the poorer sectors of the population, those with incomes lower than three minimum wages, that account for three quarters of the total need for new homes, estimated at over a million houses in 1994 (Cordiplan 1995: 20).

The new endemic lack of houses can be assessed by a glance at the spread of the metropolitan *barriadas*.

Interesting enough, against this background of intense social crisis, the chapter in the *IX Plan de la Nacion*, that deals with the factors contributing to social exclusion and the deterioration of living conditions, recognizes that the transformation of the Venezuelan family, from an extended to a nuclear one, has probably made survival under "adjustment" more difficult. Where the change has taken place, no social services have been developed to compensate for what the extended family used to provide through its cooperation and solidarity networks. One consequence is that the Venezuelan proletarians are no longer being pressured heavily, as they used to be, to enter formal nuclear marriages, once advertized as more functional to "development." (G.F. Dalla Costa 1980, 1994). Nuclear families, in fact, are confronted now with especially hard living conditions and responsibilities, either because they generally have only a single parent, most often the mother (30% of nuclear families are single parent families) or because stable couples cannot guarantee the family's reproduction, as both parents must work and receive no help from their social environment (Cordiplan 1995: 19).

It is now openly recognised that the nuclear family cannot function without a system of social services replacing those which the extended family provided (ibid.); and that the shortcomings of the social security system leave workers' families without healthcare, unemployment benefits or pension. This is an especially serious problem given that in Venezuela, over half of the workers are employed in the informal sector and are not even formally covered by the social welfare system; and, in addition, this is the very sector in which future jobs creation is planned (ibid.20).

One of the most pernicious consequences of "adjustment" has been the disintegration of family life and the increase of violence in and out of the home, which has affected particularly women. Venezuela is among the countries that have the highest number of women in poverty. Among single mothers, 39% are illiterate, three times the national average, and only 48% have a paid job, although they are responsible for supporting their families. According to the studies prepared for the Beijing UN World Conference on Women of 1995 *Venezuela Informe Preliminar Nacional* 1994: 47,106,107,125), women are being "superexploited" because of the adjustment program, and are not benefitting from the *Ley organica de trabajo*.

To correct this situation a *Defensoria Nacional de Los Derechos de la Mujer* has been planned, under the Law of Equal Opportunity (*Ley de igualdad de oportunidades*) approved by Congress in 1993. But the figures drawn from the studies mentioned above, show the degree to which women are suffering.

Maternal mortality rates continue to fluctuate between 60 and 70 deaths for every 100,000 child-births, indicating that their remarkable pre-adjustment improvement has come to a halt. Women's wages are on an average 25% lower than men's. In 1992, among "unskilled" workers, covered by the social security system, 15% of the women and 6% of the men earned less than the minimum wage. Among unskilled workers outside the social security system, 60% of women failed to reach the minimum wage, compared with 40% of the men. Again the average female wage was $202 a month compared with $259 for men, as women work primarily in the informal sector—domestic service, self-employment and other among the worst paid occupations.

It is obvious that women are heavily discriminated in the application of the adjustment program, despite the fact that Perez, in his *VIII Plan*, had urged the development of *Centros de atencion integral a la mujer*, and had shown his support for the national women's movement through the creation of the Women's National Council (*Consejo Nacional de la Mujer*) (*VIII Plan* 1990 :21). Indeed, so dramatic has been the deterioration of living conditions in Venezuela that the plight of women cannot be addressed by means of any compensatory legislation. At best , this can only improve the conditions of a female elite and build consensus in certain circles.

As for the *IX Plan*, it gives little attention to the worsening conditions of women, as it is focussed mainly on the family.

The New Social Policy Mechanisms and the Promotion of Integration. Solidarity programs, *economia solidaria*, family policy (atención integral à la familia).

Given the dramatic impoverishment of the population, the failure of the social "safety nets" and the lack of credible prospects, social conflict in Venezuela has been among the most intense in Latin America, becoming almost uncontrollable in recent years.

It is in the context of this strong opposition to structural adjustment that Caldera proposed a broad social policy program—the *Programas de solidaridad social* (Cordiplan 1995:86), supposedly trascending the limits of the traditional approach to welfare policy.[2]

The *Programas de Solidaridad* include subsidies to food and other basic necessities, the construction of houses and other infrastructures, incentives to job creation, training programs. The subsidies allocated to the poorest part of the population were decided in agreement with the World Bank, which confirmed its intention to disburse to Caldera, for the fight against poverty, for basic education, for housing for the poor and other infrastructures, the one billion U.S. dollars it had already promised to Pérez (Colomine 1994 a).

More specifically, the *programas de solidaridad social* provide for the following (Cordiplan 1995: 86):

-The promotion and strengthening of the *puntos de abastecimiento* (supply) *solidario.*

-The restructuring and expansion of work training programs.

-The extension of health and food programs managed through the educational and out-patient healthcare networks.

-Employment and wage agreements with business.

-Increase of the minimum wage.

-The reactivation of the health and education centers in the *barrios* and housing construction.

As one can see, these programs range from typical trade union objectives (the increase in the minimum wage, agreements with business about wages and employment) to broader social objectives as work training, the provision of popular housing, education, food and health programs.

This relatively new way of conceiving social politics--within a broader vision of governmental intervention[3]—has been realized through the *Economia Solidaria*, the center-piece of Caldera's policy, which was supposed to affect above all the popular sectors and have a positive impact on employment.

> The *economia solidaria* is to be created gradually to generate a large contingent of jobs, and it is to function as a complement to the subsidy policy. Its essential condition is the participation of organized communities in the management of the program against poverty, and the direct participation of the people involved. (Cordiplan 1995: 86)

The *economia solidaria* represented the third element in the program for the quick development of employment. The first was represented by housing construction, while the second was the revitalization of small and middle size firms.

The housing construction program was to provide 180,000 dwelling units in 1995, giving a stable employment to 89,000 workers. The *economia solidaria* also promised to realize by 1995 work training programs directed to youth, and to promote the development of 500 associative type firms linked to the programs of *equipamiento de barrios* and *abastecimiento solidario* and other "popular economy" activities overall providing 50,000 jobs (Cordiplan 1995:85-86).

The *programas de solidaridad social*, conceived as areas of mobilization from below, and in the context of a post-adjustment economic recovery program, are the key to understanding Venezuela's development politics. Imagined as a social network, they are supposed to ensure social participation in the development process, especially through the work-place.

In the case of welfare policies specifically addressed to the "war against poverty," the declared objective was to go beyond the traditional subsidies, and implement a more comprehensive program realized through the mobilization and self-organization of the communities themselves, in conformity with the World Bank recommendations [there are many examples in South America of services managed by communities, autonomously or with the support of international organizations, starting from the popular kitchens (*comedores populares*), where very often it is women who do the work].

The trend was towards a welfare policy where the users, in order to obtain some improvement in their standard of living, even just a daily meal, were forced to do some work and respect organizational guidelines, outside the traditional work channels. Even on the business front, there was a tendency to favor companies that, in addition to providing jobs, take on more social responsibility.

> This approach supports the formation of associative firms that promote solidarity as well as economic activities. In particular, it will support activities contributing to the satisfaction of basic needs, such as the commercialization of food and basic consumer goods, and the realization of infrastructural projects in the *barrios*. To strengthen social organization and marketing capacity a network of firms will be promoted combining production, distribution and consumption. Micro-enterprises are encouraged to organize, to generate a prosperous popular economy. (Cordiplan 1995: 159-160)

And again:

> The state will support with funds and technical assistance the opening of associative firms...similarly the state

will support the creation of a financial coordination system linked to saving and credit cooperatives and other
institutions typical of the popular economy, as a means
of channelling surpluses towards activities that are considered as priorities by these organizations. A communication network will be set up to tie together all the organisms and programs of the *economia
solidaria...*(ibid:160)

The State was supposed to give priority to associative type firms,
in the acquisition of goods and services, both in the contracting
out of public services and in the construction of public works in
the neighborhoods.[4]

On the family front, the objective was to strengthen the function of the family, through a network of community based family
organizations, from which would emanate various interventions
in the sphere of social reproduction, from the home to healthcare.
The coordination of this policy, defined as "integral intervention
on the family," was assigned to the specially created ministry for
social development. This is what the IX Plan wrote about it:

> The strategy for the family is to strengthen the decision
> making nucleus, to develop community organizations and
> promote social networks. We will try to satisfy the fam-
> ily members' social needs with respect to health, educa-
> tion and safety nets....Our intervention strategy will ini-
> tially try to contain the consequences of extreme poverty
> by strengthening and expanding the institutional network
> of public and non-governmental organizations; then we
> will proceed to the formation of family community based
> organizations that, in the long run, will have to take over
> the national and local direction of social programs, as
> part of the social promotion network. (Cordiplan 1995 :
> 145)

The goal was the formation of a community-based network of
families functioning as a link between the welfare programs and
the firms—especially small and middle size associative type

firms—in the realization of the initiatives of the *economia solidaria*, in the context of a social development politics coordinated by the minister of social development.

It was certainly not the first time in Venezuela that vast projects aiming at social and productive integration were designed on paper. For years, in the *barrios* a more coherent social policy had been called for. Thus, not too much significance could be given to policies that could have easily collapsed or be emptied out of any substance. This was all the more true in a political situation that was characterized by continual changes and reversals and by an extraordinarily strong opposition to government policies. There is no doubt, however, that the government guidelines placed a special emphasis on the formation of social networks linking production, distribution, the building of infrastructures and the provision of services, work, welfare and employment. The government clearly hoped to integrate these new forms of organization with existing neighborhood organizations, in order to strengthen their role as negotiating partners and, in the process, control the most radical opposition to the new forms of development.

Confronted by powerful anti-adjustment struggles, against which Caldera's appeals for a truce in the *barrios* remained ineffective, the government obviously felt the need to give recognition to initiatives that had already an autonomous existence in the popular economy, while extending the production and distribution centers for food and other basic necessities. As entire metropolitan neighborhoodds became no-go areas, ways had to be found to ensure that grassroots organizations did not create even more uncontrollable areas of social life, providing the population new means of subsistence, as well as new sources of antagonism and resistance to the hunger-developing programs imposed by the IMF and the World Bank.

Summing up, therefore, what has been said so far, we can observe that, on the one hand, Venezuela has imported a development model congenial with the requirements of the global economy and the recommendations of international capital and international financial organizations. At the same time, new forms of social integration have been promoted, and there has been an attempt to stimulate new forms of grassroots mobilization and grassroots responsibilization, that go beyond the traditional patterns. The aim has been to stabilize the social base, so as to contain social conflict which has exploded in the face of the new productive models introduced through the politics of adjustment.

In this context, through the new solidarity networks, not only has the housework been confirmed in its role as an "adjustment variable," (ILO 1984; G.F. Dalla Costa 1993, 1994), but there has been an attempt to strengthen the familiy organizationally as a community control and decision making center. In other words, despite the collapse of the main subsistence sources, once again the hoped for 'human development' has been anchored to a strengthening of the family, within a broader process of integration to the new development models. However, the link between adjustment, development and the family is extremely problematic, particularly in Venezuela, where the burden of adjustment is added to a family that never was consolidated, not at least according to the canons of advanced capitalism.

Women's demands concerning the quality of development and the project of 'integral intervention' on the family.

As a mirror of the state relationship with women, the project of "integral intervention" on the family can be examined both from a formal/organizational viewpoint and from the viewpoint of its substance. In formal and organizational terms, the state seems to have moved closer to women's demands, expecially with the provision of decentralized structures to be consulted, through their organizations, when new projects, the allocation of resources and local government decisions are to be approved (*Coordinadora de organizaciones non gubernamentales de mujeres* 1993). The initiative, however, has frustrated women's aspiration to have a presence at the decision making level, instead of being confined to a mobilization from below, which is the level at which they have always been encouraged to intervene, because of their recognized effectiveness in this area.

That the state is coming closer to women's demands is certainly due to the new strength of women's organizations (Coordinadora de ONG de mujeres 1988). Today, in Venezuela there are many active women's groups, collectives, coordinating committees, operating with or without autonomy, as feminist, party activists, in a broad range of initiatives and struggles, from those around subsistence and basic necessities to those against violence and for healthcare and legislative reforms.

Yet, the state has shown no support for the *substance* of women's demands, since it is evident that women have a very different perspective on the development question, one more strategically interested in people's reproductive needs and antagonistic to the impoverishment caused by the international economic policies.

Women's organizations and coordinations start from the following premises which, however, cover only partially the issues women are concerned with.

•The right of citizens to have their subsistence guaranteed, regardless of the changes produced in the labor market by structural adjustment and the external debt. From this follows the need to support the struggles of those who have been impoverished by these changes. A striking example here would be the 1989 "bread riots," against the second Pérez government, of which women were the protagonists, as they have been in thousands of struggles against hunger that have taken place all over South America (*Coordinadora de ONG de mujeres* 1993).

•The need to create and safeguard alternative forms of subsistence for the production and distribution of necessary goods, which contrast with the current promotion of the export market, especially in the agro-business sector. We refer here to initiatives, mostly led by women, designed to defend the land and to lead to the restoration of traditional crops and their independent sale. Such initiatives have acquired a special visibility in the years of "adjustment," and their importance for people's lives is now being recognized in many quarters. One example among many is found in the state of Aracuy. Ecofeminists have discussed it most extensively (see Claudia von Werlhoof 1994).

•The recognition of the central role of the process of reproduction and, therefore, of women who are those primarily engaged in reproductive work. Women, then, should be given special consideration, not as participants in development programs dominated by outside interests, but as social subjects whose needs should shape social options and values. In fact, women's struggles and organizations have tried to be the carriers of demands concerning the reproduction of the whole community. Significantly enough, over the last few years, groups of indigenous women, which previously were not involved in most of the country's political and social organizations and were not even included in the national census, have asked to join the women's coordination groups.

Under these conditions, even when the goal is social integration, social intervention essentially produces dichotomies, between those who are and those who are not in the institutions, starting with the family. This is particularly true in Venezuela, since much of the population lives with a high degree of autonomy not only from the family but also from the institutions. Today, however, there are major overlaps between women's organizing and the institutional responses as far as areas of intervention and organizational spaces are concerned. Faced with an explosive social opposition and with the growth of women's organizations, the government is striving to penetrate the formal and informal groups created by women organizationally, with stronger and more internal controls. At the productive and reproductive level, the tendency is to make the family part of the network that filters through job opportunities, the payment of subsidies and the rehabilitation of the *barrios* , through new formal and informal, institutional and non-institutional connections. The families' network thus becomes the prerequisite for the setting up of a system of welfare services and small scale production. This redefinition of the family's function presupposes, however, the stability of the family's nucleus, and the continuous presence of the woman, or if possible the couple, in view of the broad range of tasks the network is supposed to support.

Venezuelan women, however, are not easily "integrated" into such governmental policies. For a start, the traditional formal marriage has always been the choice of a minority among the poorer classes and most women continue to live in informal unions. Moreover, with the growth of the women's movement, new contradictions have emerged with respect to family relations. A broad debate has developed on the character of the family as a place of work, social subordination and loss of rights for women. The critique of housework as unpaid labor has taken hold and become an object of struggle in various South American countries. In Argentina, for instance, "wages for housework" has already become a women's demand (Fisher 1993).

Women's struggles for a complete democracy, capable of safeguarding the rights of all social sectors against the free-market based democracy (*Coordinadora de ONG de mujeres*, 1993) signals a determination to overturn patriarchal rules and related forms of violence that feed the first forms of discrimination within the family, against women above all. Significant here is the growth of a broad mobilization in the country against the violence perpetrated against women inside and outside the family. As in other South American countries, and as in Europe, North America, Africa, this has led to the creation of shelters for battered women, and *ad hoc* committees in the police stations, to take care for the victims of domestic and sexual violence, as well as legal aid centers. Many *child-birth houses* have also been set up to protect expectant mothers against the violent treatment to which they are all too often subjected in the hospitals (*Coordinadora de ONG de mujeres,* 1993).

Contrary to the trend visible in women's struggle, the tendency of the "integral intervention" policy to strengthen the family as a solidarity and tutelage institution, submerges the case of women within that of the other *"vulnerable subjects"* (above all children) (Cordiplan 1995: 154), thus maintaining the forms of discrimination present in the family set-up and expanding their functions. Women's role as unwaged workers in the family is ignored, a role which makes it impossible for the woman to be assimilated to the other members of the family except at the cost of renouncing her struggles to make visible her subordination as a housewife, wife and mother. If anything, these policies tend to strengthen women's subordination, by asking them to perform reproductive functions at the collective level, and promote new forms of social activism, this time under the guise of "integrated social development."

In this sense, considering the woman as one and the same as the group, is a way to undermine her struggles over reproduction, in all their political and organizational implications—struggles that now are on the agenda in many countries of South America (Kuppers 1994) as well as other countries. In Venezuela, in fact, women's organizations were immediately critical of the exclusive attention paid to the woman as the head of the family and mother in the "integral intervention" policy, a criticism that was also clearly voiced in the document prepared for the Beijing Conference in 1995 (*Venezuela. Informe Preliminar* 1994 : 54).

The determination of women in Venezuela, as everywhere else across the world, to proceed further down the path of autonomy—a path travelled for more than twenty years—is now evident on an incredibly large scale. Their demand to be heard and contribute to a different development makes of this an aspiration that cannot be renounced.

Notes

1. Most recently Caldera replaced VAT with a similar sale tax.
2. "The policies aimed to stabilise and incentivize employment must be coupled with a set of compensatory programs to help the most vulnerable population" (Cordiplan 1995:86)
3. The concepts of a social politics *justa and solidaria*, and of a *"popular economy"* were already present, however, in Pérez's *VIII Plan* (*VIII Plan* 1990:12) .
4. "The State will give preference to associative type of firms in the acquisition of goods and services. And the public enterprises will give priority to these firms when will contract out public services.The companies charged with realizing public works in the barrios will be expected to privilege local associative firms, according to communitarian criteria of responsibility and participation" (Cordiplan 1995:160).

Bibliography

A.A. VV., (1987), *Venezuela hacia el 2000. Desafíos y opciones*, Caracas: Editorial Nueva Sociedad.

Bailey, N.A. (1994), *Economic Analysis*, in Perry, W. and Bailey, N.A.

Banco Mundial (1993), *La Mujer en el proceso de desarrollo. Venezuela*, (draft).

Bethencourt, L. (1991), "La mujeres. La crisis y el ajuste estructural", in *Cuadernos del Cendes*, n. 17/18, Caracas: Vadell Hermanos editores.

Blanco, C. (1993), (coord*.), Venezuela, del siglo XX al siglo XXI: un Proyecto para construirla*, Comision presidencial para la reforma del estado (Copre) and Programa de las Naciones Unidas para el desarrollo (Pnud), Caracas: Editorial Nueva Sociedad.

Bowe, M. E. Dean, J.W., (1993), "Debt-Equity Swaps: Investment Incentive Effects and Secondary Market Prices", in *Oxford Economic Papers*, n. 45.

Brooke, J., (1995), "Bank Failures Undercut Venezuelan Government," in *The New York Times*, 30 March.

Cartaya, V. and D'Elia, Y., (1991), *Probreza en Venezuela: realidad y politicas*, Enfoque social, Cesap-Cisor.

Castillo, A., (1994), *Mujer y poder economico en Venezuela*, unpublished work, Caracas.

Castillo, A. (1985), *La crisis y la situacion de la mujer trabajadora en Venezuela*, Trabajo Femenino, Caracas: Ministerio de la Juventud.

Cella, G.P., and Torre Santos, J. (1994), (eds) "Lavoro e Politiche neoliberali in America Latina," *Sociologia del lavoro*, 55, Milan: FrancoAngeli.

Centro de Estudios de la Mujer (Cem), (1994), Boletin, n. 1, March.

Colomine, L. (1994a). "BM otorga 1.000 miliones de dolares al gobierno de Rafael Caldera," *Economia Hoy*, 15 January.

Colomine, L., (1994b), "En democracia, las promesas se devaluaron," in *Economia Hoy*, 3 February.

Comision presidencial para el enfrentamiento de la pobreza (1989), *Plan para el enfrentamiento de la pobreza*, Caracas.

Conasseps (Consejo nacional para supervision y seguimiento de los programas sociales del ejecutivo nacional), (1994), *Seguimiento de la ejecucion fisica y financiera de los programas sociales compensatorios 1989-1992*, Caracas.

Conasseps (Consejo nacional para supervision y seguimiento de los programas sociales del ejecutivo nacional), (Undated), *Programa Boca alimentaria. Evaluacion del proceso*.

Coordinadora de organizaciones no gubernamentales (Cong) de mujeres, (1988), Caracas, August.

Coordinadora de organizaciones no gubernamentales (Cong) de mujeres, (1993), *De las mujeres*, III, n.7. May.

Cordiplan (Oficina central de coordinacion y planificacion de la Presidencia de la republica), (1994), *De la Venezuela rentista a la Venezuela productiva. Programa de establizacion y recuperacion economica*.

Cordiplan (Oficina central de coordinacion y planificacion de la presidencia de la republica), (1995), *Un proyecto de Pais. Venezuela en consenso*.

Crisp, B. (1994), "Limitations to Democracy in Developing Capitalist Societies: The Case of Venezuela," *World Development*, Vol. 22, N.10.

Dagher, L. (1994), "El megaproyecto social no pudo detener el deterioro," *Economia Hoy*, 2 February.

Dalla Costa, G.F., (1978), *Un lavoro d'amore*, Rome: Edizioni delle Donne.

_____. (1980), *La riproduzione nel sottosviluppo. Un caso: il Venezuela*, Cleup, Padova (new edition *La riproduzione nel sottosviluppo. Lavoro delle donne, famiglia e Stato nel Venezuela degli anni '70*, 1989, Milan: FrancoAngeli).

_____. (1993). "Sviluppo e crisi economica. Lavoro delle donne e politiche sociali nel quadro dell indebitamento internazionale in Venezuela." Dalla Costa, M. and Dalla Costa G.F. (eds).

_____. (1994). " I tempi dello sviluppo: il lavoro domestico come variabile di aggiustamento', in "Tempo vincolato e tempo liberato. La riduzione del tempo di lavoro e le ambiguitá del tempo libero", *Sociologia del lavoro dell'organizzazione e dell'economia*, n. 56, Milano: FrancoAngeli.

Dalla Costa, M. (1988), "Domestic Labour and the Feminist Movement in Italy since the 1970s" *International Sociology*, vol. 3, n.1, March.

_____. (1996), "Capitalism and reproduction", *Capitalism Nature Socialism*, n.4, Vol. 7, December.

_____.Dalla Costa, M. and Dalla Costa, G.F. (eds.) (1993), 2nd ed. 1995, *Donne e politiche del debito. Condizione e lavoro femminile nella crisi del debito internazionale*, Milan: FrancoAngeli.

Ellner, S., (1995), "Left Parties in Regional Power", *Nacla. Report on the Americas*, vol. XXIX, n.1, July/August.

El Nacional, (1994), "En libertad 22 procesados por los intentos golpistas," 13 February.

Fajardo Cortez, V., (1991), "Politicas economicas y paro forzoso: Venezuela 1989-1991," Estudios del desarrollo de la Universidad Central de Venezuela, *Cuadernos de Cendes*, 17/18, Caracas: Vadel Hermanos editores.

Faria, H. (1995), "A Venezuelan Rescue: Dollarize the Economy," *The Wall Street Journal*, 6 October.

Fica, M., (1994), "Inflación en medicamentos dobla Ipc General," *Economic Hoy*, 1 February.

Fica, M. and Tovar, F., (1994), "Concertan plan de 90 dias para salvar a la Pymi," *Economia Hoy*, 3 February.

Fisher, Jo (1993), *Out of the Shadows. Women, Resistance and Politics in South America*, (Research and action). London: Latin America Bureau.

Fuentes, M., (1994a), "Impuestos internos no cubriran caida de ingreso petrolero," *Economia Hoy*, 21 January.

Fuentes, M., (1994b), "Ajuste salarial sujeto a aprobacion de nuevos tributos," *Economia Hoy*, 17 February.

Garcia, H., (1993), Centro de Investigaciones economicas y sociales (Cies), *Politica social en Venezuela: antes y despues del ajuste*, Caracas: Pnud/Unicef.

Garcia. Y., (1994a), "En Venezuela todo es objeto de consumo, hasta la politica," *Economia Hoy*, 3 February.

_____. (1994b), "Reactivaran Plan Orinoco para salvar a la Pymi," in *Economia Hoy*, 2 February.

Gonzales, F., (1992), "Paradojas de un programas de Ajuste en Marcha (a tres años del "Gran Viraje")", in *Indicadores socio economicos*, 8, Universidad Central de Venezuela, Facultad de Ciencias Economicas y Sociales, Instituto de Investigaciones, Caracas, Ediciones Faces/ UCV, Caracas.

Guanipa, T., (1993), "Inversion extranjera directa cayò en 56,35%," *Economia Hoy*, 28 December.

Gutierrez, A.T., (1991), "Las politicas publicas en la decada de los noventa: el caso de la nutricion," *Cuadernos del Cendes*, n. 17/18, April, Caracas: Vadell Hermanos editores.

Hernandez, G.A., (1994), "Disminuyen aportes petroleros al fisco en Bs. 110.000 millones," *Economia Hoy*, 17 February.

Kuppers, G., (ed.) (1994), *Compañeras. Voices from the Latin American Women's Movement*, Latin America Bureau, London (First ed. 1992, *Feministamente*, Wuppertal: Peter Hammer Verlag).

Iranzo, C., (1994), "Il processo di riconversione in Venezuela e le sue conseguenze sui lavoratori," *Sociologia del lavoro*, n.55, Milan: FrancoAngeli.

"Ley Organica del Trabajo," (1990), *Gazeta Oficial* n.4.240 extraordinario, 20 December.

Lucena, H., (1994), "Sindacati e negoziazione colletiva in Venezuela," in Cella G.P. and Torre Santos J., (eds*), Lavoro e politiche neoliberali in America Latina, Sociologia del lavoro*, n. 55, Milan: FrancoAngeli.

Maracara, C.I., (1994), "Empresas Cvg [corporacion venezolana de Guayana] que generan divisas no deben venderse," *Economia Hoy*, 8 January.

Martinez Olavarria, L., (1991), "La situacion del habitat en Venezuela: balance y perspectivas para la decada de los 90," *Cuadernos del Cendes*, n. 17/18, Caracas: Vadell Hermanos editores.

Martel, A., (1995), *Estrategias de Superacion de la Pobreza*, paper for the congress promoted by the Ministry of the Familly and Ildis (Instituto latinoamericano de investigaciones sociales) for the "Informe nacional para la cumbre mundial sobre el desarrollo social", Caracas, January, 1995.

Martner, G., (coord.), (1986), *America latina hacia el 2000*, Caracas: Editorial Nueva Sociedad.

Mi compromiso de solidaridad social, Programas para el Desarrollo So cial en el Gobierno de Rafael Caldera, (1994), Caracas.

Ministerio de la familia, Hacia el desarrollo social (1993), *Informe sobre la politica social.*

Ministerio de la familia, Hacia el desarrollo social 1994), *Familia...Inversion en el futuro.*

M.L.C., (1994), "Anuncio de Moody sobre riesgo del pais es precipitado," *Economia Hoy*, 9 February.

Naciones Unidas y Comision economica para America Latina y el Caribe-Cepal (1992), *Focalizacion y Pobreza: Nuevas tendencias en la politica social. Focalizacion de programas masivos: el caso venezolano de la beca alimentaria. Tercera conferencia regional sobre la pobreza en America Latina y el Caribe*, LC/L.714 (Conf.82 /3) Add.5, Santiago.

Organizacion Panamericana de la salud (Ops) y Instituto de desarrollo economico (Ide) (Banco Mundial), (1993), *Informe de Pais. Venexuela*, Seminario sobre focalizacion de programas de salud y nutricion para madres y niños de bajos ingresos en America Latina, (unpublished), Quito.

Organizacion Internacional del Trabajo, Oficina Regional para America Latina y el Caribe, (1984), *Mujeres en sus casas*, Lima.

Peña, G., (1994), "Medicamentos aumentaron entre 10% y 205% en enero", *Economia Hoy*, 12 January.

Perry, W., *Political Assessment*, in Perry, W. and Bailey, N.B. (1994).

Perry, W. and Bailey, N.B., (1994), *Venezuela 1994. Challenges for the Caldera Administration. A Report of the Csis Americas Program*, CSIS (The Center for Strategic and International Studies, Washington, D.C.), Causa (The Center for the analysis of the U.S.A., Caracas, Venezuela).

Pujol, J.A., (1993), "Caldera revisarà efectividad de political social," *Economia Hoy*, 27 December.

Republica de Venezuela, Consejo de Economia Nacional, (1994), *Perfil de desarrollo humano en Venezuela 1994*.

Romero Salazar, A., (1993), *Los rigores de la urgencia. El trabajo de los menores en la calle*, Maracaibo: Contextos, Fundacontextos.

Sabino, C., (1994), *De como un estado rico nos Ilevó a la probeza*. Hacia una nueva political social, Venezuela Hoy, n.5, Editorial Panapo.

Salleh, A., (1995), "La sfida nuova dell'ecofemminismo," in *Capitalismo Natura Socialismo*, n.1, January-April.

Shiva, V. (ed.), (1994), *Close to home. Women Reconnect Ecology, Health and Development Worldwide*, Philadelphia: New Society Publishers.

Silva Michelena, J.A., (1987), "Introducción", in AA. VV.

Tovar, F., (1994), "Gobierno dara prioridad a cuatro sectores productivos líderes", *Economia Hoy*, 4 February.

Unicef, (1989), *The Invisible Adjustment: Poor Women and the Economic Crisis*, Santiago: Unicef, The Americas and The Caribbean Regional Office.

Unicef, (1992), *Situacion de la mujer en Venezuela*, Cisfem (centro de investigacion social, formacion y estudios de la mujer), Caracas.

Unicef, (1994), *Situacion de la mujer en Venezuela. Actualizacion*, Cisfem (Centro de investigacion social, formacion y estudios de la mujer), Caracas.

115

Velasquez, M., (1993), "Ineficiencia del sector publico impulsò la privatizacion," *Economia Hoy*, 27 December.

Venezuela. Informe preliminar nacional. IV conferencia mundial de la mujer, (1994), Beijing (China), 4-15 septiembre 1995, "Acción para la igualdad, el desarrollo y la paz", VI conferencia preparatoria regional para America Latina y El Caribe, Buenos Aires.

Verlhof, C., von, (1994), *Through dissidence to subsistence as non-development. With recent examples from Venezuela*, (paper) xiii World Congress of Sociology, Bielefeld, 18-23 July.)

Walton, Jh., and Seddon, D., (1994), *Free Markets and Food Riots. The Politics of Global Adjustment*, Oxford: Blackwell.

World Bank, (1991), *Venezuela Poverty Study: From Generalized Subsidies to Targeted Programs*, Human resources division, country department, Latin America and the Caribbean regional office, Report, n. 9114-VE, 5 June.

Doing Housework For Pay:
Political Struggles and Legal Rights of Domestic Workers in Brazil

Alda Britto da Motta

Domestic Service in Contemporary Brazil

Payed domestic service has been traditionally the main occupation for women considered economically active in Brazil. This was historically the case also in the industrialized countries until recently in the United States, for instance, domestic service was the largest category of female employment until at least 1950 (Berch 1984)—and it is still the case in the countries of the "periphery." In Latin America, with small national variations, domestic workers averaged about 20% of the female work-force in 1980 (Motta 1985b). Yet, this large female presence in the waged work-force has not resulted in more social recognition for the women employed, nor, until recently, has it had a significant impact on their legal rights and political participation.

Quantitative and qualitative changes have, however, occurred in the domestic service sector over the past three decades, particularly in recent years. Although domestic work represents a large percentage of female employment, and is even perhaps the main form of employment for women, compared to other occupations—there has been a relative decline in the size of this sector since the 1960s. The same trend is found in other countries of Latin America (Castro 1982; Galvez and Todaro 1983; Gogna 1988).

In the case of Brazil, the number of domestic workers, among the economically active female population, was 27% in 1970, and only 19.9% in 1980. Yet, women's participation in the Brazilian work-force has greatly increased during this decade. Between 1970 and 1980, the number of women in the work-force has expanded by 92%, while the number of domestic workers has increased only by 45.9% (Mello 1984).

In Bahia, the largest state in Northeastern Brazil, despite a significant increase in the number of women present in the waged work-force, the number of domestic workers, as a percentage of the economically active female population, was 34.5% in 1970 and 27.2% in 1980, both relatively higher figures than the percentage for Brazil as a whole. Still, a relative decline was again noticeable. By Castro's calculations (1985), in 1980, domestic work accounted for only 60% of what female employment had been in Bahia in 1950. Castro and Guimaraes note other changes as well, in the Bahia work-force, with respect to the traditional forms of female employment. First, women have a greater access to traditionally male dominated occupations, while the presence of men in forms of employment considered as typically female has also increased. For instance, the number of women employed in consumer services has increased. At the same time, in recent years, in Bahia, the presence of men employed in domestic services, although still small, has substantially increased, from 5%, according to the census of 1980, to 6.2%, according to the census of 1989.

Castro and Guimarães suggest, however, that these are not radical conquests for women. Women still perform the majority of tasks traditionally considered their responsibility, especially in the areas of healthcare and childcare. Thus, despite the new trends, there has been an increase in the percentage of women employed in areas traditionally considered female.

What census statistics do not reveal, however, because they only report averages and aggregates, is the development of new job categories in the domestic service sector itself. Yet, they are of great importance for our understanding of the trends and changes that are occurring in this sector—both in terms of occupational sub-categories, and the place that domestic workers occupy in the general division of labor.

This is confirmed by studies done by other Latin American researchers: Mello (1984) for Brazil, Castro (1982) for Columbia, Galvez and Todaro (1983) for Chile, Gogna (1988) for Argentina. Beside confirming the reduced share of domestic service indicated by the census figures, all these studies indicate that the sector has become internally diversified, and that there have been important modifications in the composition of the subcategories of domestic service over recent years.

Along with the occupational sub-categories traditionally used to define tasks and pay rates (e.g. cook, nanny, housecleaning, general service), three other basic classifications for domestic work are now in use, that are based upon the work's time framework and the worker's place of residence. There is the fixed *resident*, who sleeps in the employer's home, then the *permanent external* worker, who sleeps in her own home, working less hours on the job than the resident, then the *daily rate* worker, whose work-hours and tasks are more defined and limited. In this classification, the "external workers" are those who do not reside in the employer's home, whereas the "externals" include both the permanent workers, who work 5 or 6 days a week in the same home, and the daily rate workers (or "temporaries," as referred to in this article), who are contracted for their services from day to day.

In this new situation, the traditional figure of the resident permanent worker, the universal type domestic worker until a short while ago—has slowly, but steadily, declined. While still the prevalent category, this model is giving way to one or the other of the two new types of payed domestic work. For instance, the idea that a permanent worker might not sleep "at work" was, until not long ago, something unthinkable and undesirable. Today, however, this seems to be the preferred type of arrangement both for employers and for workers. This is due to the diminishing size of apartments, the intensification of class conflict, and the growing political awareness of the domestics. There is also a significant increase in the number of both individuals who seek temporary positions and families who prefer to have a temporary domestic, who either complements the work of a resident worker (for example, cleaning or washing clothes), or is the only domestic employee, often hired for two or three days a week to do a variety of jobs, cooking included.

The spread of these new work models implies that domestic workers have new lifestyles. There is still a demand for personal services, coming, above all, from the traditional and the new bourgeoisie, and from a modern professional middle class (Guimarães 1987). Though statistically small in numbers, their luxurious mansions and condominiums represent an important market, demanding a great variety of domestic services, and employing a large number of workers. Even so, the greatest source of employment for domestic workers is the traditional middle class, which has been proletarianized, because of the current economic crisis, and has neither the extra money nor can hope to climb the social ladder. These employers and their families are forced to make constant cuts in their household budgets, and to reduce their consumption of goods and services, including domestic service.

Families that have always hired help in the home, but are now confronting the reality of financial austerity, are now having to cut the number of their employees' hours, have to let workers go, or at least reduce the number of days they work. This is reinforced by the current political situation, in which the working class is struggling to retain its rights (while the same proletarianized middle class is struggling to preserve its standard of living). In this context, domestic workers are increasingly becoming aware of their rights, and are no longer satisfied with starvation wages, sweetened by the illusion of being treated as "one of the family," or by "gifts" of clothes and other used objects. However, most employers, among the newly pauperized middle class, still refuse to pay higher salaries to their domestic servants, both because of their diminishing household budgets and also for ideological reasons. Many simply cannot imagine that a domestic worker should receive an *actual* salary. This creates new conflicts, but also facilitates new forms of awareness on both sides.

Thus the contradictions grow. The contractual nature of the services of the external domestic, mainly the temporary worker, has generated a new respect for her basic worker's rights, like the eight-hour workday, a fixed lunch break, well defined tasks and pay rates, and wages adjusted to inflation. This by no means precludes the common attempts by the employers to cut, or stretch the working day, according to their immediate needs, nor does it eliminate traditional client-patron relations. For instance, non stipulated extra meals continue to be offered by the employers, and to be expected by employees, and small services, outside the contractual agreement, often more personal in nature, continue to be demanded of external domestic workers. One temporary domestic worker puts it this way: "The majority of temporary workers eat lunch at work. Many (patrons) even offer breakfast. Midday snacks are what is rare. Many times I can finish the work before (the agreed upon hour), but the patron always finds something else for me to do. Some keep pans from the entire week, even underwear, for me to wash. If it were up to them, I would be there till 7 or 8 at night."

A small segment of the middle class, the one more intellectually aware, stimulated perhaps by its recent pauperization, tries to display a different attitude towards its employees. At any rate, the increasing political awareness of domestic workers leads them to insist upon certain rights, and this behavior tends to have a demonstrative effect on other situations as well, the ones where the families either cannot, or do not want to give in to more egalitarian demands.

The fact that on the part of both the families and the state, domestic work in Brazil has not been socialized, along with the lack of more employment opportunities in this sector, has created a persistent impasse. Relations between employing families and domestic workers limp along, in a manner that, on another occasion, I have described as "an impossible relation" (da Motta 1986). Throughout all this, the awareness among domestic workers that they are part of the working class has grown, stimulated by their professional associations and unions, and by other groups active in the community, such as religious workers, feminist and ethnic groups.

The continuing decline in the pace of employment in paid domestic service, due to the financial austerity experienced by many of the sector's traditional employers, does not imply the extinction of the sector, certainly not in the short term. In fact, given the current social and sexual division of labor in Brazil, it is improbable that this work can be extensively replaced. For this to happen the state should take on the task of socializing the access to housework equipment, and industry would have to invest more in the reproduction of its work-force, which is an unlikely prospect. Moreover, there is still a large pool of domestic workers, many of them being young migrants from the countryside, or from the neighborhoods in the peripheries of the large cities, poorly educated and without prospects for other types of employment.

For all these reasons, despite the increasing availability of industrially prepared products, allowing for the preservation and quick preparations of foodstuffs (from packaged pre-cooked meals to freezers and microwave ovens), only that sector of the population that has been less affected by the crisis makes use of these type of goods. In this latter case, the hiring of domestic workers is more a question of cultural preference than of economic need. What we are witnessing, however, is an internal reorganization of domestic work, that is both reshaping work relations and creating a new type of domestic worker: the external and/or temporary worker.

New Contexts, New Actors

It would be unrealistic to argue that there is a well defined class identity among Brazilian domestic workers. There have been, however, remarkable changes in their reciprocal relations, and in their relations with others, that point to a new direction. These novelties, significant whenever they are present, give us the measure of the change that has taken place.

The economic and political conjuncture that has caused the relative decline of domestic work in the economically active population, the transfer of part of this work-force to other sectors of the economy, the internal restructuring of the subcategories of domestic work, and the growing male presence in this occupation, have all produced a slow and gradual change in the mentality and attitude of domestic workers. The "external worker" best embodies this change; thus it his/her existential and political trajectory that must be further analysed.

The step from resident to external, to temporary worker is a difficult but significant one, in human, social and political terms. It is not only a political victory in the economic sphere, but also an emotional one. It means to overcome hesitations and fears concerning one's capacity to pay the rent, as well as the fear of loneliness and of the unknowns in the situation. Says one woman: "I used to be afraid. People would say I had to rent a room and I have always thought that it would be very difficult. I was afraid that it would not work out. But now I am quite happy. Now I know one can get by."

It is also a personal conquest that often seems to produce a growing sense of freedom and victory, necessary for the formation of a worker's identity. This is the case of an activist, belonging to a domestic workers association, who says : " If one day I don't feel like going to work, or have other things to do, I can always call or change the day. Daily workers have more freedom. "Again, speaking about shoppping for food: "It is wonderful to be able to buy your own food. It makes me feel more like other workers."

The idea of becoming an external worker is spreading slowly, but steadily, among domestic workers affiliated with the associations and unions of their category. It is becoming something of a symbol of domestic workers' struggles. We should not assume, however, that becoming an external worker is necessarily associated with the development of a political consciousness. In many cases, it is the result of a combination of different individual trajectories; it is perhaps the only option in the case of married women with small children.

It is true, however, that this occupational model is extremely representative of the activists of the movement for domestic workers' rights. Lenira, a nationally recognized leader from the Union in Recife (the capital of the Northeastern state of Pernambuco), made the following revealing declaration at the Northeastern Regional Encounter in July 1988. "No other worker lives where he works...Why it's only us...? This is a question we must discuss." This is also what one hears in the words of international leaders of the domestic workers movement, as in the case of Elvira Duran Majon (Ministerio de Cultura, Istituto de la Mujer, 1986).

> Our main struggle is to make people aware that they have the right to have their own life, the right to work eight hours a day, like everyone else, and then go home and be able to sit without having to ask for permission from anyone.

The idea of preserving one's space, separate from that of the employers' family, seems to represent, in the activists' thinking, a decisive step. It helps break the workers' dependence on their employers; and strengthens the consciousness of oneself as part of the working class. This is a development that seems initially to affect only the more politically aware groups of domestic workers, especially those organized in professional associations and unions. However, empirical observation of domestic workers suggests that this trend towards working class identification is destined to become stronger in the future and more generalized, going beyond the circle of activists.

The symbolism of an autonomous space expresses not only the changes in the domestic workers' relationship with their employers, but also the possibility of their identifying with the experiences and practices of other workers. Once again, the words of Lenira are illustrative:

> If you live in the houses of the patrons, you don't think of the problem of housing. But those who go to live in the proletarian neighborhoods, ...in the *invasões**, struggle for the improvement of public transports, like the other workers. Our world is that of the other workers. Our employer, no matter how good she may be, is not part of our family...We are part of the working class (*squatters' settlement).

We have here a new political dimension: the external worker has the possibility of gaining an experience and a political formation alternative to or, at times, complementary to that which might come from her membership in an association or union. For there are many movements in contemporary Brazil, that are flourishing in neighborhoods, and engaged in struggles theoretically linked to the reproductive sphere, or in ethnic struggles (for instance, the Black Consciousness Movement in Bahia, a state whose a population is largely of African descent). The non-resident domestic worker, above all the daily worker, has a greater opportunity to become part of this social space, to be better informed, and to gradually become more politically aware. This process is nourished by conversations with neighbors and, most important, the daily meetings with other workers at bus stops and during the trip back and forth from work. Everything is discussed while waiting long hours and travelling together: the irregular service and high cost of public transportation, the often violent popular reaction to the lack of basic services, the "garbage in front of my door that they haven't collected for six days," strikes, the low value of the minimum wage, who does or does not have the right to receive it, and other workers' rights. This discourse guarantees a continuous comparison and sharing of experiences.

Thanks to these contacts, domestic workers have often participated in neighborhood movements and struggles. External or daily workers, already belonging to their occupational associations, have been able to take unity building initiatives, mobilizing their own organizations and other urban movements.[1]

A peculiar trait of domestic workers' associations, though one rarely promoted by their members, is that they are made up almost exclusively by women. However, the strong, if not exclusive, emphasis they have placed upon their mobilizing along occupational lines, and the growth of class consciousness, has precluded their recognition of demands and issues specifically related to their members' gender. This, at times, manifests itself in curious ways, such as the use of the masculine form of the word "workers" (*empregados*) to describe those belonging to these associations, although empirical research has shown that there are no men among their members (Motta 1984). This inability to recognize themselves *also* as women's groups, confronted, therefore, with specific problems that cannot be resolved in a purely occupational or class context, is surprising, above all if one considers that domestic workers are such precisely because they are women (Motta 1987). It seems, however, that this gender dimension of the class is too hidden, to this day, to be recognized. Offers of support have come to domestic workers' associations from some feminist groups, or study groups doing research on women. But they have not been well received, for the promoters of these initiatives were frequently seen from a class viewpoint, as people belonging to the same class as the employers, and having interests different from those of the workers.

For domestic workers, then, organizing is a complex process that immediately raises a set of questions. What has been achieved so far, beside a long and slow mobilization and con-sciousness-raising process on the side of a limited number of domestic workers? What is the probability that these groups of activists, with their relatively small number of members, suc-ceed in exercizing some political power? Can domestic workers hope, in a short time, to achieve the status of political subjects, capable of influencing the events that affect them?

It is certainly premature to answer these questions, given that most domestic worker unions and associations are relatively new, have a limited number of members, and are at different stages with respect to their development, degree of mobilization, experience and access to resources, depending on the geographi-cal region to which they belong. At the same time, they have amongst their ranks some very active militants, and have the sup-port of other groups, some with ample resources and and a wide experience of political struggle, like the CNDM (National Coun-cil of Women's Rights), before it became practically extinct at the end of Sarney's government in 1989.

On balance, there can be no doubt about the contribution the domestic workers' unions and associations have given to the po-litical formation of domestic workers, to the legitimation of their rights, and the integration of their struggles in the wider context of the current political struggle in Brazil. I would argue that their political future depends on whether or not they will succeed in integrating their initiative and action with that of the organized movements that have emerged in Brazil since the 1980s, whose purpose is to democratize the country's political structure and make it more responsive to people's needs.

This potential is well illustrated by the mobilization that took place to ensure that the rights of domestic workers would be in-cluded in the new Constitution. After an initial debate on the pro-posals presented by each association, these were gathered in a common document prepared in the course of regional and na-tional encounters. The document thus prepared was given to the President of the Constitutional Commission, with a popular pro-posal for an amendment to the new Constitution that would include the rights of domestic workers. With the support of the National Council For Women's Rights (CNDM) and other progressive groups, domestic workers organized to ensure a continuous presence in Brasilia during the discussion and vote on these proposals. It was on this occasion that Benedita da Silva, the federal deputy (MP) responsible for the negotiations with the Congress, concerning the proposed amendment, rose to a position of prominence. A black woman and a spokesperson for the black people's rights movement, Benedita was a former domestic worker, with a long history of poverty as a *favelas* dweller. Thus, her role in the campaign surrounding the amendment should not be surprising. All the new developments that have intervened in the conditions of domestic workers have reflect a long history of struggle and learning that cannot be underestimated.

The Current Situation

During the preparations for the Constitution of 1988, women conducted well managed political battles. The groups that participated in them enjoyed the assistance and support of the CNDM, that, at the time, was an important organ of the Ministry of Justice. In fact, the CNDM proved so effective in the discussions about women's rights, that once the constituent period was concluded, it was stripped of its resources, representation and initiative by the very Ministry of which it was part.

Women's demands, including those of domestic workers, were as a whole accepted, however, in the constitutional text. Domestic workers were able to gain many of the rights recognized to other workers, such as the minimum wage, annual (paid) vacations, 120 days of maternity leave, and the right to a pension.

Thus, there has been a qualitative change and a political one in the area of domestic work. Most crucially, the domestic workers' presence in the unions and associations has grown. In Bahia, for instance, between 1986 and 1991, the members of these associations, still to this day quite modest, increased, from an initially small group of about fifteen activists to 150 members. In the same period, the association turned into a union.

On the social-judicial front, two controversies that were generated by the endless wrangles over the meaning of the articles concerning workers' rights in the new Constitution must be mentioned. The first was about maternity and paternity leave—an issue touching upon the socially sensitive question of gender relations and roles within the family. The other issue, that also received national attention, was that of the new and broader rights gained by domestic workers, which involved not only material gains, but also the social recognition of domestic work as a professional category.

Domestic workers were also able to have, for the first time, quick access to a large body of information concerning their rights, broadcasted daily by the mass media, especially the television. In this way, by the simple act of providing information, the media contributed to raise consciousness about workers' rights, even among domestic workers not affiliated with any organization.

With the enacting of the new Constitution, a tense and relentless dialogue was inaugurated between employers and domestic workers, that deepened the latter's awareness of their "otherness," an essential condition for the growth of self-awareness. With the new preoccupation with one's rights, previously limited to a small number of workers' associations' and union members, there has been an increase in the number of complaints and law suits against employers. Moreover, the tendency to set up domestic workers' unions, already established in some countries of South America,* and accelerated after the International Encounter of Domestic Workers' Associations and Unions, held in Colombia in 1988, has begun to take hold also in Brazil. When the fourth National Encounter of Domestic Workers Associations and Unions took place in January 1989, five associations had already made the transition to unions, while many others had expressed similar intentions. The final document of the Encounter reflected the class character which the groups intended to give to the movement, jointly affirming, on this occasion, what they had already discussed and declared separatel, at previous times:

> "In this society divided in classes, *we belong to the working class*."

Simultaneously, during the same month, the first employers associations were formed, first in Sao Paulo and, shortly after, in Rio, as a self-defense reaction on the part of those who hire domestic workers.

Meanwhile, while waiting for the definition of the complementary laws to the the Constitution, and while the State Constitutions were being debated, the new workers' rights activists prepared themselves. The goal was to create a new a framework for presenting and negotiating new forms of conflict based upon on collective interests and practices. This framework has now largely, though not completely, replaced the daily disputes and tensions, of a purely individual character, that, in another context, I have referred to, somewhat jokingly, as "body to body...class struggle" (Motta 1985a).

---

* The growth of political consciousness that has accompanied the formation of domestic workers unions is also reflected in the following statement and demands by Alesda, the Domestic Service Union in Uruguay that was formed in 1984. "We are women workers without a factory....Our union, which embraces one of the biggest, and certainly most exploited labour sectors in Uruguay is rooted in shared deprivation....We are a union of women workers with a class consciousness and the will to struggle for our dignity, like that of any other worker....We are fighting for our rights as workers and as people. Women have always been taught and brought up to to do domestic jobs, relegated to the social role of being servants in our own homes. However, we are no longer isolated....we're growing stronger all the time. Things are definitely changing." From Miranda Davis, *Third World.Second Sex*. Vol. 2, 1987, p.174. [Note of the editors]

Notes

1. This is what has happened, one day in 1988, in Salvador, Bahia, when in the same meeting the Domestic Workers Association was approached by a representative of the Popular Movement Against Bus Fare Increases—an organization in which the Association still has representation—and two members of a black cultural group seeking its participation in a debate on the theme: "A hundred years without abolition." The relationship with this latter group continued, even taking an electoral form, when, sometime later, in the course of another visit, a member of the same black group announced his candidacy as councilman in the upcoming municipal elections.

2. What has really produced these advances? The work? The activists? Of which groups? Would the new domestic workers' rights have been fully approved, had "Bené " not been a federal deputy? Perhaps not. Were these victories a product of circumstantial and individual action? Yes and no. The existence of a person like Benedita testifies to the importance of an individual ready to embody the struggle. But it also points to the existence of a social context and a class that produced and supported that individual, capable even of mobilizing the political force necessary to elect her.

3. The first months were rather stormy, as the employers would question the new rights gained by domestic workers; and the latter in turn would protest against the salary deductions and the various contractual arrangements imposed on them by the law. What followed was a tacit agreement. A good number of domestic workers, less informed or less experienced, made individual deals with their employers, giving up some of their rights, especially the right to a minimum wage. On the other hand, a growing number of employers, those more aware, more prosperous, or more prudent, began to recognize their legal responsibilities, easing the shock and tension of the initial reactions.

Bibliography

Berch, B. (1984). "The sphinx in the household: a new look at the history of household workers". In *Review of Political Economics*, vol. 16, n.1.

Castro, M. G. (1982). *"Que se compra y se vende en el servicio doméstico? El caso de Bogotá."* In León, M. (ed.) (1982).

Castro, N. A. (1985). *Força de trabalho e emprego não-agrícola no Estado da Bahia—1950-1980.* Report produced at the CRH/FINEP /UFB Conference, Salvador: Centro de Recursos Humanos (mimeo).

Castro, N. A. and Guiarães, I. (1987). "O que é que a baiana faz? (os novos padrões da divisão sexual do trabalho nas atividades urbanas do Estado da Bahia)". In Caderno CRH. n. 2. Salvador. n.2.

Chaney, E. and Garcia Castro M. (1988). *Muchachas no more (household workers in Latin America and the Caribbean).* Philadelphia: Temple University

Galvez, T. and Todaro, R. (1983). *La especificidad del trabajo doméstico la organización de las trabajadoras de casa particular (Santiago de Chile).* Report produced at the XI Congresso Internacional da Lasa, México.

Gogna, M. (1988). *"Domestic service in Buenos Aires."* In Chaney, E. and Garcia Castro, M. (eds.) (1988).

Guimarães, A. S. A. (1987). "Estrutura e formação das classes sociais na Bahia." *Novos Estudos CEBRAP*, n. 18, Sept, São Paulo.

Leon, M. (eds. (1982). *Debate sobre la mujer en América Latina y el Caribe*, Bogotà: T.L. ACEP.

Mello, H. Pereira de. (1984). *Empregadas domésticas—quantas são, suas lutas e relações com o movimento feminista,* Report produced at the VIII Encontro Anual da Anipocs, Aguas de São Pedro (mimeo).

Ministério de Cultura, Instituto de la Mujer, (1986). *Mujeres, Ano III*, n. 10. Mar. Madrid.

Motta, A. Britto da (1984). *Emprego doméstico masculino.* Report produced at the VII Encontro Anual da Anpocs. Aguas de São Pedro (mimeo).

Motta, A. Britto da (1985a). "Emprego doméstico no capitalismo: o caso de Salvador". In *Cadernos do NEIM*, n. 2, Salvador.

Motta, A. Britto da (1985b). *Emprego doméstico em Salvador*. (Final Research Report CNPQ-UFBA. Salvador).

Motta, A. Britto da (1986). "A relação impossível". In *Anais do Seminario Relaçoes de Trabalho e Relaçoes de Poder*. Fortaleza: UFCE/ Mestrado de Sociologia.

Motta, A. Britto da (1987). *Associations of domestic servants: the case of Bahia, Brazil*. Report produced at the Third International Interdisciplinary Congress on Women. July. Ireland: University of Dublin.

Oritz, R. (1980). *A consciência fragmentada*. São Paulo: Paz e Terra.

Maldevelopment in the Context of North-South Relations:

The Case of Algeria

Andrée Michel

Algeria is a classic example of "maldevelopment." For its economy, being based almost exclusively on gas and oil, the country's only significant exports, requires enormous investments, and has no adequate diversification of production. It is this type of development that has increasingly enabled the ruling elites to appropriate the oil revenues—a process that has brought the country on the verge of bankruptcy—and plunged it into the violence fomented by Islamic fundamentalism.

Algeria, a Model For Third World Countries

Today Algeria is devastated by terror; yet, until 1980, it seemed a model for Third World countries seeking emancipation. A leader

in the non-aligned world, it denounced colonialism and imperialism and supported the Third World people's liberation struggle.
Algeria launched the idea of a "New World Order" (NWO), a
term that was appropriated in 1974 by the Group of 77 which, at
the time, Algeria was chairing (Erb 1978). (A caricature of the
idea of the New World Order was later forged by George Bush at
the time of the Gulf War). It was President Boumedienne who,
before the United Nations, "demanded a better distribution of the
world's wealth, as a victory for humankind, rather than as a re-
venge of the poor against the rich"(Corm 1991). In this way, however, "he ignored that the economic development of a nation must
be gained through a struggle, and is not achieved by sitting at a
negotiating table where the rich would presumably renounce some
of their privileges in favor of the oppressed" (Corm 1991).

It was again Algeria that launched the idea of a North-South
dialogue, at a meeting of the non-aligned countries in 1975. International opinion was impressed by the country's rapid industrialization and strong economic growth. Its economic take-off
set an example for the Third World. The Algerian leaders, who
considered themselves socialists, believed that natural resources
belong to the country in which they are located and proceeded to
nationalize the oil industry, first taking over the small companies
and later the natural gas fields. In the end, Algeria had 51% of the
stocks of the French oil companies operating in its territory
(Boumedienne 1994).

In 1973, when OPEC (Organization of Petroleum Export-
ing Companies) quadrupled the price of oil, which rose from $3
to $11.60 a barrel (Gallois 1993), Algeria acquired the means to
undertake a new development program. The Algerian economy
remained in a state of euphoria until 1982 when the price of oil
reached $17 a barrel. This was a victory for Third World oil pro-
ducers. The industrialization process fueled by it was accompanied by the recognition of significant workers' rights. The only
problem was the lack of political democracy. The National Liberation Front (NLF), still enjoying the immense prestige it had
gained during the anti-colonial struggle, remained the only party

and it denied its opponents the right to express their views, except at the price of going into exile.

This caused an exodus that proved very costly for the Algerian people.

From Model Country to Crisis

Everything changed after 1983 when the oil prices began to fall to a record low. In 1985, at the lowest point in the price cycle, a Paribas Bank's report observed that:

> In real terms, oil prices have remained close to what their historic average has been since the early part of the century. In other words, oil does not cost today more than it did in 1908 when the discovery of petroleum, in Persia, by an English engineer set off the extraction of crude oil in the Middle East. (Tuquoi 1993)

By 1992, the real oil prices were still falling—the price per barrel was down to $4.2 in 1973 figures—and oil had lost half of its 1973 purchasing power (Tuquoi 1993). As a consequence, in the mid-1980s, Algeria was hit by an economic and social crisis that later only kept worsening. An important role in this crisis was played not only by North-South relations—in a few years the North was able to take back what it had been forced to concede to the oil producing countries—but also by domestic maldevelopment.

The fall of the oil price revealed the many pitfalls of the Algerian development program. It showed the failure of an industrialization model that had given priority to the production of intermediate goods over consumer goods, and imposed it on a society not ready to accept it. According to Daniel Junqua, development in Algeria also ran into problems because of its ambitious objectives, its systematic reliance on advanced technologies, the inexperience of the Algerians technicians, and the bureaucratic mentality of both executives and workers, who had little interest for profitability.

All of this was aggravated by the unscrupulousness of the foreign companies with which Algeria had contracts (Junqua 1976).

Too much had been sacrificed to the myth of a certain industrialization model. Agriculture had been neglected in favor of industry, despite the efforts made by the government in 1972 to contain the exodus from the rural areas through the introduction of an agrarian reform. As a consequence, Algeria, which had fed France during the French Revolution, had to depend on the world market and in 1979 had to import 70% of its food, compared with 27% in 1969, 45% in 1973 and 59% in 1977 (Karsenty 1979). In 1994, a quarter of Algerian imports consisted of foodstuff (*El Watan* 1995. 23. 03).

Throughout these years, an unprecedented rural exodus emptied the countryside and swelled the cities beyond all measure.

Farmers, drawing their livelihood from the cultivation of small parcels of land in hilly and mountainous areas, could not get ploughs, while "scythes and shovels were wanted and were objects of speculation," because the Algerian industry did not produce them. (Judet 1979). Fishing too was neglected, its development being hindered by the lack of trained personnel and funding, so that Algeria, with a coastline of 1, 200 km, "is the country with the lowest consumption of fish per person." (Tiemçani 1995). Algerian industry was not even able to produce enough jobs to match population growth, as it relied on imported, highly automatized "key-in hand" plants that used little labor. In 1979, moreover, it was found that "the increase in the number of jobs in the non-agricultural sectors has been accompanied by stagnation and the prospect of decline in agricultural employment, while the rural population continues to grow in absolute terms" (Judet 1979). Lastly, inadequate professional training prevented the production of quality goods and placed limits on plant capacity, which fluctuated between 40% and 60% in the late1980s, and between 25% and 30% by the early 1990s (Yahiaoui 1995).

Services (housing, education, healthcare), catering to people's basic need, were sacrificed to megaprojects. Imposing steel or engineering works were built, for instance, at the expense of low-cost housing, despite a serious housing crisis that dated back to the time of independence. As Judet writes:

> In 1966, the Algerian planners entered a blind alley with regard to low-cost housing, as with other sectors of the economy considered 'non-productive.' The state believed that the existing housing stock and the other infrastructures available in 1967 were sufficient, and that it was, therefore, possible to wait...However, numerous investigations have shown that the housing shortage is one of the main causes of absenteeism and instability in the factories and other work-places. (Judet 1979)

Algeria devoted a substantial amount of financial resources to education and healthcare, but in both these sectors there has also been an enormous waste. Thus, despite the efforts made by the state to help the Algerians overcome the state of illiteracy in which French colonialism had left them, a recent study has shown the presence of a 32% illiteracy rate in the country, 54% in the case of women (Iqra Association, 1994). Nevertheless, in 1980, the literacy centers were closed, while a substantial amount of funds was earmarked for the construction of mosques and universities. Similarly, hospitals were built, but in some regions there was a shortage of medical and para-medical staff, and the available staff lacked training. In the name of population growth, the provision of family planning units was neglected and so was the training of personnel catering to the needs of women and their families. The Algerian healthcare system is a classic example of waste. In the 1970s, the main concern was prevention and a network of healthcare centers were set up. But, starting with the 1980s, hospital building took precedence over the provision of light infra-structures, like polyclinics or day hospitals, and preventive care ceased to be given priority even on paper (*El Watan* 1994.23.03.)

In this as in other cases, the desire to copy the countries (capitalist or socialist) with a long history of industrialization played a role. Thus, preference was given to megaplants, key-in hand factories and cutting-edge technologies, while the professional training, the funding and structural diversification necessary to provide consumer goods and basic services were ignored. This mimetic type of development has also led Algeria to purchase goods that have become emblems of modernity, power and technological prestige in the Third World. Two nuclear reactors, for instance, were acquired from Argentina and China.

Debt, Social Inequalities and the Growth of Fundamentalism

The process described above well illustrates the pitfalls of the mimetic development programs that many Third World countries adopted after independence, under political and economic pressure by the officers, banks and multinational companies of the industrialized countries. As long as the price of oil was high, the serious problems inherent to these programs were masked; but they became visible when the crisis started. It then became evident that favoritism, kickbacks, waste and corruption had created an economic muddle, and were responsible for the excessive public debt, the embezzlement of the oil revenues by the ruling élite, and the growth of religious fundamentalism.

The enormous efforts which the government had made to invest in heavy industry and the energy sector (gas and oil) had required a significant recourse to foreign borrowing, guaranteed against future oil revenues (Adda 1993), in order to pay for massive imports of technology and consumer goods. Thus, as Corm writes, starting from 1975,

> only one year after the quadrupling of the price of oil, Algeria (like Iran) registered a heavy balance of payment deficit, and was forced to take considerable loans

on the international capital market to face her debts.
(Corm 1991)

By January 1995, Algeria's foreign debt was a crushing burden of $27 billion, amounting to 59% of the Gross National Product, and involving servicing charges equal to 82% of the country's exports (Yahiaoui 1995).

The oil revenues and the possibility to import key-in hand plants and luxury products also contributed to the creation of a national élite, further stimulating luxury spending by the privileged at the expense of the provision of basic necessities for the lower income groups. Thus, social inqualities deepened, as "what was left from the oil and gas revenues [was] confiscated by the minority that controlled the main companies and the state." (Yahaioui 1995). As in other Third World countries, a privileged class was created in this process, that has formed a bulwark in support of capitalism, as it depends on it for its survival, its lifestyle and its luxury consumption.

This situation has been the cause of an immense frustration among the popular classes who have become aware of the huge gap between the luxury in which their leaders live and their own poverty, which is worsening every year. The popular uprisings that took place in the streets of Algiers in 1988 revealed the anger that many Algerians felt, in seeing themselves excluded from all the fruits of development. The very growth of religious fundamentalism was a direct response to this injustice, a protest against the Algerian leaders' inability to address the unemployment problem and the economic and social crisis afflicting the country.

We cannot, in fact, blame the growth of fundamentalism on the speeches that President Boumedienne delivered before international organizations. For on such occasions he always maintained that

> The Koran's verses are not enough to feed hungry people.
> A devout Muslim must be above all a fanatic supporter
> of liberation and emancipation, and these can be achieved

only through the conquest of modern science. (Corm 1991).

Boumedienne also argued that "these days, whether you like it or not, power, in the world, is founded on the economy and oil." (Corm 1991).

However, already during his presidency, democrats were denied the right of expression, while the fundamentalists were allowed to indoctrinate the youth in the mosques, and their followers had the certainty of impunity when they went on the attack, for example, by killing women not conforming to Sharia Law. Later, under the presidency of Chadli Benjedid (1990-1991), the Algerian leaders promoted a politicized Islam in order to contain popular malcontent, exploiting the widespread misogeny which, in many societies, makes of women the scapegoats for popular frustration. By convincing some sectors of the population that their misfortunes stemmed from women's behavior, in violation of Koranic law and teaching, rather than from social inequalities and corruption, the Algerian ruling class managed to delay a settling of accounts for a few years. As Hayane writes,

> The Chadli regime could only thwart the democratic forces by promoting the rise of an anti-democratic fundamentalist trend, in this case an Islamic fundamentalist movement functioning as a political ideology. (Hayane 1994)

Chadly preferred to use the Islamic fundamentalists to prevent the birth of a socially rooted movement, that might have challenged the corruption and the shameless enrichment of his 'court,' his family and his entourage's salons. He reckoned that it was preferable to come to an agreement with an opportunistic and thus more ideologically 'manageable' fundamentalism, by giving it moral control over society (S.G. 1994).

To this end, the Algerian state allowed the fundamentalists' politicized version of Islam to invade the schools, the universities, the mosques (*El Watan* 1994. 9. 03) and the television, all of which became instruments of ideological manipulation and propaganda.

The press has revealed that the mosques were used as deposits for secret arms caches and bases for terrorists (S.G. 1994), while the schools became nurseries for a new breed of "killer-children" (Berkani 1994). People have also denounced both the content of the school books, that are "manifestly steeped in fundamentalist ideology," and "the fundamentalist cloud that hovers over the schools, traumatizing the pupils' imagination." (Ghazi 1994). Ghazi, in making these charges, added that " the danger is deep and does not allow any longer for the complicity of silence" (Ghazi 1994).

Showing greater foresight, women were the first to expose the complicity of the government with the fundamentalists, when the Algerian state refused to stop the violence perpetrated against them. This is what Mme. Meraoun, president of the Women's Association for Personal Development and the Exercise of Citizens' Rights (AFEPEC), told the press, after recalling the various phases of the violence unleashed against women from 1970 on :

> In 1980, the Islamic fundamentalists moved to a new level of social infiltration, when they started organizing, in full daylight and without being disturbed, training camps on some of the country's beaches. The schools and the mosques have become platforms for courses that foment hatred against against women and places for the indoctrination of the youth. In 1984, the most serious attack against women was the adoption of a family code that has legalized the worse forms of violence against them. (Meraoun 1994)*

None of this would have been possibile without the complicity of a state that claimed to be secular but, according to the Egyptian ambassador to Algeria, had made a deal with the leader of the

Islamic Salvation Front (FIS) Abassi Madani, in Saudi Arabia, through the office of President Chadli (S.G. 1994).

In the same vein, under pressure by the fundamentalists, the government made Arabic the official language. This linguistic reform was considered legitimate by many, but was introduced in haste and, given the lack of competent teachers, it deepened the gap between French-speaking and Arab-speaking Algerians, lowering the latter's educational level, exacerbating their frustrations and making it more difficult for them to find work and a place in society.

In order to preserve class privileges, freedom of expression, in vain demanded by democratic citizens, was denied. Corruption was institutionalized, and when President Boudiaf came to power to fight it, in 1988, he was assasinated. A brief liberalization followed in the wake of the tragic events of 1988, but soon there was a return to authoritarian practices. The power struggle between different factions has now reached a frantic level and is accompanied by an infernal spiral of repression and assassinations, as the Islamic fundamentalists have unleashed a campaign of terror in the attempt to build an Islamic state.

As any hope for a better political and economic future has vanished, the Islamic fundamentalists preach a return to the original purity of Islam, of which they offer, however, a caricature version. In their propaganda the source of all evil is "modernity," whose main symbol, vilified in the eyes of a largely illiterate population, is the emancipated woman, who exercises a profession and goes out of the home without the veil.

By making women the scapegoats, the fundamentalists have both spared the ruling class, whose political and economic power they want to share, and precluded any questioning of class inequalities. This is, arguably, an incontrovertible proof that their goal is the struggle for power not for social equality. The failure of the western model of development in Algeria has generated a terrorism that uses the political perspective of Islam and assassination for the conquest of power.

Andrée Michel

What is at Stake for the Algerian People and Algerian Women in the Struggle for Democracy

In the current debates on Algeria, both the western media and the politicians portray the country's situation as if only two political subjects were present on the scene. On one side they place the state, which responds to and represses the fundamentalists' terror campaign; on the other, the FIS and the fundamentalist armed groups, which are supposed to have the support of the majority of the population. In reality, in the parlamentary elections of 1992, which the government cancelled, about half of the electorate did not vote.

What is not being acknowledged by the press is the presence of a third social-political force: the Algerian democrats, who are committed to the formation of a society built upon tolerance, freedom and a different development model. Unfortunately, due to factional quarrelling, the opposition parties have not been able to give expression to this popular demand. Many have avoided taking a position; or have been slow to condemn the assassinations carried out by the armed groups supported by the fundamentalists, while some have refused to take part in the street demonstrations organized against the terrorists's brutal violence.

By contrast, Algerian women have been the first to go to the streets to demonstrate against religious fundamentalism, demanding that the government take a firm stand against the assassins and stop dialoguing with those refusing to condemn them. Showing a greater awareness than the politicians, many Algerian journalists have paid homage to the women's courage and struggles. One reason for women's resistance is certainly the fact that they are the favorite target of the fundamentalists, whose main objective is to force them not only to wear the veil but to go back to the home. One tactic they have used has been to blame the unemployment crisis on women's presence in the labor market, despite the fact that out of 14 million Algerian women, only 317,000, less than 5% of the female population of working age, have a job outside the home (Bendouba-Touati 1995).

Women, meanwhile, have continued to pressure the Algerian leaders to convince them that they must support the democratic forces in the country, if fundamentalist terror is to be stopped. They have also appealed to the opposition parties whose leaders have refused to take a position or make a common front against terrorism, because of their divisions and lack of courage.

What is at stake for the Algerian people in the outcome of this mobilization is the very future of democracy. Even before the 1992 elections were cancelled, the FSI had declared that, if it should gain power, there would be no more voting, because it did not need representatives and only a theocracy, based upon the divine word, as interpreted by the Ayatollahs, could legitimately hold power. The Algerian women's resistance to this horrendous attempt to set the clock backward has been exemplary. Will they and the other democratic forces, that are organizing in the cities and neighborhoods, or through professional associations, prove strong and united enough to prevent the fundamentalists from taking over? This is the crucial question today.

It is to be hoped that the opposition parties will overcome their divisions and unite in the struggle against their common enemy. Women's struggles have scored a first victory in that, under pressure, the government has reasserted its commitment to the elimination of terrorism, declaring that "Algeria will not retreat," and has asked "all citizens to equally assume their responsibilities" (*La Liberté* 1994.12.07). Moreover, despite the restrictions placed by the International Monetary Fund (IMF) and the World Bank on the state's management of the economy, the government has tried to move beyond a social policy exclusively based upon security considerations and has set up projects that should make jobs available for the unemployed youth.

What is at Stake in the Algerian Conflict from the Viewpoint of the North: Capitalism and Democracy

For international capital, what is at stake in the Algerian conflict are obviously profit, business expansion, access to a market of

28 million people and complete control over gas and petroleum prospecting as well as speculation in oil revenues. It is calculated that

> between 1986 and 1990, on the basis of 1985 oil prices (that fell on an average from $28 to $15 in 1986, and subsequently failed to top $20) the OPEC countries lost $263 billion, the main beneficiaries of this loss being the rich countries. (*Solidarieté Internationale*, January 1991)

Strangled by debt the Algerian state has been forced to request a rescheduling of its payments with the IMF and the World Bank, while the state companies have been forced to open their doors to foreign capital. Shortly before their talks with the IMF, the Gozhali government offered foreign oil companies the possibility of investing in the existing national oil companies in exchange for an entry fee. This was the first step taken by multinational capital in the recolonization of Algeria's oil's wealth. However, before proceeding further and starting to make investments, international capital is demanding the guarantee of social and political *stability*, which is synonymous with security for foreign companies. The great powers are not interested in who rules the state in Algeria. A lesson here should be learned from the behavior of the multinationals towards China and Iran. In the face of intense competition to expand their international market shares, their pledges that they would stop dealing with China because of the Tien-An-Men Square massacre, and they would place a ban on Iran, because of its human rights violations, have fallen by the wayside. Thus, it is not surprising that, at the end of 1994, the United States was encouraging the Algerian government to negotiate with the fundamentalists. Convinced that the FIS would gain power and

> burned by the Iranian experience, Washington want[ed] to avoid attracting thunderbolts from another set of fundamentalists, this time Algerian, should they gain power. (*Le Monde* 1994.21.05)

Business is business. Thus, it is no coincidence that an Algerian newspaper should ask "Is Clinton playing the FIS card?" (*Le Matin* 1994. 23. 05). More recently, the U.S. position has changed. Faced with the general indignation aroused by the fundamentalists' assassination of foreigners in Algeria, the Group of Seven meeting in Naples in 1994, condemned terrorism and rejected all negotiations with the assassins. Time will tell if this was a concession to world opinion or a commitment to the advent of a democratic society in Algeria. It would not be the first time, however, that a condemnation of human rights violations by the great powers is accompanied by tolerance and behind the scenes dealings when profit is at stake.

For western democrats the stakes in the Algerian conflict are very different from those of business, as they will have to take a stand against the export of a development model that has failed in the Third World, showing its devastating consequences for people's lives, and has exacerbated rivalries and social inequalities. Far from allowing the state and the multinational companies to impose such development programs, western democrats should help block the propagation of this recipe for disaster. Asking for the cancellation of the external debts is not enough. It is important to ensure that the debt is not reproduced, as it will happen if a development model is reintroduced that is based upon the looting of raw materials, through the fixing of low prices for exports (oil in this case) and high prices for imports. For this model favors the enrichment of the Northern banks and multinationals and gives support to corrupt élites in the Third World.

Obviously, it is the pople of the Third World who must decide what development model they want to pursue, if their sovereignty is to be respected. But no effort should be spared to convince the Algerian policy makers that the economic model imposed by the IMF and theWorld Bank will not succeed in rescuing the Algerian economy from its crisis. As for us in France, we must mobilize to prevent the French nuclear lobby from selling nuclear reactors to Algeria (as it has offered to do according to the French radio), when the Algerian manufacturing industry opcratcs at 25% or 30% of its capacity, and the Algerian people's need for food and other basic commodities is not being met.

Coordinatcd, cross-border action by Algerian and western democrats must be organized in support of alternative models of development and to block the megalomania of some Third World states. For such joint action to be possible, however, solidarity networks must be developed among social groups on both shores of the Mediterrancan. The citizens of the industrialized countries should also question their ostentatious and wasteful consumption models and object to nuclear as well as conventional arms expenditure. In this way, the industrialized countries would cease to provide a spurious model of consumption for the Third World. It is important here to stress that the people of the industrialized countries contributc to the exploitation of Algeria when they allow the importation of petrolcum that is " practically free," even though they pay dearly for it at the pump. For the low price fetched for petroleum, equivalent, in constant values, to its price in 1908, prevents the Algerians from buying the food, the machinery and the spare parts they need.

This practically free petroleum has been the result of the political and economic strategy pursued by the states of the North, which bear the main responsibility for the situation in Algeria. For without the active support of the Unitcd Statcs and other western powers (including France and, after the fall of the Berlin Wall, Russia), Saudi Arabia and Kuwait would not have been able to exceed their OPEC quotas and cause the price of oil to fall so low. The economic and political annihilation of Iraq, by the coalition put together by George Bush, was a direct consequence of the fact that Iraq was the only country of the region that resisted the attempt by western powers to establish a total control over petroleum.

For western democrats, then, the crucial question is devising a development model that will not ruin the other regions of the planet. To this end we must look at the earth as a whole, and recognize that the damage inflicted on any one of its parts affects every other part as well. In other words, we must steer away from the vague, but often cherished notion of "citizenship," towards a more planetary perspective, a planetary citizenship requiring respect for everybody's rights, regardless of what part of the globe they inhabit. These rights must include, in addition to the traditional political rights, the right to adequate social and economic resources. People must receive a "fair price" for the resources that they sell on the international market, and an adequate pay in exchange for their labor, or, in the absence of a wage, adequate means of survival. The first concrete application of this concept must be the reduction of the enormous inequalities that characterize not only North-South relations, but also class and gender relations within each country, whether industrialized or "developing."

The concept of a planetary citizenship challenges the model of conspicuous and wasteful consumption that prevails in the industrialized countries, since its counterpart is the economic and social misery of the Third World. A classic example of policies that produce social misery is the way in which petroleum is managed, in planetary terms, by western powers and the oil producing countries acting on their behalf.

The call for a planetary citizenship, then, is an invitation for the industrialized countries to make structural changes that some people will undoubtedly find disturbing: changes in the way of living, in the concept of daily comfort and in the model of consumption, at least until alternative sources of energy are developed. These changes must take place now, otherwise they will be realized in the context of an intensifying violence, from which no one will emerge unharmed. There can be no doubt, in fact, that the present world leaders, who plan underdevelopment and the death of millions in other parts of the world, are equally capable of imposing the same underdevelopment and death on their own compatriots, as demonstrated by the existence of millions of unemployed in France, the six million victims of Chernobyl and the 37 million Americans who are deprived of even the right to health insurance. Sickness and death can easily become the lot of the French and other European populations, who are already destined to live subject to the senseless risk of accidents at nuclear plants, whose closure is prevented only by the quest for profit and corporate megalomania.

Notes

* The "Family Code" is the term commonly used for the "Law on Personal Status." It was drafted in great secrecy and then passed, under the Chadli regime in 1983, amidst intense protest and mobilizatiion by Algerian women. It stipulates, in the name of the Koranic law, that women have no right to marry and must be *given* in marriage, that the purpose of marriage is reproduction and sterility can be a cause for divorce, that only the husbands can divorce; that after a divorce a woman must live in the vicinity of her husband so that he can check on her; that as far as legal evidence the testimony of two women is equal to that of one man.

For a discussion of the "Family Code," of the process by which it was passed, and of women's mobilization against it, see Marie-Aimee Helie Lucas "Bound and Gagged by the Family Code." In Miranda Davis ed., *Third World, Second Sex.* Vol. 2. London : Zed Books, 1987, pp. 3-15. Marie-Aimee Helie-Lucas is an Algerian feminist and a founding member of the organization "Women Living Under Muslim Law." [Note of the editors]

Bibliography

Adda, J. (1993). "Pétrole: la manne illusoire." In *Alternatives Economiques* n. 3.

Association Iqra (1994). "L'Analphabetisme en Algérie." In *El Watan*, 17 January.

Bendouba-Touati, A. (1995). *Les Femmes au coeur du drame algérien.* Document of the Association Pluri-Elles-Algérie.

Berkani M. (1994). "Les 'nouveaux monstres'." In *El Watan*, 9 March.

Boumedienne, A. (1994). "Le pétrole Saharien." In *Algérie Actualités*, 15-21 May.

Corm, G. (1991). *Le Proche Orient éclaté. 1956-1991.* Paris: Gallimard.

Erb, G.F. (1978), "*L'Afrique et l'économie internationale: les grandes lignes d'une politique américaine,*" in S.J. Whitaker, (ed.) (1978).

Gallois, D. (1993). "Pétrole: vingt ans après." In *Le Monde,* 21 December

Ghazi, S. (1994). "La chappe intégriste." In *El Watan*, 3 May.

Hayane, A. (1994) "Médias et Terrorisme." In *El Watan*, 10 March.

Judet, P. (1979). "La stratégie d'industrialisation: un refus et un défi." In *Le Monde*, 2 November.

Junqua, D. (1976). "L'Ouest algérien à l'heure industrielle". In *Le Monde*, 16 October.

Karsenty, J.C. (1979). "L'agricolture de l'autogestion à la révolution agraire." In *Le Monde*, 2 November.

La Liberté (1994. 12.07). "L'Algérie ne reculera pas."

Le Matin (1994. 23.05)."Clinton joue-t-il le Fis?"

Meraoun, M. (1994). "Les pires violences pour les femmes." In *El Watan*, 10 March.

Le Monde (1994. 21.05).

S.G. (1994). "Les trois trahisons." In *El Watan*, 24 March.

Solidarité Internationale, (1991 January), n. 18, "Impérialisme et main d'oeuvre."

Tiemçani, S. (1995). "Pêche, un secteur toujours en létargie." In *El Watan,* 27 May.

Tuquoi, J.P. (1993). "Le pétrole quasi-gratuit." In *Le Monde*, 27 February.

Yahiaoui, H. (1995). "Un appareil productif paralysé." In *Alternatives Economiques.* January.

El Watan (1994. 9.03). "Culte."

El Watan (1994. 29.03). "Les défaillances du système de soins."

El Watan (1995. 23.03). "Importations."

Whitaker, S.G. (ed.), (1978). *Les Etats Unis et l'Afrique.* Paris: Karthala.

ON THE NOTION OF A CRISIS OF SOCIAL REPRODUCTION:

A THEORETICAL REVIEW

C. George Caffentzis

What is the role of extra-market relations in the process of social reproduction, when market relations become the paradigm of social exchange? Are "extra-market" relations and activities (e.g. having a friendly conversation, parenting a child) just a shadow of the central, radiating presence of the market, or are they the bulk of social matter? Is paying exclusive attention to market phenomena—the tip of the social iceberg—justified, or is this a prescription for conceptual and practical disaster? These questions have long been essential to the self-definition of sociology, as opposed (until recently) to economics.

To get a concrete idea of the issues evoked by these questions imagine the telephone calls made in a day, in any city of the United States. We may label them as market exchanges, as most calls are bought from the telephone company, and many are made in the context of market activities. But what about the non-marketable exchanges made possible by them? What about the calls that people make, not to buy or sell, but in the context of family relations, love affairs, struggles, including those against the telephone company? These calls certainly have a "use value." Can we say that it is irrelevant to social wealth?

As Marx writes, "The wealth of those societies in which the capitalist mode of production prevails, presents itself as 'an immense accumulation of commodities' (Marx 1967, Vol. 1 : 35)." In the case of the telephone company, wealth presents itself in the form of the company's revenues. But revenues do not reveal the web of information and social coordination that moves through the wires. What is the relation between this informing, imaginative wealth and the commodity form? We know that a telephone workers' strike, or an increase in the interest rate will affect how many calls are made and their price. But what about the social wealth produced in these exchanges? Can all be measured by market means?

If we extend the example of the telephone calls to include all material exchanges (e.g., conversations, amorous encounters), we begin to discover the great "Other" of the market. This realm, subsisting outside the circulation of commodities and money, has been, since the late 1960s, a pole of attraction for the social sciences. For there has been a growing realization that non-market exchanges can challenge and disrupt the formal economy, and yet are essential to its existence (Swedberg 1987; Swedberg 1990; Smelser and Swedberg 1994). Thus, measuring their quantity, and assessing their potential have become crucial problems in social theory. This is especially true in the study of societies in many areas of Africa, Asia and the Americas, where the commodity form is not dominant, and in the study of housework and the other activities involved in the reproduction of labor-power, which are mostly performed outside the space of formal market exchanges in most of the planet.

To describe the sphere of non-market relations new terms have been developed by the last generation of political theorists: the "unwaged work" sector (Dalla Costa and James 1972), the "social factory" (Tronti 1973), the "shadow economy" (Illich 1981), the "general economy" (Bataille 1988), the "moral economy" (Thompson 1991), the "informal economy" (Latouche 1993). With them, a new set of social-economic polarities has emerged: formal/informal, production/reproduction, market/moral, rational/customary, modern/post-modern, and a deconstruction of social forms has begun. For no sooner were apparent dichotomies identified, than their presumed positive and negative poles were displaced, or inverted, to reveal new fields of relations. Once, for instance, reproductive work, including subsistence farming, was made visible, it could no longer be ignored that the quantity of unwaged labor dwarfs the mass of wage labor, which was previously given pride of place in economic analysis, Marxist and non-Marxist alike.

The first question this theoretical revolution poses for us concerns the status of the older concepts in light of these developments. How has the reappraisal of the importance of non-market relations in social life transformed the concept of social reproduction, previously analyzed by political economy on the basis of the market alone? More specifically, how does the notion of a "crisis of social reproduction," intended as a break in "normal" market exchanges, and associated (by Marx and the classical economics tradition) with depressions, panics, and bubbles, relate to this realm? Can we develop a more general notion of such crises, by analogy to those rooted in commodity exchanges? Can famines, genocides, and other breaks in social reproduction be explained through a generalization of the classical notion of crisis?

These questions are the focus of this essay, as they have been for social theory since the 1980s, when it was recognized that famines, and many other catastrophes are by no means natural disasters, but are socially imposed consequences of the negation of entitlements—to food, land and other factors of subsistence—as the work of A. K. Sen and others has demonstrated [cf., (Sen 1981); (Macrae and Zwi 1994); (De Waal 1989)].

My discussion starts with an analysis of Marx's theory of social reproduction, still the most sophisticated classical economic theory on the matter. I then identify three alternative approaches that acknowledge the importance of non-market relations, but differ in the way they account for them. The first approach explains non-market exchanges by generalizing the commodity form, the second generalizes the social-exchange relation, the third stresses the value-producing aspects of non-market phenomena. Each also provides a different perspective on the concept of a crisis of social reproduction, which, in my view, is a test of their explanatory power. I conclude that the third approach has the greatest potential for explaining crises of social reproduction like famines.

Social Reproduction: Genealogy and Crisis, A Marxian View

"Social reproduction" is an odd term. "Reproduction" evokes naturally reoccurring biological cycles, while "social" connotes a set of intentional and voluntary interactions. Nevertheless, the belief that modern capitalist societies have natural reproductive cycles has been central to the development of economics and sociology. The tension present in the concept is evident in the continuing tension between these disciplines. The reasons for it can be illustrated etymologically. "Sociology" is rooted in the Latin *socius,* that stands for a freely chosen companion with whom there are no blood ties. "Economics" derives, instead, from the ancient Greek word *oikos* ("hearth and home"), that describes the bonds of blood and slavery. One could talk about the reproduction of the *oikos,* because the household was not seen as a terrain of choice and freedom, but as the threshold between nature and convention, *physis* and *nomos,* thus sharing the automaticity and repetitiveness of the physical world. From this viewpoint, economic relations were in the realm of necessity. They occurred between husband and wife, parents and children, masters and slaves, and their reproduction was rooted in seemingly "natural" rhythms. Social relations, instead, were in the realm of freedom, being established by mutual agreement among equals, free from "natural" bonds. It was inconceivable that these unique relations, built on desired coincidences, could be reproduced. At best (as in Aristotle's *Ethics*), rules could be set for their preservation.

The Greco-Roman distinction between *socius* and *oikos* eroded, however, with the development of capitalism, as familial, subsistence production was replaced by dependence on monetary exchanges (which is the foundation of the bourgeois concept of "freedom"). From this development, that affected both the proletariat (after the enclosures) and the rentiers (who had been accustomed to consume goods produced on their estates),— originated the very concept of "society," as a term describing human togetherness, and later the concept of "political economy," where the Greek *politikos* was made synonymous with the Latin *socius*. Locke's "social contract" theory formalized the perception, widespread among the 17th century bourgeoisie, that the "natural" relations of the *oikos* (husband-wife, father-children, master-servant) were becoming "social," that is, a matter of individual decision and contract among equals. But a converse recognition was also taking shape, revolving around the idea that society too has a biological metabolism and reproductive cycle. This recognition led to the concept of "social reproduction," the main object of study for political economy in the period of the Enlightenment.

The first theory of social reproduction was presented by Quesnay in the *Tableau économique,* in the mid-18th century. Quesnay asked how a collection of associated individuals, members of specific classes (rentier, capitalist, worker) and connected only by contract, could reproduce itself in such a way that, after a cycle of production and circulation of commodities, the same individuals and classes would reappear. As Marx was to point out, the analytic power of Quesnay's approach derived from the fact that he rooted his analysis in the old locus of the *oikos*: land and agricultural production. Yet, this was also the limit of the *Tableau,* as manufacturing appears in it only as an embarrassing "miscellaneous," though, by the late 18th century, industrial production, in Western Europe, was beginning to overshadow agriculture.

In the trajectory from Quesnay to Marx, the most important development in the analysis of social reproduction, was Adam Smith's theory that value production must include industrial labor.[1] But it was Marx, the theorist of the capitalist crisis and proletarian revolution, who was to elaborate the most definitive analysis of the conditions for the reproduction of capitalist society.

This subject is treated in Volume II of *Capital*, where Marx shifted from the class struggle (the focus of Volume I) to the analysis of those social phenomena of capitalist society that return to themselves: circulation, rotation, turnover, circuit, reproduction. Instead of changes in linear variables (e.g., rises in wages, falls in profit), in Volume II, Marx examined those changes that return a system to its starting point, showing how the transformations it undergoes in the process are crucial for both the reproduction of the system as well as its subversion.

The model Marx used to analyze the reproduction of capital, in Vol. 2, was the mechanical theory of heat, developed by mid-19th century physics, that explains macroscopic phenomena as the products of millions of microscopic events and entities.[2] In conformity with this method, Marx described the macroscopic aspects of capitalism as the product of millions of micro-events, and accounted for the reproduction of social capital on the basis of the circuits of individual capitals, with their microphysical orbits, different velocities and periods. Marx gave a graphic account of the movement from the micro-to the macro-level in the Introduction to Part III, that deals with "The Reproduction and Circulation of Social Capital":

> ...the circuits of individual capitals intertwine, presuppose and necessitate one another, and form, precisely in this interlacing, the movement of the total social capital. Just as in the simple circulation of commodities the total metamorphosis of a commodity appeared as a link in the

series of metamorphoses of the world of commodities, so now the metamorphosis of the individual capital appears as a link in the metamorphoses of the social capital. (Marx 1967b: 357-358)

Marx's vision of capitalist economy is that of an immense collection of exchanges, with individually coherent circuits, where value is conserved, increased or decreased, and where commodities and money leap back and forth to other circuits in the course of each exchange, transmitting impulses in every direction.[3] It is an image reminiscent of the play of the atoms in the organic chemistry diagrams so popular in Marx's time. For we can imagine capitalist A (i) selling the produced commodity to another capitalist B who uses it as means of production, (ii) taking part of the money so realized and buying some luxury goods from capitalist C, (iii) buying labor power from worker D and new means of production from capitalist E who, in turn energizes, new circuits of other individual capitals.

However, exchange must be profitable for the system to reproduce itself, on the micro-and macro level. Thus, "[a]ll three circuits have the following in common: the self-expansion of value as the determining purpose." (Marx 1967b:103). But no exchange is necessary or guaranteed; each connection can be broken, or its purpose may not be realized; hence the permanent possibility of micro-crises and even the dissolution of the system as a whole.[4] Marx attributes a tremendous importance to the possible breaking of the exchange symmetry. The breaking of the micro bonds of capital's circuit, intimates for him the possibility of the crisis and the end of capitalism, as we can see from the following passages published (respectively) in 1859 and 1867. "The division of exchange into purchase and sale...contains the general possibility of commercial crises...because the antithesis of commodity and money is the abstract and general form of all contradictions inherent in the bourgeois mode of labor (Marx 1970: 96)." And again:

> If the interval in time between the two complementary
> phases of the... metamorphosis of a commodity become
> too great, if the split between the sale and the purchase
> become too pronounced, the intimate connexion between
> them, their oneness, asserts itself by producing a crisis.
> The antithesis, use-value and exchange value; the con-
> tradictions that private labor is bound to manifest itself
> as direct social labor, that a particularized concrete kind
> of labor has to pass for abstract human labor; the contra-
> diction between the personification of objects and the rep-
> resentation of persons by things; all these antitheses and
> contradictions, which are immanent in commodities, as-
> sert themselves.... in the antithetical phases of the meta-
> morphosis of a commodity. (Marx 1967a: 113-114)

For Marx the crisis brings to the surface the truth of the capitalist system of social reproduction. For the metamorphosis of the commodity into money and profits, requires a continuous suppression of needs and glaring contradictions. But once the bond between the commodity and money temporally loosens, a gap grows that can explode all the contradictions of capitalist life. As we know, the main contradiction for Marx is in "the bourgeois mode of labor." This may appear irrelevant in the sphere of circulation, since people generally buy goods to satisfy their needs, not because of who made them. But the primary objective of market-exchanges is the expansion of value, and here the labor that goes into the commodity becomes the key factor. For its "contradictions," beginning with workers' struggles, can cut into the capitalists' profits, and put the circulation process into crisis.

As Marx pointed out, the process of social reproduction brings everything back—Money, Commodity, Production—to the starting point. But this return is not guaranteed, since in reproducing itself, capitalism also reproduces its contradictions. "Capitalist production, therefore,.......produces not only commodities, not only surplus-value, but it also produces and reproduces the capitalist relation; on the one side the capitalist, on the other the wage-laborer" (Marx 1967a: 578). Far from being natural, the reproduction of the contradictory, conflictual capitalist relation, is permanently vulnerable to the possibility of crises and catastrophe.

The Crisis of Marx's Theory of Social Reproduction

Not surprisingly, then, from the publication of *Capital*, Vol. I, in 1867, to the late 1960s, "crisis theory" has been a key component in the development of Marxist thinking, while the attempt to exorcise the danger of the crisis, in theory and practice, has been the driving force of bourgeois economics. Marxists largely accepted and often revisited Marx's account of social reproduction (Palloix 1973; De Brunhoff 1976). But their main concern was to establish the possible causes of capitalist crisis, and here Marx's explanation was of little help. Did crises arise from a disproportion in the production of consumer-goods versus producer-goods? Were they caused by a chronic insufficiency of aggregate demand, or were they a response to the falling rate of profit during periods of expansion and investment (Foley 1986)? Though many times reinterpreted, the text of *Capital* could not resolve the matter.

Still, "crisis theory" generated provocative hypotheses. From Luxemburg's, Hilferding's, Lenin's and Bukharin's underconsumptionist explanations of imperialism, to Kalecki's "political business cycle" theory, during World War II, to Baran and Sweezy's "realization" hypothesis, and Paul Mattick's "rate of profit" retort in the 1960s, the field of crisis theory was contentious (Luxemburg 1968; Bukharin 1966; Kalecki 1971; Baran and Sweezy 1966; Mattick 1969).[5]

Soon after the publication of Volume I of *Capital*, bourgeois political economy itself underwent a major change. Under the newly adopted name of "economics," it ceased all attempts to explain the totality of social exchanges, and turned its attention to the way in which fields of desire and modes of rational calculation lead to the maximization of utility in individual subjects (whether consumers or firms) at any particular time. Older questions of social reproduction were either refracted in the categories of the new discourse, or became meaningless for economists. For late 19th century economists—such as Walras, Pareto, Jevons and Menger—there could not be such a thing as a crisis. The market was supposed to tend toward an equilibrium, assuring the full employment of all factors of production, and maximizing every one's desires (although under budget constraints). Thus, any movement away from equilibrium had to take the form of a "shock," i.e. it had to be a phenomenon exogenous to the sphere of economic relations, as, e.g., a change of customs and tastes, an earthquake, or a government decree. The result, for the most part, was that a century of oblivion enwrapped the Marxian problematic of reproduction and crisis in economics. This state of affairs came to an end, however, in the 1960s, when the growth, worldwide, of new social movements, threatening the foundations of capitalist society, forced a reappraisal of both the Marxist analysis of the reproduction/crisis nexus, and its evasion in bourgeois economics.

The problem with Marxist theory was that it could only explain the reproduction of the capitalist-waged-worker relation. But the revolutionary subjects of the '60s were mostly unwaged. They were subsistence farmers in the Third World, housewives, students, and all the "minorities" that make up the bulk of the world's population. Marx's theory was practically silent about these figures, leading many Marxists to underestimate the political potential of the anti-colonial movement, the welfare mothers and black power movements, the student movement, the women's movement, and, today, the indigenous peoples' movements.

A similar problem confronted bourgeois economics, as the "unemployed," the "underemployed," the "non-productive" of the neoclassical economic synthesis were making history and were becoming the subjects of government policies and corporate investment. New paradigms were needed; governments and corporations demanded new reports; and obligingly, the economists came to the rescue with new theories reappraising the economic significance of non-market spheres, from the family, to sexuality, racial discrimination, education, and health. In both the Marxist and bourgeois research programs, the analysis of what had been left to the rest of the social sciences, especially sociology, now became a priority. The core of this new activity was the re-examination of the concept of social reproduction.

Three new theories of social reproduction emerged in this period, in response to the shortcoming of bourgeois and Marxist political economy. Each can be understood as a generalization of one, or another, moment of the commodity-money-production circuit, as presented in Marx. As we know, this process begins with the commodity, C, that is exchanged for money, M, with which the means for producing the commodity are bought and put into action in the production process, P, leading to a new commodity, C', that incorporates more value than the money invested in the production process. Each moment of this process, that moves from the commodity (C), through a series of exchanges (M and P), to the commodity C', as increased by the surplus value, allows for a generalization of the economic into the social. The new theories of reproduction and crisis differ from each other with regard to what part of the social reproduction circuit they generalize.

The Totalization of the Commodity Form: the market is all

The first approach explains social reproduction through a generalization of the commodity form. Classical political economy defines a commodity as something that is owned and can legally be exchanged. But even in "advanced" money economies, where the commodity form seems to dominate all aspects of life, there is much that escapes its grip. Much housework is unpaid, and so are many instances of sexual intercourse, most babies are not produced in exchange for money, most votes are not directly bought. Moreover, a large part of the U.S. population is not made up of wage earners nor of private capitalists, and most of the average person's day is not directly involved in wage or profit-earning activities. The vast terrain of love, friendship, sleep and dreams, sickness and death, as well as much religious, scientific, or artistic activity are crucial aspects of social reproduction, though they escape the hold of the commodity form. Or so it seems. For there are economists, who are ready to dispute that we can ever exit from the world of commodities.

As Blaise Pascal showed in the 17th century, a market logic can be applied even to the question of the salvation of the soul, as he argued that a reasonable person should believe in God and wager his/her energies in living a Christian life, even if there is only an infinitesimally small probability that Christian beliefs may be true. For the infinite pain of going to Hell multiplied by the small probability that Christian beliefs may be true is still much greater than the discomfort of leading a moral life multiplied by the large probability that Christian beliefs may be false.

Pascal's famous wager provides a model for what some have called "the economic approach to human behavior," or "rational choice theory," and still others have described as a form of "economic imperialism" [(McKenzie and Tullock 1978), (Tullock 1972), (Boulding 1969)]. For if the soul can be treated as if it were a commodity to be invested in, then our leisure time, our children, sexual desires, even our taste for revolution are open to the same treatment under the dominance of capitalism. This, at least, has been the contention of Nobel Prize winner Gary S. Becker, who claims that his economic approach stems from: "The combined assumptions of maximizing behavior, market equilibrium, and stable preferences, used unrelentlessly and unflinchingly, form the heart of the economic approach as I see it" (Becker 1976: 5).

The ideal object of Becker's analysis is the "behavior" of a set of "agents" (e.g., a married couple who behaves like an ideal firm), who treat every decision they make (whether or not to have a child, sleep or stay up, brush their teeth) as if they were rational consumers choosing to buy a car. Becker's model, in effect, applies the logic of commodities to things and activities that are legally or morally inalienable, e.g., children, votes, life, sexuality, or are not given an explicit economic value (rarely, e.g., anyone is paid to dream). Becker and other "rational choice" theorists, explain how people make choices about their personal lives, by taking the market as the model. A "rational agent" would treat all the alternatives "as if" they were commodities with a price attached, calculated by how much time and money it would take (for instance) to bring up a child, or spend an evening with one's lover, where the value of one's time is measured by the amount of money one could earn in the formal labor market in the same time period. The "rational agent" would likely have a budget constraint, that would be calculated as a quantity of time, valued at its market value; and s/he would have, then, to choose the combination of "as if" commodities that would maximize his/ her utility. Becker does not claim that actual human beings behave according to these "economic assumptions," but he believes that every actual "behavior" can be compared to what an ideally rational being, embodying the "economic" assumptions of the market, would do, and that the distance between the actual and ideal results can be computed.

The "rational choice" approach has allowed economists to apply their analyses to regions of social life that economics had largely ignored (because it considered them economically irrelevant or because of legal restrictions on their commodification). The growing hegemony, in the 1980s, of a neoliberal perspective that makes of the market the arbiter of all social decision-making has given this theory a new use. Surrogate mothering, the adoption market, the legal traffic in organs— all have drawn upon it, in their attempt to acquire a legal status.[6] Pure Neoliberals want these new "trades" to be fully legalized, they want polices devised so that bottlenecks in these areas (e.g. the resistance of a surrogate mothers to relinquishing "her" commissioned child) are eliminated, and the social utility of these exchanges maximized. They also want to erase the stigma still attached to the commercialization of these spheres of life, and this is where "rational choice theory" becomes important. The logical conclusion and aspiration of neoliberal politics is to apply Becker's "economic approach" to every aspect of social and individual life, so that commodity logic can prevail even in fields where moral or psychological prejudices have so far barred its application (Posner 1992: 3-4).

Once "rational choice" theory is applied to such fields as demography, then it can claim to provide a general theory of social reproduction, taking into account non-formal as well as formal exchanges. Thus, it is no coincidence that this generalization of commodity logic has led to a "new institutional economics" that tries to provide a "rational explanation" (and justification) for the very existence of commodities, money, firms and capitalism itself (in this way, it gives capitalism the same boost that medieval philosophy gave to the Church, when it devised proofs for the existence of God).

One of the key questions for "institutional economics" is how to account for the existence and reproduction of super-individual structures, given the dramatic changes in the preferences of the individuals who create them (Williamson 1994). If every aspect of social life is determined by a commodity logic, based on atomized human desires, and if human preferences are continually changing, why (it is asked) do some institutions, for example, the monetary system, survive over long historical periods? The answer given rests on the concept of "transaction costs," these being the additional costs involved in the carrying out of exchanges, production and consumption. A classic example of "transaction costs" are transport costs, but there are other costs as well, e.g., the cost of acquiring information about market prices. A now classic account argues that the "transaction costs" of monetary exchange are lower than those of the alternative, the barter system, because the transportation and information costs of finding someone who has what we want, and wants what we have, in a barter system are very high (Clower 1967). A monetary system, enabling us to exchange commodities for money, short-circuits these costs, and this (we are told) is what makes the institution of a money system reasonable for all market participants. According to this "institutionalist" approach, once a monetary system comes into being its positive features become evident to all, and this is why it survives and is reproduced through time.

It is easy to see why this "economic approach" is a perfect expression of neoliberal ideology. By explaining super-individual structures as the result of rational choices among individuals, it generalizes the commodity form to all aspects of life, and presents the basic components of capitalism as the embodiment of Reason in the social world. However, this approach ignores the beliefs and desires of the very subjects whose behavior it supposedly explains. Many women e.g. have demanded wages for housework, but not to become little entrepreneurs, but to refuse more work and economic dependence (Federici 1982). Similarly, subsistence farmers have struggled, throughout this century, under the slogan "Tierra and Libertad". But this did not mean "Real Estate and Cash Crops." The demand for land, as in the Mexican revolution of 1910-1917 and the Zapatista movement of 1994, expressed the desire to decommodify the earth, and disentangle it from real estate and the grip of agribusiness (Collier and Quaratiello 1994).

A further problem with "rational choice" theory is that it cannot conceptualize the crises of social reproduction except as shocks exogenous to the commodity system. The shocks must come from "outside," because every process "inside" the system is driven by the decision of rational agents facing budget constraints, and by a predetermined commodity distribution that is supposed to lead to an equilibrium. This explanation is similar to the way in which crises are explained in neoclassical economics. According to the latter, changes in tastes and in the natural or social environment (from a craze for chocolates to the discovery of new oil fields) transmit, through the price mechanism, information concerning new desires, new commodity stocks, or new restrictions. As the explanation goes, rational economic agents interpret the new price structures with their budgets in mind, and then shift their pattern of exchanges. As it filters through the market, this shift, at first, can cause catastrophic results, e.g., sudden pockets of unemployment, or large stocks of unsold commodities. But, in time, the equilibrium is presumably restored : the unemployed move to areas of high employment, or accept a lower wage at their present jobs; and the unsold commodities are reduced in price or destroyed, if storage costs are greater than any likely future return on their sale. A new equilibrium is reached, with all the market participants (or, at least, those who managed to survive) maximally satisfied, at the end of the adjustment, as they were prior to it.

However, once this neoclassical model is generalized to encompass *all* areas of social life previously excluded from the study of formal market relations, a logical problem appears. Once the commodity logic is generalized, e.g. to the realms of psychology and politics, then changes in these realms cannot be treated as exogenous, nor can they function as the source of shocks to account for the origin of crises. If a new set of desires, or a new governmental policy, are the product of rational choice, then they cannot be an extra-systemic source of crisis. They become part of the formal market. Consequently, one has to either invent a new extra-systemic sphere, or accept the possibility that the system of rational choice is not equilibrium tending, but creates within itself perturbational forces. In other words, *the generalization of commodity logic to the realm of social reproduction puts the logical framework of neoclassical theory itself into crisis.*

Exchange Generalized

The second approach to social reproduction sees commodity exchange as a special case of a more general social exchange relation. The main spokesmen for this theory are Granovetter and Foucault, who argue that market relations are "embedded" in a wider network of social relations. Granovetter, echoing the work of Karl Polanyi, emphasizes the importance of trust and obligations as essential conditions for the existence of market relations and the formation of markets. He argues that without some protection against generalized malfeasance and opportunism, and some guarantees of mutual confidence, even the simplest market transactions would not be possible. How could we go to a market—the argument runs—if we could not obtain any trust-worthy information, or ever turn our eyes from our possessions without fear of losing them?

The claim is that protection and guarantees are provided by the "embeddedness" of market relations in "networks" of concrete personal relations (Granovetter 1992: 60). In other words, social reproduction rests on relations of reciprocity and redistribution, as well as market exchanges (Polanyi 1992). According to Granovetter, only in the context of non-utilitarian personal relations of loyalty and mutual recognition, can we understand the "altruistic" behavior required for the operation of a commodity market driven by egoistic buyers and sellers. Paradoxically, the existence of an economic agent capable of "standing true" to a contract depends on non-economic forms of social behaviors that can be learned only in an environment pre-existing outside the market. In effect, Granovetter "humanizes the market" by claiming that trust, community solidarity, and reciprocity are preconditions, not consequences, of a market society. This position, however, faces a major contradiction: inherent to the advance of market relations is the tendency to destroy the very relations of trust, solidarity and reciprocity the market presumably depends upon.

For both Granovetter and Polanyi it is this tendency that is responsible for crises of social reproduction. Polanyi, for example, has described how the rise of capitalism in the 16th and 18th centuries—the "Great Transformation" of Land, Labor and Money into commodities (Polanyi 1944/57)—destroyed the sociality that was at the root of market relations in medieval Europe. But how could the "Great Transformation" occur, and why, would the market destroy what is vital to its survival? If we accept Granovetter's and Polanyi's assumptions, such phenomena are bound to remain incomprehensible.

This impasse is evident in the politics of "communitarianism," the movement in which the theories of Granovetter and Polanyi have found their political expression. With its revaluation of volunteerism, its praise of "non-governmental organizations," and its fore grounding of the "non-profit sector" (Etzioni 1988, 1995; Rifkin 1995), communitarianism takes a stand in favor of a market economy, but with a "human face." Like Granovetter, the communitarians believe that a triumph of commodity logic—as in the aspirations of the neoliberals—undermines the very market society it wants to consolidate. Thus, their organizations have rushed into the various catastrophes caused by neoliberal structural adjustment policies around the planet (from Detroit to Somalia) to save "humanity." But, in this process, they have also helped save "the market" and, by the same token, the very policies which allowed for the development of such catastrophes.

These contradictions may in part explain why, in the intellectual tides of the post-1968 period, Granovetter's (and Polanyi's) analyses have been overshadowed by the work of Michel Foucault. Like other theorists of the "sociology of economic life," Foucault agrees that non-commodifiable relations condition the possibility of capitalist exchange. But, while Granovetter highlights the moral virtues necessary to the life of *homo economicus*, Foucault questions the very concept of "rationality" and the "rational economic agent." In a series of historical works, written between the early 1960s to the early 1980s, he argues that not only is rationality a social construct, but it is shaped in a field of power relations, forming a "general economy," that does not function according to the calculations of a pre-existent rational ego (as believed by the theorists of commodity logic), because it is precisely these power relations that define what "rationality" and the "ego" must be in any particular epoch (Foucault 1971a; Foucault 1971b; Foucault, 1973; Foucault 1977; Smart 1983: 123-137).

Power relations are as essential to Foucault's account of social reproduction as they are to Marx's. In place of the optimistic picture presented by Granovetter and Polanyi, of a network of reciprocity relations surrounding any economic agent, his work confronts us with a somber scenario, where economic rationality is genetically the offspring of regimes organized to produce pain, confinement, control, and of technologies by which power is exercised over its Others (the mad, the ill, the criminal, the sexually deviant).

Foucault rejected, however, the traditional view of power. First, he criticizes the "juridical/monarchical" model of power which poses a central stabilizing axis (the Rule of Law, or the Divinely Sanctified King) at the peak of the social hierarchy legislating, and repressing any deviations from the norm. Echoing Nietzsche's slogan "God is Dead," he asserted that there is no Ruling Class, Judge or King imposing the law on all social agents and punishing its transgressions with death. Nor is there an opposing class struggle against its rule and prohibitions. In the place of the "binary and all-encompassing opposition between rulers and ruled" serving as a "general matrix" for all power relations, he identified a manifold of omnipresent "relationships of force" that "come into play in the machinery of production, in families, groups, institutions, and are the basis for wide-ranging effects of cleavage running through the social body" (Foucault 1981: 94).

Foucault also rejected the assumption that "power" operates only, or primarily, through a structure of prohibitions, and emphasized instead its productive character. Power relations do not only forbid or restrict social or individual possibilities, but produce new strategies, techniques of control (as exemplified by the development of "Reason" and "economic rationality") and, correspondingly, new capacities in the social individual.

As is well-known, much of Foucault's work is concerned with the description of the emergence of new regimes of Power. Particularly influential, in this context, has been his analysis of the development of "bio-power," which he identifies as the distinguishing feature of European societies in the "modern era," beginning with the 18th century. Through this term Foucault describes the forces upon which the social reproduction of capitalist relations has historically depended, and capitalism has in turn developed. Thus, "bio-power" is largely reminiscent of the Marxian "labor-power" and, indeed, Foucault admitted that capitalism would not have been possible without the controlled insertion of bodies into the machinery of production and the adjustment of the phenomena of population to economic processes (Foucault 1981: 140-141). But he adds that "this was not all it required, it also needed the growth of both these factors, their reinforcement as well as their availability and docility; it had to have methods of power capable of optimizing forces, aptitudes, and life in general without at the same time making them more difficult to govern" (ibid.).

Thus, while Marx concentrated on power relations in the factory, Foucault looked at the development of the sciences of sexuality (from demographics to psychoanalysis) that arose in the 19th century to control and develop that main component of bio-power: sex. In this way his theory anticipated some of the insights of the feminist and gay movements that equally have stressed sexuality and the family as terrains of power relations. This is, undoubtedly, one of the reasons for the popularity his theory has enjoyed among post-1968 radicals. However, his concern with disentangling power relations from any specific political and economic structure, his insistence on the omnipresence of power relations, and above all his suspicion towards any liberationist project have prevented him from playing for the post-1968 generation the role Marcuse played for the activists of the 1960s.

There is the further problem that in his effort to stress the productive (rather than repressive) character of power relations, Foucault has often seemed oblivious to the fact that (a) the "production of life" in the "modern era" has had a purely instrumental character, being finalized to the development of the capacity of work; (b) the production of death has been a permanent component of the capitalist political economy, in all of its stages, being as essential to its goals as the "production of life," as proven by the history of colonial conquest, the mechanized slaughters of the First and Second World War, the continuing threat of atomic annihilation, and the economic and ecological catastrophes today plaguing, with increasing frequency, people all over the planet.

By contrast, in his account, so firm is the assumption that, starting from the 18th century, the goal of the state became the "production of life" that his description of the emergence of bio-power on the historical scene, almost recalls a myth of origin, if not the textbook tales still so often rehearsed to establish the progressive character of capitalism:

> ...the pressure exerted by the biological on the historical had remained very strong for thousands of years; epidemics and famine were the two great dramatic forms of this relationship that was always dominated by the menace of death. But through a circular process, the economic—and primarily agricultural—development of the eighteenth century, and an increase in productivity and resources even more rapid than the demographic growth it encouraged, allowed a measure of relief from these profound threats: despite some renewed outbreaks, the period of great ravages from starvation and plague had come to a close before the French Revolution; death was ceasing to torment life so directly. (Foucault 1981: 142)

No trace is to be found here of the famines, massacres, executions that have been the stigmata of capitalism from its beginning to the present. Of the slave trade, of imperial conquest in the ancient and new world, which transferred to Europe tremendous amounts of vital resources nothing is said, instead, "productivity" has the lion share in the alleged displacement of death from history; again no mention is made of the Irish famine of 1846. Unacknowledged is also the fact that concern with population growth and the techniques to stimulate it was already rife under the Ancient Regime, as the mercantilists well realized (Heckscher 1955).

Foucault's theory also fails to explain crises of social reproduction, because for him crisis and discontinuity are permanent conditions of social reproduction. As mentioned, Foucault rules out both the neo-classic assumption that social reproduction is governed by a centripetal, equilibrium-tending market, and the Marxian view of crisis as a product of class conflict. Rather, he pictures it as the result of "unbalanced, heterogeneous, unstable, and tense force relations." This means that crisis is literally everywhere; it is another name for Power itself, it is the norm in a society where, *à la* Hobbes, war is omnipresent, so that war itself needs no special explanation.

However, this nominalist view leads to logical difficulties. How are the great breaks, "the radical ruptures, [and] massive binary cleavages" possible? How, e.g., did the great transformation of the 18th century from "the Right of Death to the Power over Life" take place? How did the regime of bio-power begin to reproduce itself?

Foucault does not say. Instead, he resorts to Heideggerian statements that project the whole problematic into the realm of metaphysics. Such are the claims that the emergence of bio-power represents "The entry of life into history..."(Foucault 1981:141-142), and that "modern man is an animal whose politics places his existence as a living being in question" (Foucault 1981: 143). We are here reminded of the Heracliteans of old, who forced to explain the large-scale features of the universe, reverted to "harmonies in tension" and the Logos.

The Production Process Generalized

The third approach, that I describe as resulting from a generalization of the Marxian idea of production, is the one developed by the feminist theorists and activists politically associated, in the 1970s, with the "wages for housework" campaign and the "housework debate" (Malos 1982).[7]

Fundamental to this approach is the argument that value is created not only by the work needed for the production of commodities, but also by the work needed to produce and reproduce labor-power (Dalla Costa and James 1972). This contrasts with Marx's view that value is only created in the process of commodity production.

For Marx the value of labor-power was measured by the value of the commodities consumed in its production, i.e., by a bundle of "wage goods." Marx refused to give an ontological determination to the value of labor and rejected any supply-and-demand theory of wages. The value of labor-power is for him the product of a "historical and moral" struggle, like that over the length of the working day. Marx, however, did not recognize the unwaged labor that is consumed in the production of labor-power and did not include it in the realm of "productive labor." Aside from a few exceptional passages, he barely took note of the labor involved in child birth, child rearing, housework, the care of the sick and elderly. This aversion to recognizing the productivity of housework has persisted for almost a century in the Marxist tradition, although the "Woman's Question," was crucial in the development of socialist and communist ideology and state planning.

While not the first to challenge this Marxist omission, feminists like Dalla Costa and James, in the early 1970s, forcefully argued that housework is a value producing activity (Dalla Costa and James 1972). For labor-power is not a natural given, but has to be produced and reproduced as an essential condition for social reproduction. This early work was subsequently developed by James, Dalla Costa and others within the same political and theoretical framework (Dalla Costa M. 1974, 1981, 1983; James 1975b; Fortunati 1995, Federici and Fortunati 1984; Dalla Costa G F 1978, 1989, 1995). This perspective was hotly debated within feminist circles throughout the 1970s, and many of its insights have become the starting point for feminist economics and social theory (Picchio 1992; Berch 1982). But though this approach was developed at the same time as Becker's and Foucault's theories of social reproduction, there was very little direct confrontation between them (with the exception of [Federici and Fortunati 1984]).

Dalla Costa and James argue that the primary subjects of the reproduction process—commonly referred to as "housework"—are women, who do not receive any direct payment for their work, although this work is directly productive of value. These facts explain the invisibility of housework, the dependent status of women in capitalist society, the persistent concern by both employers and the state with the stability of "the family." Since housework has largely been unwaged and the value of workers' activities is measured by their wage, then, women, of necessity, have been seen as marginal to the process of social production.

The invisibility of housework hides the secret of all capitalist life: the source of social surplus—unwaged labor—must be degraded, naturalized, made into a marginal aspect of the system, so that its producers can be more easily controlled and exploited. Marx recognized this phenomenon in the case of the 19th-century European proletariat. But the post-1968 generation of feminists, who identified the work of reproducing labor-power as an unpaid source of value, generalized his analysis to encompass the work of housewives. In time students, subsistence farmers, child laborers, the increasing number of workers, especially sex workers, in near slave conditions were included in the same category [Cf. (James 1975a), (Mies 1986), (Caffentzis 1992: 265-268), (Federici 1992), (Dalla Costa M. 1995)]. All the unwaged reproductive activities that orthodox economic theory had either ignored, included in the "wage bundle," or put in the realm of "indirect costs," were introduced by feminist theorists as hidden variables essential to explaining the process of social reproduction.

This is not to say that social reproduction is reducible to the reproduction of labor-power. The reproduction of commodities, C, of money, M, and of the production processes themselves, P, require labor power, but are not defined by it. The complex circuits of exchanges that Marx described in *Capital II* remain crucial for an explanation of social reproduction. However, adding the production and reproduction of labor power to Marx' theory of social reproduction, changes the whole Marxist paradigm on a practical and theoretical level. Practically, it changes the concept of "workers' struggles." In Marx, the site of class conflict is the factory, the exemplary place of value production. But if the unwaged also produce value, then their struggles are a key aspect of the class struggle, and can threaten the production of value.

Consequently, "social movements"—whose negotiations/antago- nism with capital (public and private) have comprised much of the overt social struggle of the last twenty years (from welfare women's , to gay rights, indigenous people's, environmental and anti-nuclear movements)—become *class movements* .

Theoretically, the "addition" of housework and the circuit of labor-power reproduction changes our perspective on social re- production. It is well-known that money (M), commodities (C) and the commodity production process (P) can have dichotomous meanings for waged workers and capitalists (Cleaver 1979). For the capitalist, money is a means for investment, while money for the waged worker is the primary access to the means of subsis- tence. But the inclusion of the housework circuit, L, brings a new "perspective" on M, C. and P: the perspective of the unwaged, mostly female worker. This perspective reveals the power rela- tions and divisions within the working class. For example, money is a means of control of her behavior by waged workers who do not recognize housework as an object of exchange. The "house- hold money" the houseworker spends does not give her the au- tonomy that wages—the result of a socially recognized exchange between capitalist and worker—provide. A network of "infor- mal," but determining, often violent power relations among work- ers themselves is inscribed in this money with "strings attached,"

The exploration of the power relations operating in the gen- eralized process of social reproduction (C, P, M) from the per- spective of the unwaged worker transforms Marxist class analy- sis and makes it possible to analyze racism and sexism (in all their material embodiments) as class phenomena. It also provides a more subtle foundation to the explanation of crises of social reproduction. A classical Marxist can easily explain how a series of successful strikes in the large plants of a capitalist country can lead to an "economic crisis." But the labor-power production approach allows one to see how "the subversion of the commu- nity," through, for example, women's mass refusal to conceive children or to train their children to accept certain kinds of work and wages, can also lead to a crisis of social reproduction as well.

For a break in the L circuit brought about by a large-scale (though often silent) struggle of the unwaged houseworkers can have more serious effects on capitalist society than a thousand strikes. The great factory struggles of the late 1960s and 1970s in Italy undoubtedly affected capital, but the decision of Italian women since the late 1960s to struggle for a family size below replacement levels has had probably a much greater impact (Dalla Costa 1974).

The problem of this approach to crises of social reproduction is that the methodology needed to apply it is more subtle and the data it requires are not found in the standard volumes of national economics statistics gathered by governments or international bodies. The UN Development Program is only beginning to record the amount of unwaged housework done in many countries as part of its "human development index." And, there has been little study of the relationship between variables, like the length of the "labor-power reproduction work day," and other more well-known measures of economic and social crisis.

But these practical problems are outweighed by the contribution of this approach to an understanding of crises of social reproduction. First, it does not need to find an exogenous source of crisis. For crisis is endogenous to the capitalist system not only because of the asymmetry between buying and selling (as noted by Marx), caused by the inability of individual capitalists to satisfactorily complete the metamorphoses of their capital at a proper rate of profit, i.e., due to a contradiction between expectations in the orbit of circulation and the realities of conflict in the terrain of production.

There is also another conflict within capitalism that the labor-power approach brings out, but one that Marx ignored, i.e., the conflict between the needs of capitalist production and the demands of those whose work is centered in the arena of the social reproduction of labor-power. This conflict can lead to major crises of reproduction appearing as dramatically falling (or rising) birth-rates, urban riots, or agrarian revolts. These crises are often seen from the point of view of the market as exogenous, but once the activities of social reproduction are introduced into the cycle of capitalist society they become as relevant as the strikes of unionized workers. The reproduction of labor-power is not a variable that can be determined by Keynesian "manpower planning" or neo-classical theories of the labor market; for just as the regular commodity market has the struggle of their producers inscribed within it, so too the labor market has the struggle of those who produce labor power inscribed within it. And that struggle is not dictated by the commodity status of its results nor by the demands of its purchasers. Certainly there is no pre-established harmony leading to the best of all possible worlds when buyer and seller meet, even if it is over the kitchen table.

The labor-power production approach, then, shares with Foucault's the recognition of the permanent *possibility* of crisis, but it rejects Foucault's claim for the permanent *actuality* of crisis. For capitalism has laws, material preconditions and class divisions that are standard to the system, and therefore it has a historical form which is reproducible over centuries and continents. Indeed, much of the social standardization that is such a marked aspect of contemporary reality (and is mistakenly called "westernization") is simply the repetition of this form throughout the planet on many different scales. Specific forms of capitalism are so reproducible that international agencies like the World Bank and the IMF are applying a prepackaged template of neoliberal capitalism for its realization in locales as widely divergent as Equatorial Guinea and Tajikistan. The apparent reality of infinite micro-variations of the power model that Foucault employs is vacuous, for there is a drive to totalization within the capitalist mode of production that makes these variations extinct even before they can take on a virtual existence. One of capital's laws, of course, is to make the reproduction of labor-power completely dependent upon the wage form and hence to keep the reproducers of labor-power both invisible to and controlled by the system. That is the reason for the relentless attack on any guarantees of subsistence, especially to those who reproduce labor-power, that has been recently termed "the New Enclosures" (Midnight Notes Collective 1992: 317-333). Foucault's theory of polyvalent, decentered and fragmented force relations cannot account for the crises caused by the ability of workers to successfully struggle against their expropriation from the commons of subsistence.

Thus the labor-power production approach escapes the metaphysical flaws of both Becker's Parmenideanism and Foucault's Heraclitianism and can give endogenous accounts of crisis because it posits the antagonism between circulation/production, accumulation/reproduction as a essential to the existence of capitalism.

Notes

1. See Schumpeter (1967) for further discussion of the relation between the Physiocrats and Smith.

2. Physicists like Maxwell demonstrated that one can mathematically explain why a gas noticeably heats up when its volume is decreased by assuming that the gas is made up of millions of invisible, microscopic molecules in constant motion, colliding with other molecules and the walls of the gas' container.

3. Marx's study of this network of micro-circuits of value led to many important insights concerning capital, e.g., the deduction of the mathematical relation of turnover-time and the rate of profit. But at the heart of the model was a retelling of the story of society and its reproduction. Marx rejected Locke's tale of rational individuals tacitly agreeing to exchange their natural rights for a system that is to protect their property. He substituted a more complex, but realistic story of millions of daily commodity exchanges between capitalists and workers weaving society together.

4. J.B. Say ruled out the possibility of a crisis of social reproduction of the sort later described by Marx. He expressed what was later called "Say's Law" in his *Treatise on Political Economy or The Production, Distribution and Consumption of Wealth* with the following words: "It is worth while to remark, that a product is no sooner create, than it, from that instant, affords a market for other products to the full extend of its own value. When the producer has put the fin-

ishing hand to his product, he is most anxious to sell it immediately, lest its value should diminish in his hands. Nor is he less anxious to dispose of the money he may get for it; for the value of money is also perishable. But the only way of getting rid of money is in the purchase of some product or other. Thus the mere circumstance of the creation of one product immediately opens a vent for other products." (Say 1964: 134-135).

5. A brief description of these crisis theories is in order. Underconsumptionist explanations identified the cause of capitalist crisis in the inability of the working class to purchase consumption goods, and the overproduction of the means of production. Rosa Luxemburg's version of this theory is the most resonant for the late 20th century. She argued that capitalism needs a non-capitalist world to absorb its surplus production (and realize the surplus value embodied in it). In her view, the control of the non-capitalist regions of Africa, Asia, and Oceania was crucial for the survival of various national capitals. Thus, inter-imperialist war was an inevitable outcome of a capitalism that had largely subsumed the land and labor of Europe and the Americas. For Luxemburg capitalist accumulation enters in a final crisis when the last non-capitalist world regions are absorbed into the capitalist mode of production. "Just as soon as reality begins to correspond to Marx's diagram of enlarged reproduction, the end of accumulation is in sight, it has reached its limits, and capitalist production is *in extremis*. For capital, the standstill of accumulation means that the development of the productive forces is arrested, and the collapse of capitalism follows inevitably, as an objective historical necessity."(p. 417) Luxemburg's theory will be decisively tested in the next decade of "globalization." By contrast Kalecki's business cycle theory sees crisis as a political choice of the state used to control wage demands.

6. For a discussion of a neoliberal approach to the "organ shortage" see (Menzel 1990: 182-186) and (Caplan 1988).

7. In the 1960s and early 1970s a number of French Marxist anthropologists applied a "mode of production" analysis to African societies in ways parallel to the work of Dalla Costa and James. Chief among them was Claude Meillassoux who saw two systems of pro-

duction coexisting in colonial Africa. One was a system of do-mestic production whose result was the production and reproduc-tion of labor-power exploited by the colonial regime and the other was a mode of commodity production (Meillassoux 1981).

Bibliography

Baran, P. and Sweezy, P. (1966). *Monopoly Capital. An Essay on the American Economy and Social Order.* New York: Monthly Review Press.

Bataille, G. (1988). *The Accursed Share.* New York. Zone Books.

Becker, G. S. (1976). *The Economic Approach to Human Behavior.* Chicago: University of Chicago Press.

Berch, Bettina (1982). *The Endless Day: The Political Economy of Women and Work.* New York: Harcourt Brace Jovanovich.

Bonefeld, W. et al. (1995). *Emancipating Marx, Open Marxism 3.* London: Pluto Press.

Boulding, K.(1969). "Economics Imperialism." In *Behavioral Science.* Vol. 14, n. 16.

Bukharin, N. (1966). *Imperialism and World Economy.* New York: Howard Fertig.

Caplan, Arthur L (1988). "Beg, Borrow, or Steal: The Ethics of Solid Organ Procurement," in (Mathieu 1988).

Cleaver, Harry Jr. (1979), *Reading Capital Politically.* Austin, Texas: University of Texas Press.

Clower, R.W. (1967). "A reconsideration of the microfoundations of monetary theory." In *Western Economic Journal,* n. 6, December.

Collier, George A. and Quaratiello, Elizabeth Lowery (1994). *Basta! Land and the Zapatista Rebellion in Chiapas.* Oakland, California: Food First.

Dalla Costa, G.F. (1978). *Un lavoro d'amore*, Roma: Edizione delle donne Roma.

Dalla Costa, G.F. (1989), 2nd ed. 1991, *La riproduzione nel sottosviluppo. Lavoro delle donne famiglia e Stato nel Venezuela degli anni '70,* Milano, FrancoAngeli. (first edition. 1980. Padova: Cleup).

Dalla Costa, G.F. (1995). "Development and Economic Crisis: Women's Labor and Social Policies in Venezuela. In the Context of International Indebtedness". In Dalla Costa, M. and Dalla Costa, G.F.(eds) 1995.

Dalla Costa, M. (1974). "Riproduzione e emigrazione". In Serafini A. (ed.) (1974).

_____. (1981) "Emigrazione, immigrazione e composizione di classse in Italia negli anni 70," in: *Economia e lavoro*, No. 4 ott-dic.

_____. (1983). 3rd ed. 1997. *Famiglia, Welfare e Stato tra Progressismo e New Deal.* Milan: FrancoAngeli.

_____. (1995). "Capitalism and Reproduction." In Bonefeld, W. *et al.* eds.) (1995).

_____. and James, S. (1972). *The Power of Women and the Subversion of the Community.* Bristol: Falling Wall Press.

_____. and Dalla Costa, G.F. (eds.) (1995). *Paying the Price. Women and the Politics of International Economic Strategy.* London and New Jersey: Zed Books.

De Brunhoff, Suzanne (1976). *Marx on Money.* New York: Urizen Books.

De Waal, Alexander. (1989). *Famine that Kills: Darfur, Sudan, 1984-1985.* Oxford: Clarendon Press.

Devereux, Stephen (1993). *Theories of Famine.* New York: Harvester/ Wheatsheaf.

Edmonds, W. and Fleming, S. (eds.) (1975). *All Work and No Pay.* Bristol: Falling Wall Press.

Engels, F. (1964). *Dialectics of Nature.* Moscow. Progress Publishers.

_____. (1967). "Preface." In Marx (1967b).

Etzioni, Amitai (1988). *The Moral Dimension: Towards a New Economics.* New York: Free Press.

Etzioni, Amitai ed. (1995). *New Communitarian Thinking: Persons, Virtues, Institutions and Communities.* Charlottesville: University Press of Virginia.

Federici, S. (1982). *"Wages Against Housework."* In Malos, E. (ed.) (1982).

_____. (1988). The Great Witch Hunt of the Sixteenth and Seventeenth Century. *Maine Scholar* 1.

Federici, S. (1992). "The Debt Crisis. Africa and the New Enclosures." In Midnight Notes Collective (1992).

———.(ed.)(1995). *Enduring Western Civilization.* Westport, CT: Praeger.

———.and Fortunati, L. (1984). *Il Grande Calibano.* Milan: Franco Angeli.

Foley, D. K. (1986). *Understanding Capital: Marx's Economic Theory.* Cambridge Mass.: Harvard University Press.

Fortunati, L. (1995). *The Arcane of Reproduction. Housework, Prostitution, Labor and Capital.* New York: Autonomedia.

Foucault, M. (1971a). *Madness and Civilization: A History of Insanity in the Age of Reason.* New York: New American Library.

———. (1971b). *The Order of Things: An Archaeology of the Human Sciences.* New York: Random House.

———. (1973). *The Birth of the Clinic: An Archeology of Medical Perception.* New York: Pantheon Books.

———. (1977). *Discipline and Punish.* London: Allen Lane.

———. (1981). *The History of Sexuality.* vol. 1. Harmondsworth: Penguin Books.

———. (1996a), *Foucault Live: Collected Interviews, 1961-1984.* Edited by Sylvere Lotringer. New York: Semiotext(e), 1996.

———. (1996b), "The Ethics of the Concern for the Self as a Practice of Freedom," In M. Foucault (1996a).

Granovetter, M. (1992). "Economic Action and Social Structure. The Problem of Embeddedness," In Granovetter and Swedberg (1992).

———. and Swedberg, R.(1992). *The Sociology of Economic Life.* Boulder: Westview Press.

Heckscher, Eli F. (1955). *Mercantilism. Volume Two.* 2nd revised edition. London: George Allen & Unwin Ltd.

Illich, I. (1981). *Shadow Work.* London: Marion Boyers.

James S. (1975a). "Wageless of the World." In Edmonds, W. and Fleming, S. (eds.).

James, S. (1975b). Sex, Race, and Class. Bristol: Falling Wall Press.

Kalecki, M. (1971). *Selected Essays on the Dynamics of the Capitalist Economy, 1933-1970.* Cambridge: Cambridge University Press.

Laslett, B. and Brenner, J. (1989). "Gender and Social Reproduction". in Scott, W.R. and Blake, J. (eds.) *Annual Review of Sociology,* vol. 15.

Latouche, S. (1993). *In the Wake of the Affluent Society: An Exploration of Post-Development.* London and New Jersey: Zed Books.

Luxemburg, R. (1968). *The Accumulation of Capital.* New York: Monthly Review Press.

Macrae, Joanna and Zwi, Anthony (eds.) (1994). *War and Hunger: Rethinking International Responses to Complex Emergencies.* London: Zed Books and Save the Children (UK).

Malos, E (ed.) (1982). *The Politics of Housework.* London: Allison and Busby.

Marx, K. (1967a). *Capital: A Critique of Political Economy.* vol. 1. Moscow: Progress Publishers.

———. (1967b). *Capital: A Critique of Political Economy.* vol. 2. Moscow: Progress Publishers.

———. (1970). *A Contribution to the Critique of Political Economy.* New York: International Publishers.

Mathieu, Deborah (1988). *Organ Subsitution Technology: Ethical, Legal, and Public Policy Issues.* Boulder: Westview Press.

Mattick, P., (1969). *Marx and Keynes: The Limits of a Mixed Economy.* Boston. F. Porter Sargent.

McKenzie, R B and Tullock, G. (1978). *The New World of Economics: Explorations into the Human Experience.* (2nd edition) Homewood, Illinois: Richard D. Irwin Inc.

Meillassoux, Claude (1988). *Maidens, Meal and Money: Capitalism and the Domestic Community.* Cambridge: Cambridge University Press.

Menzel, Paul T. (1990). *Strong Medicine: The Ethical Rationing of Health Care.* New York: Oxford University Press.

Midnight Notes Collective (ed.) (1992). *Midnight Oil: Work, Energy, War, 1973-1992.* New York: Autonomedia.

Mies, Maria (1986) *Patriarchy and Accumulation on a World Scale: Women in the International Division of Labour.* London: Zed Book.

Palloix, Christian (1973). *Les firmes multinationales et le proces d'internationalisation.* Paris: Francois Maspero.

Picchio, Antonella (1992). *The Political Economy of Social Reproduction*. Cambridge: Cambridge University Press.

Polanyi, K. (1992). "The Economy as Instituted Process." In Granovetter, M. and Swedberg, R. (eds.) (1992).

_____. (1944/57). *The Great Transformation: The Political and Economic Origins of Our Times*. Boston: Beacon Press.

Polanyi, Karl (1968). *Primitive, Archaic and Modern Economies: The Essays of Karl Polanyi*. George Dalton, ed. Boston: Beacon Press.

Posner, R. A. (1992). *Sex and Reason*. Cambridge, Mass.: Harvard University Press.

Rifkin, Jeremy (1995). *The End of Work: The Decline of the Global Labor Force and the Dawn of the Post-Market Era*. New York: G. P. Putnam's Sons.

Say, Jean-Baptiste (1964). *A Treatise on Political Economy or the Production, Distribution and Consumption of Wealth*. (New York: Augustus M. Kelly Reprints of Economic Classics.

Schumpeter, J. (1967). *Economic Doctrine and Method*. New York: Oxford University Press.

Sen, A.K. (1981). *Poverty and Famines: an Essay on Entitlement and Deprivation*, Oxford: Clarendon Press.

Serafini, A. (ed.) (1974). *L'operaio multinazionale in Europa*, Milan: Feltrinelli.

Smart, Barry (1983). *Foucault, Marxism and Critique*. London: Routledge and Kegan Paul.

Smelser, Neil J. and Swedberg, Richard (1994a). "The Sociological Perspective on the Economy," in (Smelser and Swedberg 1994b).

Smelser, Neil J. and Swedberg, Richard (eds.)(1994b). *The Handbook of Economic Sociology*. Princeton: Princeton University Press.

Swedberg, R. (1987). "Economic Sociology: Past and Present." In *Current Sociology,*. n. 35, pp. 1-221.

Swedberg, R. (ed.) (1990). *Economics and Sociology: Redefining Their Boundaries, Conversations with Economists and Sociologists*. Princeton: Princeton University Press.

Swedberg, R., (1991), "Major Traditions of Economic Sociology," in *Annual Review of Sociology*, n. 17, pp. 251-276.

Thompson, E.P. (1991). *Customs in Common*. New York: The New Press.

Tronti, M. (1973). "Capitale Sociale," in *Telos*, n. 17, pp. 98-121.

Tullock, G. (1972). "Economic Imperialism," in Buchanan, J.M. and Tollison, R.D. (eds). *The Theory of Public Choice*. Ann Arbor: University of Michigan Press.

Williamson, Oliver E. (1994). "Transaction Cost Economics and Organization Theory," in (Smelser and Swedberg 1994b).

NOTES ON CONTRIBUTORS

MARIAROSA DALLA COSTA is associate professor in Political Sociology and Professor of History of the promotion of Women's condition at the Faculty of Political Sciences, University of Padua (Italy). A historical figure of the international feminist movement, she opened at the beginning of the seventies the debate about housework and women as reproducers of labor-power. She spent her theoretical and practical activity in Europe, America and Africa. Her reserach interests have been devoted to the relationship between reproduction, and capitalist development. Her works have been translated into six languges, Japanese included. Among the most known: *Famiglia, Welfare e Stato tra Progressismo e New Deal* (Milan: FrancoAngeli, 1983, 1997). A collection of her writings is available in Japanese: *Kajirodo ni Chingin-o Feminizumu no Aratana Tenbo* (Tokyo: Impact Shuppankai, 1986, 1990). She has coedited with Giovanna F. Dalla Costa *Paying The Price. Women and the Politics of International Economic Strategy* (London and New Jersey: Zed Books, 1995) translated also in Japanese as *Yakusokusareta Hatten?* (Tokyo: Impact Shuppankai, 1995). In these years she has focussed her analysis on the dramatic problems and crucial questions concerning human reproduction deriving from the devastating policies investing land as well as the physical and social body of the humanity. In this context she has produced, "Capitalism and Reproduction" published in Bonefeld W. et al. (ed.), *Open Marxism* 3, (Pluto Press, London, 1995) that appeared in many languages and "The Native in Us, the Land We Belong to" in *Common Sense*, n. 23, 1998. In the same path of discourse calling for the respect of the reproductive powers of land and bodies, she raised in Italy for the first time the problem of the abuse of Hysterectomy editing, *Isterectomia. Il problema sociale di un abuso contro le donne* (*Hysterectomy, The Social Problem of an Abuse Against Women*) (Milan: Franco Angeli, 1998).

SILVIA FEDERICI has for many years combined teaching, research work and political activism, first in the feminist movement and more recently in the campaigns for academic rights and against the death penalty. She has taught in the United States and Nigeria, and is presently an associate professor in International Studies and Political Philosophy at New College, Hofstra University. Her research work has been in the fields of women's studies and cultural studies. She has written several essays on feminist politics, education, multiculturalism and has contributed to the analysis of the condition of women and social reproduction. Her main work in this field is *Il Grande Calibano. Storia del Corpo Sociale Ribelle nella prima fase del capitale* (*The Great Caliban. History of the Rebel Social Body in the First Phase of Capitalism*) co-authored with L. Fortunati, (Milan, FrancoAngeli,1984). Her main contribution to cultural studies is her recently edited work *Enduring Western Civilization. The Construction of the Concept of Western Civilization and Its "Others"* (Westport (CT), Praeger Publishers, 1995). She is one of the coordinators of the Committee for Academic Freedom in Africa (CAFA) and a member of the Radical Philosophy Association's Anti-Death Penalty Project.

GIOVANNA FRANCA DALLA COSTA is professor in Sociology and Industrial Sociology at the Faculty of Psychology,

Department of General Psychology, University of Padua (Italy). She has been among the founding members and the main activists of the feminist network "wages for housework" in Italy. Her field is the working conditions of women in relation to development issues. Her best known works are: *Un lavoro d'amore* (Rome: Edizioni delle Donne, 1978), a major theoretical contribution to an analysis of the function of men's physical violence against women as an instrument of discipline of housework, translated into Japanese as *Ai no Rodou* ('A Labour of Love') (Tokyo: Impact Shuppankai, 1991), soon available in English as well; *La riproduzione nel sottosviluppo. Lavoro delle donne, famiglia e Stato nel Venezuela degli anni '70* (Milan: FrancoAngeli, 1989, 1991) (original edition Padua: Cleup, 1980); *Paying the Price. Women and the International Economic Strategy* (London and New Jersey, Zed Books, 1995) co-edited with M. Dalla Costa. She is co-author with M. Dalla Costa of a collection of essays (provisional title *Women, Work and Policies*) forthcoming in Japanese (Tokyo: Impact Shuppankai).

ALDA BRITTO DA MOTTA is associate professor in the Department of Sociology and Centre for Interdisciplinary Studies on Women (Núcleo de Estudos Interdisciplinares sobre a Mulher, Mestrado em Ciências Sociais, NEIM), Federal University of Bahia, Salvador, Bahia (Brazil). Her research work is in the field of labor studies and women's studies. One of her main contributions to this field is the study of women's participation in contemporary social movements. Her most important recent publications are *Espaço e Tempo de Mulher* (ed.) (Bahia: NEIM, 1987), *Caderno do NEIM*, n. 4; and Familiarizando (-se com) o Publico e Politizando o Privado, in Tereza Ximenes, (ed.), *Novos Paradigma e Realidade Brasileira* (Universidade Federal de Parà, 1993). She is a co-author of *Paying The Price. Women and the Politics of International Economic Strategy,* ed. Dalla Costa M. and Dalla Costa G.F. (London and New Jersey, Zed Books, 1995).

ANDRÉE MICHEL, honorary director at the CNRS in France, is a scholar internationally known for her research on women and the family, especially in developing countries. In recent years, her research has focussed on the impact of war and militarization on the condition of women. Her work includes: "Multinationales et inégalités de classe et de sexe," in *Current Sociology*, 31, 1 (1983); 'La Militarisation et les violences à l'égard des femmes', in *Nouvelles Questions Féministes*, 11-12 (Winter, 1985) (editor); *Femmes et multinationales* (Paris: Karthala, 1981), co-authored with Agnès Fatoumata-Diarra and Hélène Agbessi-Dos Santos; *Le Féminisme* (Paris: Presses Universitaires de France, 1979) (third edition 1986, various translations); *Les Femmes dans la société marchande* (Paris, Presses Universitaires de France, 1978) (collective work, also translated into Spanish); *Paying The Price. Women and the Politics of International Economic Strategy* ed. by Dalla Costa, M. and Dalla Costa G.F.(London and New Jersey: Zed Books, 1995) (co-author); *Surarmement pouvoirs démocratie* (Paris: L'Harmattan, 1995).

C. GEORGE CAFFENTZIS has been for many years active in radical politics and collaborated to two journals of political theory, Zerowork and Midnight Notes. He has taught for several years in Nigeria and is presently associate professor in the Department of Philosophy, University of Southern Maine. His research work is in the field of political philosophy, Marxist theory, and the philosophy of money. His main works include *Abused Words, Clipped Coins and Civil Government: John Locke's Philosophy of Money* (New York, Autonomedia/Semiotext, 1989); "The Work/Energy Crisis" in "Midnight Notes Collective," ed. *Midnight Oil. Work, Energy, War, 1973-1992* (New York: Autonomedia,1992); "The Fundamental Implications of the Debt Crisis for Social Reproduction in Africa," in *Paying The Price. Women and the Politics of International Economic Strategy* (London and New Jersey, Zed Books, 1995); "The Scottish Origin of Civilization" in S. Federici (ed.), *Enduring Western Civilization. The Construction*

of the Concept of Western Civilization and Its "Others" (Praeger
Publishers, Westport, CT, 1995); "Why Machines Cannot Cre-
ate Value; or Marx's Theory of Machines" in J. Davis, T. Hirschl,
M. Stack (eds.), *Cutting Edge Technology, Information Capital-
ism and Social Revolution* (London: Verso, 1997). He is a coor-
dinator of the Committee For Academic Freedom in Africa
(CAFA) and a member of the Radical Philosophy Association's
Anti-Death Penalty Project.

INDEX

Wedlocked

y wedded, passion

...er there's a debt to
...obeyed or a business
...got no choice but to sa...

...ionaire bridegrooms h...
...f they think marriage w...

...convenient brides beco...
of an *inconvenient* desir...

...out what happens after the

e Billionaire's Defiant Acqu...
by Sharon Kendrick

One Night to Wedding Vows
by Kim Lawrence

Wedded, Bedded, Betrayed
by Michelle Smart

l
see
d. T

t was
arry m
full view

ll announc
his brother,

great idea! I
or your brawn

felt every muscle
ng jibe. He was g
r insolence.

rince is hardly goin

Convenient

Wheth
a will to be
She's

But these bill
think coming i

Soon their

Find
Th

BOUND BY HIS
DESERT DIAMOND

BY
ANDIE BROCK

MILLS &
BOON

First Published in Great Britain 2016
By Mills & Boon, an imprint of HarperCollins*Publishers*
1 London Bridge Street, London, SE1 9GF

© 2016 Andrea Brock

ISBN: 978-0-263-92388-9

Andie Brock started inventing imaginary friends around the age of four and is still doing that today—only now the sparkly fairies have made way for spirited heroines and sexy heroes. Thankfully she now has some real friends, as well as a husband and three children, plus a grumpy but lovable cat. Andie lives in Bristol, and when not actually writing might well be plotting her next passionate romance story.

Books by Andie Brock

Mills & Boon Modern Romance

The Shock Cassano Baby
The Sheikh's Wedding Contract
The Last Heir of Monterrato

Visit the Author Profile page at millsandboon.co.uk for more titles.

To Roger.

Who has spent far more time discussing
manly emotions and reactions and romance in general
than he ever signed up for!

Thank you, Con. x

CHAPTER ONE

CLASPING THE COLD metal railings, Annalina stared down at the swirling black depths of the River Seine. She shivered violently, her heart thumping beneath the tight-fitting bodice of her evening gown, her designer shoes biting into the soft flesh of her heels. Clearly they had not been designed for a mad sprint down the bustling boulevards and cobbled back streets of Paris.

Oh, God. Anna dragged in a shuddering lung full of cold night air. *What had she just done?*

Somewhere behind her in one of Paris's most grand hotels, a society party was in swing. A glittering, star-studded occasion attended by royalty and heads of state, the great, the good and the glamorous from the world over. It was a party being thrown in her honour. And worse, far worse, a party where a man she had only just met was about to announce that she was to be his bride.

She let out a rasping breath, watching the cloud of condensation disperse into the night. She had no idea where she was or what she was going to do now but she did know that there was no going back. The brutal fact was she couldn't go through with this marriage, no matter what the consequences. Right up until tonight she had genuinely believed she could do it, could commit to

this union, to please her father and to save her country
from financial ruin.

Even yesterday, when she had met her intended for the
first time, she had played along. Watching in a kind of
dazed stupor as the ring had been slipped onto her finger,
a perfunctory gesture performed by a man who had just
wanted to get the deed over with, and witnessed by her
father, whose steely-eyed glare had left no room for second thoughts or doubts. As King of the small country of
Dorrada he was going to make sure that this union took
place. That his daughter would marry King Rashid Zahani, ruler of the recently reformed Kingdom of Nabatean,
if it was the last thing she ever did.

Which frankly, right now, looked like a distinct possibility. Anna gazed down at the ring on her finger. The
enormous diamond glittered back at her, mocking her
with its ostentatious sparkle. Heaven only knew what
it was worth—enough to pay the entire annual salaries
of the palace staff, no doubt, and with money to spare.
She tugged it over her cold knuckles and held it in her
palm, feeling the burden of its weight settle like a stone
in her heart.

To hell with it.

Closing her fist, she raised herself up on tiptoes, leaning as far over the railings as she could. She was going to
do this. She was going to fling this hateful ring into the
river. She was going to control her own destiny.

He came from out of nowhere—an avalanche of heat,
weight and muscle that landed on top of her, knocking the
breath from her lungs, flattening her against the granite wall of his chest. She could see nothing except the
darkness of him, feel nothing except the strength of the
arms that were locked around her like corded steel. Her
body went limp, her bones dissolving with shock. Only

her poor heart tried to keep her alive, taking up a wild, thundering beat.

'Oh, no, you don't.'

He growled the words over the top of her head, some-where in the outside world that, until a couple of moments ago, she had quite taken for granted. Now she panicked she would never see it again.

Don't what?

Anna forced her oxygen-starved brain to work out what he meant. Shouldn't it be her telling this mad man what he shouldn't be doing? Like crushing her so hard against him that she was almost asphyxiated. She tried to move inside his grip but the ring of steel tightened still further, pinning her arms to her sides. Her mouth, she suddenly registered, was pressed against flesh. She could touch him with the tip of her tongue, taste the very mas-culine mix of spice and sweat. She could feel the coarse-ness of what had to be chest hair against her lips. Forcing her mouth open, she bared her teeth, then brought them down as hard as she could. *Yes!* Her sharp nip connected with a small but significant ridge of his flesh. She felt him buck, then curse loudly in a foreign tongue.

'Why, you little…' Releasing her just enough to be able to see her face, her captor glared at her with fero ciously piercing black eyes. 'What the hell are you? Some sort of animal?'

'Me!' Incredulity spiked through the terror as Anna stared back at him, squinting through the dark shadows to try and work out who the hell he was, what the hell he wanted. He seemed somehow familiar but she couldn't pull back far enough to see. 'You call me an animal when you've just leapt out on me from the shadows like some sort of crazed beast!' The jet-black eyes narrowed, glint-ing with all the menace of a brandished blade. Perhaps it wasn't such a good idea to goad him. 'Look.' She tried for what she hoped was a conciliatory tone, though her voice was too muffled from being squeezed half to death to be able to tell. 'If it's money you want, I'm afraid I don't have any.'

This much was true. She had fled the party without even thinking to snatch up her clutch bag.

'I don't want your money.'

The rush of fear returned. Oh, God, what did he want, then? Terror closed her throat as she desperately tried to come up with something to distract him. Suddenly she remembered the ring that was still digging into her palm. It was worth a try. 'I do have a ring, though—right here in my hand.' She tried unsuccessfully to free her arm to show it to him. 'If you let me go you can have it.'

This produced a mocking snort from above her.

'No, really, it's worth thousands—millions, for all I know.'

'I know exactly what it's worth.'

He did? Anna gasped with relief. So that was what this brute was after—the wretched ring. Well, he was welcome to it. Good riddance. She just wished she could get out of her engagement as easily. She was struggling to thrust it upon him when he spoke again.

'I should do. I signed the cheque.'

Anna stilled. *What?* This wasn't making any sense. Who on earth was this guy? Twisting in his arms, she felt his grip loosen a fraction, enough to let her straighten her spine, tip her chin and gaze into his face. Her heart thundered at what she saw.

Fearsomely handsome features glowered down at her, all sharp-angled planes of chiselled cheekbones, a blade-straight nose and an uncompromising jut of a gran-ite-hewn jaw, all highlighted by the orange glow of the

Victorian street lights. He exuded strength and power, and his sheer forcefulness shivered its way through Anna's body, settling somewhere deep within her core.

She recognised him now. She remembered having seen him out of the corner of her eye somewhere amid the flurry of guests at the party, amid the endless introductions and polite conversations. A dark yet unmissable figure, he had been looming in the background, taking in everything—taking in her, too, before she had haughtily turned her profile to him. Some sort of bodyguard or minder—that was who he had to be. She remembered now the way he had hovered at the side of Rashid Zahani, her new fiancé, always a step behind him but somehow in charge, controlling him, owning the space, the glittering ballroom and everyone in it.

But a bodyguard who picked out engagement rings?

Somehow she couldn't see this towering force of a man lingering over a tray of jewels. Not that that mattered. What mattered was that he took his brutish hands off her and left her alone to carry on making the hideous mess of her life that she seemed so hell-bent on doing.

'So, if I am not being mugged, perhaps you would be kind enough to tell me exactly why you have leapt out of the dark and scared me half to death. And why you're not letting me go now, this instant. Presumably you know who I am?'

'Indeed I do, *Princess*.'

The word 'princess' hissed through his teeth, curdling something in Anna's stomach. Loosening his arms from around her back, he moved his hands to her shoulders, where they weighed down on her with searing heat.

'And, in reply to your question, I'm stopping you from doing something extremely foolish.'

'Flinging this into the river, you mean?' With a contemptuous toss of her head, Anna opened her hand to reveal the hated ring.

'That and yourself along with it.'

'*Myself?*' She scowled up at him. 'You don't mean…? You didn't think..?'

'That you were about to leap to your death? Yes.'

'And why exactly would I want to do that?'

'You tell me, Princess. You flee from your own engagement party in a state of high anxiety, position yourself on a bridge with a thirty-foot drop into a fast-flowing river and then lean forward in an extremely dangerous way. What was I supposed to think?'

'You weren't supposed to think at all. You were supposed to mind your own business and leave me alone.'

'Ah, but this *is* my business. *You* are my business.'

A wave of heat swept over Anna at the possessiveness of his words.

'Well, fine.' She fought to stand her ground. 'Now you can go back to your boss and tell him that you prevented a suicide that was never going to happen by leaping on an innocent woman—a woman who just happens to be a princess, may I remind you?—and scaring her half to death. I'm sure he will be very pleased with you.'

Piercingly dark eyes held hers, flicking over her like the flames of a newly lit fire, mesmerising with a promise of deadly heat. There was something else there too, an amused arrogance, if Anna wasn't mistaken. If 'amused' could ever be used to describe those forbidding features.

'In fact I may decide to press charges.' Anger hardened her voice. 'If you don't get your hands off me within the next second, I will make sure everyone knows of your behaviour.' She jerked at her shoulders to try and dislodge his leaden hold.

'I'll take my hands off you when I am good and ready.'

His voice was as dark and menacing as the river that flowed beneath them. 'And when I do it will be to personally escort you back to the party. There are a number of very important people there waiting for a big announcement, in case you had forgotten.'

'No, not forgotten.' Anna swallowed. 'But, as it happens, I've changed my mind. I've decided I won't be marrying King Rashid after all. In fact, perhaps you would like to go back and inform him of my decision.'

'Ha!' A cruel laugh escaped his lips. 'I can assure you, you will be doing no such thing. You will accompany me back to the ballroom and you will act as if nothing has happened. The engagement will be announced as planned. The wedding will go ahead as planned.'

'I think you are forgetting yourself.' Anna fired back at him. 'You are in no position to speak to me like that.'

'I'll speak to you any way I want, Princess. And you will do as I say. You can start by putting that ring back on your finger.' His hand moved to Anna's, picking up the ring and sending a jolt of awareness through her. For one crazy moment, she thought he was going to slip it back on her finger himself, like some sort of deranged suitor, but instead he handed it to her and waited as she did as she was told, the sheer force of his presence giving her no choice other than to obey.

With her ring in place, he took hold of her arm with manacle-like force and Anna found herself being turned away from the railings, presumably to be marched back to the party. This was outrageous. How dared he treat her like this? She wanted to spell out in the clearest possible terms that she did not take orders from bodyguards, or ring-choosers, or whoever this arrogant piece of work thought he was. But presumably he was working on the orders of King Rashid...

With her mind racing in all directions, she tried to think what on earth she could do—how she could get herself out of this mess. Physically trying to get away from him was clearly not an option. Even if she managed to escape his iron grip—which was highly unlikely, as the forceful fingers wrapped around her cold skin could testify—she would never be able to run fast enough to get away from him. The image of him chasing and finally capturing her flailing body was strangely erotic, given the circumstances.

She would have to use the only thing she had left in her armoury—her feminine wiles. Drawing herself up to her full height, she let her shoulder blades slide down her back, which had the desired effect of pushing her chest forward, accentuating the fullness of her breasts as they spilled over the tight bodice of her gown. Ah, yes, she had his attention now. She felt her nipples harden beneath his veiled scrutiny, sensing rather than witnessing his eyes delve into the valley of her cleavage. Her breath stalled in her throat, a tingling warmth spreading through her entire body, and she fleetingly found herself wondering who was supposed to be seducing who here.

'I'm sure we can come to some sort of mutual agreement.' Her voice came out as a sort of husky burr, more as a result of the sudden dryness of her throat than an attempt at sexiness. Still, it seemed to be working. Bodyguard man was still staring fixedly at her and, even if his granite expression hadn't softened, there was no doubt she was doing something right.

Raising her arms, Anna went to link them behind his neck. She had no clear thought of what she was doing except that maybe she could persuade him with flattery, or perhaps blackmail him after a kiss—he was certainly getting no more that—so that she could make her escape.

It went against her feminist principles but desperate times called for desperate measures.

But before she had the chance to do anything of the sort this hateful man snatched at her wrists, easily clasping them in one hand and bringing them down to her chest at the same time as swinging his other arm around her waist to pull her snugly against him. Anna gasped, the contact with his body, *that* part of his body, the particular *swell* of that part of his body, ricocheting through her with clenching waves. Granite-faced he may be, but that wasn't the only part of his body she had managed to harden.

And, judging by the look on his face, her captor had been taken by surprise too. He was glaring at her with a mixture of horror and hunger, the hand clasping her wrists shaking very slightly before he tightened its grip. Controlling the tremble of her own body, Anna stared back. If this was a small victory, though small was hardly the right word, she was going to make the most of it. Tipping back her head, she trained her eyes on his, forcing his to meet them, to see the temptations that they held, temptations that burned so brightly, even if she had no intention of honouring them. She could sense the quickening of his heartbeat beneath his white shirt, hear the faint rasp in his exhaled breath. She had got him.

'Princess Anna!'

Suddenly there was a blinding flash of light, illuminating their bodies, freezing them against the backdrop of darkness.

'What the hell?' A low growl rumbled from Anna's captor as he spun around to face the photographer that had crept out of the shadows, the shutter of the camera clicking furiously.

Blinking against the glare, Anna felt her wrists being

released as this warrior man lunged towards the photographer, clearly intent on murder. But when she went to move, to make her escape or save the photographer's life—she didn't know which—he was right back by her side again, pulling her forcefully into his arms.

'Oh, no, you don't. You're not going anywhere.'

'Come on, Anna. Show us a kiss!' Bolder now, the photographer took a step closer, the camera flashing all the time.

Anna had a split second to make a decision. If she wanted to get away from this man, avoid being frog-marched back to her own engagement party and forced to announce her betrothal to a man she could never, ever marry, there was one sure way to do it. Standing on tip-toes, she raised her arms to link them behind her captors head, shoving her fingers through the thick swathe of his hair and pulling against his resistance to bring him closer. If this was what the photographer wanted, this was what he was going to get.

With one final, terrifically brave or wildly foolish breath—Anna had no idea which—she reached up to plant her lips firmly on his.

What the hell?

Shock sucked the air from Zahir Zahani's lungs, numbing his senses, closing his fists. Plump and firm, her lips had swiftly turned from cold to warm as they sealed his own, the pressure increasing as she raked her hands through his hair to pull him closer. Her breath rasped between them, her delicate scent filling his nostrils, temporarily freezing his brain yet heating every other part of his body. Zahir went rigid, and the arms that were supposed to be restraining her were no more than useless weights as Annalina continued her relentless assault on his mouth. With the blood roaring in his ears, he found his lips parting, his body screaming to show her just where this could lead if she carried on this very dangerous game.

'Fantastic! Cheers for that, Anna.'

The camera flashes stopped and Annalina finally released him, letting her arms fall by her side. Meanwhile the photographer was already on his scooter, his camera slung over his shoulder.

'I owe you one!'

Turning the scooter around, he noisily zoomed off into the Paris streets, giving a cheery wave over his shoulder.

Zahir stared after him, suffering a split second of silent horror before his brain finally kicked into action again. Reaching into his jacket pocket, he grabbed his mobile phone. He'd have been able to catch the low life on foot if he didn't have this vixen to deal with. But his security team would pick him up—get him stopped and get the camera tossed into the Seine, the photographer along with it, if he had any say.

'No.' Her cold, trembling fingers closed over the phone in his hand. 'It's too late. It's done.'

'The hell it is.' Shaking off her hand, he started to punch in numbers. 'I can get him stopped. I *will* get him stopped.'

'There's no point.'

He stopped short, the cold determination in her voice halting his hand. 'And what exactly do you mean by that?' A trickle of dread started to seep into his veins.

'I'm sorry.' Dark-blue eyes shone back at him. 'But I had to do it.'

Hell! Realisation smacked him across the head. He'd been had. The whole thing was a set-up. This deceitful, conniving little princess had set a trap and he had walked right in. Fury coursed through him. He had no idea what her motive was but he did know that she would live to regret it. *Nobody* made a fool of Zahir Zahani.

'You will be sorry, believe me.' He kept his voice deliberately low, concentrating on controlling the rage that was pumping adrenaline dangerously fast around his veins. 'You will be more than sorry for what you have done.'

'I had no choice!' Her voice was full of anguish now and she even reached out a trembling hand to touch his arm before demurely lowering her eyes to the ground.

Nice try, Princess. But you don't get to fool me more than once.

Roughly grasping her chin, Zahir tipped back her head so she couldn't escape his searing gaze. He wanted her to look at him. He wanted her to know exactly who she was dealing with here.

'Oh, you had a choice, all right. You've chosen to bring scandal and disrepute to both our countries. And, trust me, you are going to pay for that, young lady. But first you are going to tell me why.'

He saw her slender body begin to tremble, her bare shoulders hunch against the shiver that ran through her. Bizarrely he itched to touch her, to warm that tantalisingly goose-bumped skin with his hot hands. But he would do no such thing.

'Because I am desperate.' Clear blue eyes implored him.

'Desperate?' He repeated the word with disgust.

'Yes. I can't go back to that party.'

'So that's why you set up this little charade?'

'No, I didn't set it up, not in the way you mean. I just took advantage of the situation.' Her voice lowered.

'You tricked me into following you. You arranged for that photographer to be there.'

'No! I had no idea that either of you had followed me.'

'You're lying. That guy knew you.'

'He didn't know me. He knows who I am. There's a difference. The press have been following me around all my life.'

'So you are telling me this wasn't planned?'

Annalina shook her head.

'Think carefully before you speak, Princess. Because, I have to warn you, to lie to me now would be very foolish indeed.'

'It was a spur-of-the-moment decision. And that is the truth.'

Despite everything, Zahir found himself believing her. He dragged in a breath. 'So that…that little display you just put on…?' He curled his lip against the traitorous memory of the way she had leant into him, the way she had messed with his head. 'What exactly did you hope to achieve? What makes you so desperate that you would bring disgrace upon your family? Fabricate a scandal to rock the foundations of both of our countries?'

'Disgrace I can live with. I'm used to it.' Her voice was suddenly very small. 'And the scandal will die down. But to be forced to marry Rashid Zahani is more than I can bear. That would have been a life sentence.'

'How dare you disrespect the King in this way?' Defensive anger roared in his voice. 'The engagement will still be announced. The marriage will still go ahead.'

'No. You can force me to go back to the party, even force me, with the help of my father, to go ahead with the announcement of the engagement. But, once those photographs go online, I'll be dropped like a stone.'

Zahir stared into the beautiful face of this wilful princess. Her skin was so pale in this ghostly light, so delicate, it was almost translucent. But her lips were ruby-red and her eyes as blue as the evening sky.

He knew with a leaden certainty that she meant what she said. There was no way she was going to go through with this marriage. He could still find that photographer, destroy the photos, but ultimately what good would it do? What was to be gained?

Hell and damnation. After all the planning that had gone into this union, the careful handling, the wretched party… It had taken all his powers of persuasion to get Rashid to agree to marry this European princess at all. Months of negotiations to get to this point. And for what? To have the whole thing thrown back in their faces and Rashid humiliated in the most degrading way. No, he could not let that happen. He *would* not let that happen. He had been a fool to trust this wayward princess, to believe the empty promises of her desperate father. But the situation had gone too far now—he had to try and salvage something from this mess. He had to come up with a clever solution.

Decision made, he took hold of Annalina's arm.

'You will accompany me back to the party and we will seek out the King and tell him what has happened. Then we will announce your engagement.'

'Didn't you understand a word I said?' The fight was back in her eyes. 'The King won't marry me now. That's the reason I just did what I did.'

'We will announce your engagement—not to the King, but to his brother, the Prince.'

'Yeah, great idea! I take it you must be employed more for your brawn than your brains.' Zahir felt every muscle in his body stiffen at her mocking jibe. He was going to enjoy punishing her for her insolence. 'The Prince is hardly going to want to marry me either, is he?'

'As of five minutes ago, the Prince has no choice.'

Narrowing his eyes, Zahir watched defiance turn to confusion turn to a creeping realisation. A strangely perverse sense of pleasure stole over him.

Her trembling hand flew to her mouth then made a fist as she stuffed it between her lips, biting down onto her knuckles to stifle her cry.

'Ah, yes, Princess, I see the truth is dawning.' Zahir threw back his shoulders, almost enjoying himself. 'I am Zahir Zahani, Prince of Nabatean, brother of King Rashid. And, as of five minutes ago, your future husband.'

CHAPTER TWO

ANNA FELT FOR the railings of the bridge behind her, grabbing at the bars to stop herself from sliding to the ground.

'You…you are Prince Zahir?'

One arrogant, scowling dark brow raised fractionally in reply.

No. It wasn't possible. The full horror of what she had done gnawed away at her brain. Being caught in a clinch with a bodyguard to get out of her engagement was one thing, but for the 'bodyguard' to be the fiancé's brother was quite another. This went far beyond the realms of scandal. This could cause an international incident.

'I…I had no idea.'

He shrugged. 'Evidently.'

'We need to do something—quickly.' Panic caught up with her, squeezing her vocal cords, spinning her brain around in her head. 'We must stop that photographer.'

Still Zahir Zahani didn't move. What was wrong with him? Why wasn't he doing anything? Anna felt as if she were in a terrible dream, running and running but getting no further away from the monster.

Finally he spoke. 'To use your phrase, Princess, *it's too late. It's done.*'

'But that was before I knew… There's still time to find him, pay him off, stop him.'

'Possibly. But I have no intention of doing any such thing.'

'Wh…what do you mean?' Confusion and frustration held her in their grip, hysteria not far behind. 'I don't understand.'

'Because, like you, I intend to take advantage of the situation. We will go back to the party and we will announce our engagement. Just as I said.'

Horror now joined the bedlam in her head. He wasn't serious. Surely he didn't mean it? She stared into his cold, forbidding features. *Oh, God.* He did—he really did!

Releasing the railings, she pushed herself upright, immediately dwarfed by this towering figure of a man who was blocking her way, her vision, her ability to think clearly. 'No! We can't. The idea is preposterous.'

'Is it, Princess Annalina? He glowered down at her. 'How will you feel tomorrow when those photographs are published? When you have to face your father, your people and the rest of the world? Are you prepared for the consequences?'

Her face crumpled.

'As I thought.' His mocking voice echoed in the dark around them. 'Not quite so preposterous now, is it? You have no alternative but to do as I say.'

'No. There has to be another way.' *Think, Anna, think.* Why did her poor brain seem to have turned to sludge? 'If the photographs are published I'll simply explain that it was all a misunderstanding—that I didn't know who you were…that it meant nothing.'

'And that would achieve what, exactly? Apart from prove that you are the sort of tramp who goes around seducing total strangers on the eve of your engagement and that your fiancé's own brother was caught in your trap. I would never subject Rashid to such humiliation.'

There was a second of silence.

'But we can't just swap!'

'We can and we will. The arrangements are all in place. A commitment has been made between our two countries—between your father and the Kingdom of Nabatean. He has offered your hand and it has been accepted. Nothing will stand in the way of that.' His shadowed face was as hard as stone. 'The commitment will be honoured.'

'But the commitment was to your brother—not you.'

'Then perhaps you should have thought of that before you ran away and started this whole debacle, betraying the trust my brother had put in you.' Anna lowered her eyes against the force of his biting scorn. 'Fortunately for you, it makes no difference which brother honours the commitment. The same objectives will be achieved either way.'

'And that's it? Honouring the commitment is all that matters to you?' She thrashed about, trying to find a way out. 'How can you be so unemotional? This is a marriage we are talking about, a bond that has to last a lifetime.'

'Don't you think I know that, Princess?' Lowering his head, Zahir hissed into her ear, sending a bolt of electricity through her. 'Don't you think I am fully aware of the sacrifice I am making? But, if it is emotion you are looking for, I must warn you to be careful. To expose my opinion of you would be straying into a dark and dangerous territory indeed.'

Cloaked in menace, his words settled over her like a shroud. Anna bit down hard on her lip to control the shiver. She didn't entirely know what he meant by that chilling statement. She wasn't sure she wanted to.

'And if I refuse?' Still she tried, squirming like a worm on a fish hook.

'All I can say is, to refuse would be extremely stupid.'
He paused, weighting his words with care. 'I'm sure I
don't have to remind you that you already have one failed
engagement behind you. Another might cause consider-
able speculation.'

A sharp jab of pain went through her. So he knew
about that, did he? About her humiliating broken engagement to Prince Henrik. Of course he did. Everyone did.

Tears were starting to build now, blocking her throat,
scratching at her eyes. Tears of frustration, self-pity and
wretched misery that her life had come to this. That she
should be forced to marry a man who clearly despised
her. A man who was as terrifying as he was alien—an
arrogant, untamed brute of a man the like of which she
had never come across before. She hadn't begun to process the extraordinary reaction between them when she'd
kissed him, the shockingly carnal way his body had re-
sponded. That would have to be for another time. But she
did know he would never make her happy—that was a
certainty. He would never even try.

'You have brought this upon yourself, Princess Annalina.' Somewhere outside the buzz of her head she heard
him relentlessly press home the point. 'You have forced
my hand, but I am prepared do my duty. And, ultimately,
so must you.'

His damning statement was the final nail in the coffin.

And so it was that Anna found herself being uncer-
emoniously marched back to the hotel to meet her fate.
With Zahir's arm around her waist, propelling her forward, she had had no choice but to stumble along beside him, needing two or three stiletto-heeled steps to
match his forceful stride as he rapidly navigated them
through the Parisian streets. Her heart was thumping
wildly, her dry breath scouring her throat as she tried to

come to terms with what she was about to do—tie herself to this man for ever. But with the heat of his arm burning through the sheer fabric of her dress she found herself trying to fight that assault, the whole shimmering force of his nearness, his muscled flesh, his masculine scent, leaving her brain no space to cope with anything else.

Finally outside the hotel Zahir turned her around to face him, his gaze raking mercilessly over her pale face. With the light spilling from the hotel, they could see each other more clearly now, but Anna had to tear her eyes away from his cruelly handsome features, afraid of what she might see there. Her gaze slid down the broad column of his neck to the open buttons of his shirt, the grey silk tie tugged to one side. And there, plainly visible against the exposed olive skin, was the livid red mark—the bite, where she had sunk her teeth into him. Instinctively her hand flew to her chest.

Alerted by her stare, Zahir swiftly moved to do up his shirt and straighten his tie, his knowing glare spelling out exactly what he thought of her barbarism.

'We will go in together,' he began coldly. 'You will talk to our guests and behave in the appropriate manner. But say nothing to anyone about the engagement. I will find my brother and tell him of the new arrangement.'

Anna nodded, swallowing down her dread. 'But shouldn't I be there when you speak to your brother? Don't I owe him that?'

'I think it's a little late for the guilt to kick in now, Annalina. We are way past that. *I* will deal with Rashid and then explain the situation to your father. Only then can we announce our engagement.'

Her father. In her frenzied state Anna had almost forgotten the man who had brought about this hideous debacle in the first place. It had been King Gustav who had insisted that his only child should marry King Rashid of Nabatean, leaving her no room to argue. Not after she had already let him down once, let her country down, by failing to secure a successful match between herself and Prince Henrik of Ebsberg—something that still both humiliated and swamped Anna with relief in equal measure.

A cold, heartless man, King Gustav had never recovered from the death of his wife, Annalina's mother, who had suffered a fatal brain aneurysm when Anna had been just seven years old. The shock had been too much for him and it seemed to Anna that a part of her father had died with her mother. The loving, caring part. It seemed that just when she had needed him most he had turned away from her. And had never turned back.

He would be utterly furious to find out that she had messed up again—that she was refusing to marry Rashid Zahani and was chucking away the chance to provide financial stability for Dorrada. At least, he would have been, if she hadn't had an alternative plan to offer him. For the first time Anna felt a tinge of relief about what she was doing. Zahir might be the second son but everything about him suggested power and authority, far more so than his elder brother, in fact. She suspected that her father would have no problem accepting the new arrangement. Somehow she had to find it inside herself to do the same.

She looked down, concentrating on arranging the folds of her dress, all too aware of the fire in Zahir's eyes as they licked over her, missing nothing.

'You are ready?'

She nodded, not trusting herself to speak.

'Very well, then, we will do this.'

The arm snaked around her waist again and together

they ascended the red-carpeted steps, the hotel doorman ushering them in with a polite bow.

The scene inside the ballroom appeared even more daunting than when Anna had fled less than an hour ago. More people had arrived, swelling the numbers into the hundreds, and they were milling around beneath the magnificent domed ceiling of the gilded room, illuminated by dozens of huge chandeliers and watched from above by carved marble statues. The air of anticipation had increased too. Anyone who was anyone was here, the great and the good from a host of European and Middle Eastern countries gathered at the invitation of King Gustav of Dorrada for a celebration that had yet to be disclosed.

Not that it took much working out. Presumably everyone in the room knew what this party was in aid of—or at least thought they did. It was common knowledge that King Gustav had been trying, and failing, to make a good marriage for his only daughter for some time. And the newly formed kingdom of Nabatean desperately needed entrée into the notoriously closed shop of 'old' Europe. The fact that the party was being held here, in one of the oldest and most exclusive hotels in Paris, right at the heart of Europe, bore testament to that and was certainly no coincidence.

Anna looked around her, the heat and the noise thundering inside her head, shredding her nerves, fuelling her panic. Zahir had left her side and gone in search of his brother, which should have been a relief, but bizarrely only made her feel more vulnerable and exposed. She could see her father in the distance and her heart took up a shaky beat at the thought of what he was about to be told. Of what they were about to do.

Grabbing a glass of champagne from a passing waiter, she took a deep gulp, followed by a deep breath, and, pulling on what she hoped was the suitably starry-eyed expression of a fiancée-to-be, set about mingling with her guests.

It was not long before Zahir was by her side again. Taking her arm, he steered her away from the curious stares of the small group of people she had been trying to converse with, guests who were clearly starting to wonder what was going on. Anna didn't know who else had witnessed it, but a few minutes ago she had caught sight of Rashid skirting around the edge of the room. Their eyes had met for a fleeting second before he had lowered his head and hurried from the ballroom.

'The necessary arrangements have been made.' Zahir's voice was steely with determination. 'It's time for the announcement.'

So this was it, then. Part of her thought she might wake up at any moment, that this was some sort of crazy dream—no, correction, nightmare. But as she slipped her arm through his, felt herself being pulled to his side, her whole body lit up to his nearness. Her heart thumped as the smooth fabric of his dinner jacket brushed against her bare arm, pinpricks of awareness skittering across her skin. This was real all right. This was actually happening.

As they moved across the floor of the ballroom the guests parted to let them through, something about the purposefulness of Zahir's stride or maybe the mask-like expression on Annalina's face, halting their conversations as they turned to look at them, curiosity glinting in their eyes.

Silencing the orchestra with a raised hand, Zahir waited a second for complete quiet to descend before he began.

'I would like to thank everyone for coming this evening.' Anna heard his calm words through the roaring of her ears. She could feel hundreds of pairs of eyes trained on her.

'We are here to celebrate the coming together of two great nations—Dorrada and the Kingdom of Nabatean. Our countries are to be joined together by the age-old tradition of matrimony.' He paused, scanning the room, which had gone deathly quiet. 'I would like to formally announce that Princess Annalina and I are to be married.'

There was a collective gasp of surprise, followed by furtive whisperings. Obviously Princess Annalina was not marrying the brother the guests had been expecting. Then a small cheer went up and people started to applaud, calling out their congratulations.

Anna's father appeared by her side and she felt for his hand, the little girl in her suddenly needing his reassurance. The smallest squeeze of encouragement would have done. Anything to show that he was pleased with her. That he loved her. He leant towards her and for one hopeful moment Anna thought he was going to do just that, but all hopes were dashed when he whispered in her ear, 'Don't you dare let me down again, Annalina.' Extricating his hand, he took a glass of champagne from the proffered silver tray and waited for Anna and Zahir to do the same. Then, refusing to meet his daughter's eye, he cleared his throat and proposed a toast, instructing everyone to raise their glasses to the happy couple and the future prosperity of their joined nations.

Anna gripped the stem of her glass as their names were chorused by the guests. Beside her she could sense Zahir, all rigid authority and unyielding control, while the false smile she had plastered across her face was in danger of cracking at any moment. In terms of appearing to be a happy couple, she doubted they were fooling anyone. But that wasn't what this was about, was it? This betrothal was a straightforward business deal. Anna just wished that someone would tell her stupid heart.

The next hour was a torturous round of introductions and small talk as Zahir swept her around the room, making sure she was welded to his side at all times. He moved between the ministers and ambassadors of Nabatean, the diplomats and high-ranking officials of Dorrada. It was blatantly nothing more than a networking exercise, making contact with the people that mattered. Congratulations were swiftly swept aside in favour of discussions about policies and politics, Anna left smiling inanely at the wives of these important men, and forced to display the stunning ring on her finger for them to coo over yet again.

Finally finding themselves at the entrance to the ballroom, Zahir announced in lowered tones that they had done their duty and it would now be acceptable for them to leave.

Anna gave a sigh of relief but, looking up, she was immediately caught in the midnight black of Zahir's hooded gaze. Suddenly she felt awkward, like a teenager on her first date. 'I will say goodnight, then.' She went to turn away, desperate to escape to her hotel room, to be free of her captor, at least for a few hours. More than anything she wanted to be alone, to have time to try to come to terms with what she had done.

'Not so fast.' With lightning speed, Zahir laid a restraining hold on her arm. 'This day has not ended yet.'

Anna's heart skipped a beat. What did he mean by that? Surely he wasn't expecting…? He didn't think…? Heat flared across her cheeks, spreading down her neck to her chest that heaved beneath its tight-fitting bodice. Somewhere deep inside her a curl of lust unfurled.

'I can assure you that it has, Zahir.' She touched

primly at her hair. 'I don't know what you are suggesting, but for your information I intend to go to bed now—alone.'

'You flatter yourself, young lady.' Scorn leeched from his voice. 'For your information, I do not intend to make any claims on your body.' He paused, eyes flashing with lethal intent. 'Not tonight, at least. But neither will I be letting you out of my sight. Not yet. Not until I feel I can trust you.'

'What do you mean?' Desperately trying to claw back some composure, she folded her arms across her chest. 'You can hardly keep me prisoner until our marriage.' Even as she said the words the terrible thought struck her that maybe he could. He was a man of such power, such authority, it was as if his very being demanded to be obeyed. The glittering lights of the ballroom had only accentuated his might, his towering height, the long legs and the broad, muscled shoulders that refused to be tamed by the fine material of his dinner jacket. Anna had noticed several women openly staring at him, their refined good manners deserting them in the face of this ruggedly handsome man.

'Not a prisoner, Princess. But let's just say I want to keep you somewhere that I can see you.'

'But that is ridiculous. I have given you my word, made the promise to my father. We have announced our engagement to the world. What more do I have to do to convince you?'

'You have to earn my trust, Annalina.' His eyes roamed over her, flat and considering. 'And that, as I'm sure you won't be surprised to hear, may take some time.'

'So what are you saying?' Anna bristled beneath his harsh scrutiny. 'That until I've earned this so-called trust you're not going to let me out of your sight? That hardly seems practical. Not least because we happen to live on different continents.'

Zahir shrugged. 'That is of little consequence. The solution is simple—you will return with me to Nabatean.'

Anna stared back at him. His knowing gaze was doing strange things to her head—making it swim. She must have drunk too much champagne.

'That's right, Princess Annalina.' Cold and authoritative, he confirmed what she feared. 'We leave tonight.'

CHAPTER THREE

ANNA PEERED OUT of the window as the plane started to descend, the sight of the dawn sky making her catch her breath. Below her shimmered Medira, the capital city of Nabatean, glowing in the pinks and golds of a new day. Her first glimpse of the country that would be her new home was certainly a stunning one. But it did nothing to lighten Anna's heart.

The little she knew about Nabatean had been gleaned during the first panicked days after she had been informed that she was to marry King Rashid Zahani. There had been a bloody civil war—that much she did know—when the people of Nabatean had fought bravely to overthrow the oppressive regime of Uristan, eventually winning independence and becoming a country in its own right again after more than fifty years.

There had been mention of Rashid and Zahir's parents, the former King and Queen of Nabatean, who had returned after living in exile, only to be murdered by rebel insurgents on the eve of the country's independence. Details of the horrifically tragic event were few and far between and in part Anna was grateful for that. There was frustratingly little documented about the new country at all and she realised just how ignorant she was about the place that she would somehow have to learn to call home.

Just as she knew so little of the man who was bringing her here, who intended to make her his wife. The man who had taken himself off to the office area of the luxury private jet and had spent the long journey so immersed in work, either glued to his laptop or reading through documents, that he had paid her no attention at all.

But what did she expect? When they had boarded the jet he had suggested that Anna retire to the bedroom, making it quite clear that the space would be her own. But stubbornness, or the fact that she knew she would never be able to sleep, or the hope that they might be able to have some meaningful discussion, had made her decline his offer.

Now she knew just how futile that hope had been and, staring at her own anxious reflection in the glass, found herself wondering how it was that her life had always been so controlled by others. First her father and now this dark, brooding force of nature that was to be her husband. Her destiny had never been her own. And now it never would be.

'We land in ten minutes.' With a start, Anna turned around to see that Zahir was standing right beside her, his hand on the back of her seat. For such a large man he moved surprisingly quietly, stealthily. Even his voice was different—raw and untamed, as if capable of sinful pleasure or brutal destruction. 'The distance from the airport to the palace is not a long one. Your journey is almost over. I trust you haven't found it too arduous?'

'No, I'm fine.' That was a lie. She was totally exhausted. But, having turned down his offer of an in-flight bedroom, she wasn't going to admit that.

'I think you will find the palace is most comfortable. You can rest assured that your every need will be catered for.'

'Thanks.' Anna didn't know what else to say. Who did he think she was? A princess from a fairy tale who would be unable to sleep should a pea be placed under her mattress? Or, worse still, some sort of prima donna who expected her every whim instantly to be obeyed?

If so, he couldn't be more wrong. She might have been raised in a palace but it had been as echoing and draughty as it was ancient, with crumbling walls, peeling paint-work and plumbing that only worked when it felt like it. And, as for expecting her every need to be catered for, well, she had been brought up to have no needs, no special treatment. Since her mother's death a succession of nannies—each one more severe, more cold-hearted than the last—had been at pains to point that out to her. Whether it was because they'd been handpicked by her father for that very reason—King Gustav believed his daughter needed a firm hand—or because the chilly conditions of the palace somehow had rubbed off on them, Anna didn't know.

She did know that she had never found anyone who had been able to replicate the warm feeling of her mother's arms around her, or the soft cushion of her breast, or the light touch of her fingers as she'd swept Annalina's unruly hair from her eyes. Which was why she held on to those feelings as firmly as her seven-year-old's grip would allow, keeping them alive by remembering everything she could about her beloved mother, refusing to let the memories fade.

A fleet of limousines was there to whisk Zahir and Anna, plus Rashid and assorted members of staff who had accompanied them on the plane, on the final leg of their journey to the palace. Once inside the palace, they were greeted by more deferential staff and Anna was shown to her suite of rooms, the bedroom dominated by an enormous gilded bed that was surmounted by a coronet and swathes of luxurious, deep-red silk.

It looked incredibly inviting. Finally giving way to her tiredness, Anna headed for the bathroom for a quick shower, taking in the huge, sunken marble bath with its flashy gold fittings and the veined marble walls. Then, climbing into the bed, she closed her eyes and let herself sink into deep, dream-filled sleep.

She was awoken by a tap on the door. Two dark-haired young women appeared, each bearing a tray laden with fruit, cheese, eggs, hummus, pitta bread and olives. She sat forward as they silently plumped up the pillows behind her, then one started to pour a cup of coffee whilst the other one held a plate and a pair of tongs, presumably waiting for Anna to make her selection.

'Oh, thank you.' Pushing the hair out of her eyes, Anna smiled at them, wondering how on earth she was ever going to do justice to this feast. What time was it anyway? A gilded clock on the wall opposite showed it to be just past one o'clock. So, that would be one in the afternoon? She looked back at the food. She was going to have to choose something. Judging by the earnest look on the young girls' faces, she wouldn't have been surprised if they had offered to feed her themselves. 'I think I'll try the eggs—they look delicious.'

Immediately an omelette was set before her and two pairs of eyes watched as she tentatively dug in her fork.

'Do you speak English?' Anna took a mouthful of omelette followed by a mouthful of coffee. The latter was strong, dark and utterly delicious.

'Yes, Your Highness.'

'Does everyone in Nabatean speak English?'

'Yes, Your Highness, it is our second language. You will find everyone can speak it.'

'It's the second language in my country too, so that's handy.' Anna smiled at these two pretty young women. 'And please, call me Annalina. "Your Highness" sounds far too stuffy.'

The women nodded but something told Anna that they would struggle with such informality. 'Can I ask your names?'

'I am Lena and this is Layla.'

'What pretty names. I'm guessing you are sisters?' She tried another forkful of omelette.

'We are. Layla is my younger sister by two years.'

'Well, it's very nice to meet you. Have you worked here in the palace long?' If she couldn't manage to eat much, at least she could distract them with conversation.

'Yes, for nearly two years. Ever since the palace was built. We are very lucky. After our parents died we were given a home in return for serving the King and Prince Zahir.'

So their parents were dead. Anna suspected there were going to be many tales of death and destruction in this country once ravaged by war. She wanted to ask more but Lena's lowered eyes suggested to pry further would be insensitive. Layla, however, had edged closer to the bed, staring at her as if she had been dropped down from another planet.

'I like your hair.'

'Layla!' Her sister admonished her with a sharp rebuke.

'That's okay.' Anna laughed, looking down at the blonde locks that were tumbling in disarray over her shoulders. 'Thank you for the compliment. It takes a lot of brushing in the morning, though, to get the tangles out.'

'I can do that for you,' Layla replied earnestly.

'Well, that's very kind of you but...'

'We are honoured to be able to serve you, Your Royal Highness,' Lena said. 'Prince Zahir has instructed us to attend to your every need.'

He had? Anna found it hard to believe that he would concern himself with such trivialities as her every need. 'Well, in that case, I will take you up on your kind offer. Prince Zahir...' Anna hesitated. She wanted to ask what sort of an employer he was, what sort of a man they thought he was, but suspected that they wouldn't be at liberty to tell her and it would be unfair to ask. 'Do you see very much of him?'

'No. He is away from the palace a lot. And, even when he is here, his needs are very few.'

'Do you have many visitors, here in the palace?'

'Not so many. Mostly foreign businessmen and politicians.'

'We've never had a visitor as pretty as you before,' Layla offered conversationally. 'Do all the women in your country look like you?'

'Well, the women of Dorrada tend to be fair-skinned and blue-eyed. The men too, come to that. Your dark beauty would be much prized in my country. As I'm sure it is here.'

'So, Prince Zahir...' Layla continued. 'You think him handsome?'

'Layla!'

'I am only asking.' Layla stuck out her bottom lip.

'Obviously she thinks him handsome. She wouldn't be marrying him otherwise.'

Anna suppressed a smile as the two sisters set about one another in their own language, waiting for them to finish before speaking again.

'The answer to your question is yes—I do think him handsome.'

The sisters exchanged an excited glance.

'And it is true that you will be marrying and coming to live here in the palace?' This time Lena asked the question, her curiosity overcoming her sense of decorum.

'Yes, that is true.' Saying it out loud didn't make it seem any the less astonishing.

Lena's and Layla's pretty faces broke out into broad smiles and they even reached to clasp each other's hands.

'That is very good news, Your Royal Highness. Very good news indeed.'

Staring at the screen, Zahir cursed under his breath. He had braced himself for a small photograph of the two of them on the bridge, prepared to suffer the mild humiliation of being caught kissing in public, or rather being kissed, when it was put in the wider context of the engagement party. But this wasn't a small photograph. This was a series of images, blown up to reveal every minor detail. With his finger jabbing on the mouse, Zahir scrolled down and down, his blood pressure rocketing as more and more pictures of him locked in a passionate embrace with Annalina flashed before his eyes. There were even several close-ups of the engagement ring, worn on the slender hand that was threaded through his hair, before finally the official photographs of the party appeared, the ones he wanted the world to see. The ones where he and Annalina were standing solemnly side by side, displaying their commitment to each other and to their countries.

And it wasn't just one newspaper. The whole of Europe appeared to be obsessed with the beautiful Princess Annalina, the press in France, the UK, and of course Dorrada itself taking a particular interest, feasting on the titbits that the photographer had no doubt sold to them for a handsome fee.

A rustle behind him made him turn his head and there stood the object of the press's attention, Annalina. At last—it was over an hour since he had sent servants to her room to find out what she was doing, giving orders that she should meet him here in the stateroom at her earliest convenience. Clearly he was going to have to be more specific. Dressed in a simple navy fitted dress, she looked both young, chic and incredibly sexy at the same time. Her ash-blonde hair was loose, tumbling over her shoulders in soft waves, falling well below the swell of her breasts.

Zahir felt his throat go dry. He hadn't been prepared for such hair, only having seen it secured on top of her head in some way before. He had had no idea it would be so long, so fascinating. He had had no idea that he would be fighting the urge to imagine how it would feel against his bare skin.

'Have you seen this?' Angry with himself, with his reaction and this whole damned situation, his voice rasped harshly. He hadn't been able to concentrate all morning, hadn't got through half the work he'd intended to.

She glanced at the laptop, screwing up her eyes. 'Is it bad?'

'See for yourself.'

A soft cloud of floral scent washed over him as she sat down next to him, tucking her hair behind one small, perfect ear. He almost flinched as she reached across him to touch the mouse, quickly scrolling through the images and scanning the text as she moved from one website to the next.

'Well.' She turned in her seat to look at him, her eyes a startling blue. 'I guess it's no worse than we were expecting.'

'You, maybe. I certainly wasn't expecting such mass coverage.'

'Well, there's nothing we can do about it now.' She exhaled, the light breath whispering across the bare skin of his forearm and raising the hairs, raising his blood pressure. 'Are the photos in the Nabatean newspapers too?'

'Fortunately not. The official photographs from the engagement party are all that they will see. My people would not be interested in such a sordid spectacle.'

He watched as she wrinkled her small nose. Her skin was so pale, so clear, like the finest porcelain.

'What?' He didn't want to ask, he hadn't even meant to ask. But her disrespectful gesture refused to be ignored.

'I'm just wondering how you know that—if they aren't given the chance, I mean. That sounds like censorship to me.'

Temper snaked through him, slowing his heart to a dull thud. He narrowed his eyes, the thick lashes blurring his image of this infuriating woman. 'Let me make something clear right from the start, Princess Annalina. I may, or may not, seek your views on matters to do with European culture and traditions that I am not familiar with. That is your role. However, you do *not* attempt to interfere with the running of my country. Your opinions are neither needed nor wanted.'

'If you say so.'

'I do.'

'All I'm saying is…' she raised finely shaped eyebrows '…you can't have it both ways.' It seemed she was determined to stand up to him. To have the last word. 'If you are marrying me solely because I am a Western princess, because you want entrée into Europe that my family, my country, can give you, then you are going to have to accept this sort of media attention. It comes with the job. It comes with me.'

Zahir scowled. Was this true? If so he was going to have to put a stop to it. He had no intention of becoming part of some celebrity circus. But then twenty-four hours ago he had had no intention of marrying at all.

'I have to say, I am somewhat surprised that you would be happy for the first sighting the people of Nabatean have of their new princess to be a grubby little paparazzi shot of you wantonly pressing your body up against mine.' He wished he hadn't reminded himself of that now. Not when she was so close. Not when he knew he wanted her to do it again.

'It doesn't bother me.' She tossed her head, her hair rippling over her shoulders, deliberately countering his pomposity with a throwaway remark. It felt to Zahir as if she was throwing his weakness for her back in his face too, even though he had gone to great pains to cover it up.

'Well, it should bother you. It is hardly becoming.' The pomposity solidified inside him, holding him ram-rod-straight.

'Look. The paparazzi have been following me all my life. I'm used to it—it's part of the role I was unwittingly born into. There are probably hundreds of images of me being *unbecoming*, as you put it.'

Zahir felt himself pale beneath his olive skin. This was worse than he'd thought. In his haste to arrange a suitable match for his brother it appeared he hadn't been thorough enough in his research. He knew there had been a broken engagement but what was she telling him now? That she had a history of debauched behaviour? This woman who he now had to take as his wife.

'It's okay!' Suddenly she let out a laugh, a light-hearted

chuckle that echoed between them, seeming to surprise the cavernous room as much as it did him. 'There's no need to look like that.' Now she was reaching for his hand, laying her own over the top of it. 'I haven't done anything really terrible! And, who knows, maybe now that I'm officially engaged the paparazzi will lose interest in me, find someone else to train their zoom lenses on. Especially as you are not well known in Europe.'

'Unlike your last fiancé, you mean?'

Annalina withdrew her hand, all traces of humour gone now, colour touching her cheeks at his mention of her former partner. If he had wanted to snuff out her sunshine, he had achieved it.

'Well, yes, Prince Henrik was well known to the gossip columnists. When that relationship ended it was inevitable that there was going to be a feeding frenzy.'

There was silence as Zahir refilled his coffee cup before returning his gaze to Annalina's face.

'I expect you want to know what happened.' She twisted her hands in her lap.

'No.'

'I will tell you if you ask.'

'I have no intention of asking. It's none of my business.' And, more than that, he didn't want to think about it. She continued to stare at him, a strange sort of expression playing across her face, as if she was trying to decide where to go from here.

'I suggest we concentrate on making plans for the future.' There, he could be sensitive, moving her on from what was obviously a painful subject.

'Yes, of course.'

'I see no reason for a long engagement.'

'No.' Now she was chewing her lip.

'A month should be ample time to make the arrangements. I'm assuming you'll want some sort of society wedding in Dorrada? If we follow that with a blessing here in Nabatean, that should suffice.'

'Right.'

'So I can leave you to organise it? The wedding, I mean? Or hire people to do it, or however these things work.' At the mention of the wedding she seemed to have gone into some kind of stupor. Wasn't the idea of arranging your wedding day supposed to be appealing to a young woman? Clearly not to Annalina. A thought occurred to him and he leant back in his chair. 'If it's money that is concerning you, let me assure you that is not a problem. No expense is to be spared.'

But instead of lessening her worry his statement only furrowed her brow deeper and was now coupled with a distinct look of distaste in her eyes. Perhaps talking about money was distasteful—he had no idea, and frankly he didn't care. Or perhaps he was the thing that she found distasteful. He didn't want to care about that either. But somehow he did. Abruptly scraping back his chair, he pushed himself to his feet, suddenly needing to end this meeting right now.

'Perhaps you will inform me of the date of the wedding as soon as you know it.'

He looked down on Annalina from the superior position of his height. He heard himself, cold and aloof.

CHAPTER FOUR

'YOUR ROYAL HIGHNESS?'

Anna was wandering around the palace when one of the servants came to find her. She had spent the last hour pacing from one room to the next, still fuming too much over Zahir's abrupt departure from their so-called meeting to pay much attention to her opulent surroundings. The way he had just got up and walked out, ending their discussion with no warning, no manners!

She had thought she would try and distract herself by finding her way around this grand edifice but it was all too huge, too daunting, each room grander than the last, all domed ceilings, brightly coloured marble floors and micro-mosaic decorations. But there was nothing homely about it. In fact it had a new, unlived-in feel to it, as if no laughter had ever echoed through its stately rooms, no children's feet had ever raced along its miles of corridors or young bottoms slid down its sweepingly ornate banisters. Which, no doubt, they hadn't. This was a show home, nothing more. A monument erected as a display of wealth and power, a symbol of national pride for the people of Nabatean.

'Prince Zahir has instructed that you are to meet him at the palace entrance.' The servant bowed respectfully. 'If you would like to follow me?'

So that would be right now, would it? This was how it was to be—Zahir issued his orders and she was expected to obey. Just like any other member of his staff. Instinctively Anna wanted to rebel, to say no, just to prove that she wasn't at his beck and call. But what would that achieve, other than deliberately antagonising him? Something which she strongly suspected would not prove to be a good idea. Besides, she had nothing else to do.

A wall of heat hit her when she stepped out into the searing afternoon sun. Shielding her eyes, she could see Zahir standing by the limousine, waiting for the chauffeur to help her inside before getting in beside her.

'Can I ask where we're going?' She settled in her seat, preparing herself to turn and look at him. It still gave her a jolt every single time her eyes met his, every time she stared into his darkly rugged features. It was like a cattle prod to her nervous system. He had changed into a sharply cut suit, she noticed, so presumably this wasn't a pleasure trip.

'The Assembly House in the town square.' He returned her gaze. 'I have arranged a meeting with some officials, members of the senate and the government. It will be an opportunity to introduce you to them, so they can put a face to the name.'

A face to the name? His cold phrase left her in no doubt as to her role here—she was nothing more than a puppet, to be dangled in front of the people that mattered, jiggled around to perform when necessary and presumably put back in her box when she wasn't required. It was a depressing picture but she had to remember that this was what their union was all about, a mutually reciprocal arrangement for the benefit of both of their countries. Nothing more. She needed to catch her sinking stomach before it fell still further.

Breaking his gaze, Anna turned to look out of the window as the limousine swept them through the streets of Medira. It was a city still under construction, enormous cranes swinging above their heads, towering skyscrapers proudly rocketing heavenwards. The place certainly had a buzz about it. Lowering her head, Annalina peered up in awe.

'I hadn't realised Medira was such a metropolis. Is it really true that this whole city has been built in under two years?'

'It has, in common with several other major cities in Nabatean.'

'That's amazing. You must be very proud.'

'It has been a great responsibility.'

Responsibility. The word might as well be indelibly etched across his forehead. In fact it was, Anna realised as she turned to look at him again. It was there in the frown lines that crossed his brow, lines that furrowed into deep grooves when he was lost in thought or displeased. Which seemed to be most of the time. There was no doubt how heavily responsibility weighed on Zahir Zahani's shoulders, that his duty to his country knew no bounds. He was prepared to marry her, after all. What greater sacrifice was there than that?

'But you have achieved so much.' For some reason she wanted to ease his burden. 'Surely you must allow yourself a small acknowledgement of that?'

'The acknowledgement will come from the people, not me. They are the judge and jury. Everything we are doing here in Nabatean is for them.'

'Of course.' Anna turned to look out of the window again. It was pointless trying to reason with him. Through the shimmering heat she could now make out a mountain range, grey against the startling blue of the sky. She was used to mountains—Dorrada had plenty of them—but these were not like the familiar snow-capped peaks of home...these were stark, forbidding.

'The Jagros Mountains.' Zahir followed her gaze. 'They form the border between us and Uristan. They look deceptively close but there is a vast expanse of desert between us and them.'

Just as well. Annalina had no desire to visit them. She remembered, now that he said the name, that they were the mountains that had been the scene of terrible fighting during the war between Nabatean and Uristan.

'If you look over there...' With a jolt of surprise, Anna realised that Zahir had moved across the leather seat and was now right next to her. She registered the heat of his body, his scent, the sound of his breathing as he stretched one arm across her to point at an oval-shaped structure in the distance. 'You can see the new sports stadium. It's nearing completion now. Soon we will be able to host international sporting events. We intend to make a bid for the Olympics.'

Now the pride had crept into his voice. This might be all about the people but there was no doubt what this country meant to Zahir.

'That's very impressive.' His nearness had caught the breath in her throat and she swallowed noisily. How was it that this man affected her so viscerally, so earthly? In a place deep down that she had never even known existed before?

She was grateful when the limousine finally pulled up outside the Assembly House and she was able to escape from its confines. Escape the pull of Zahir's power.

The meeting was as long as it was boring. Having been introduced to large numbers of dignitaries and advisors,

Anna was then given the option of returning to the palace whilst the men—because it was all men—continued with the business of the day. But stubbornness and a vague hope that she might understand some of what they were discussing, that she would get a small insight into the running of Nabatean, made her say she would like to stay. In point of fact, even though the meeting was conducted in English, the items on the agenda were far too complicated for her to get a grip on, and she ended up staring out of the window or sneaking sidelong glances at Zahir as he controlled the proceedings with masterful authority. There was no sign of his brother at the meeting, or even any mention of him. It appeared that Zahir was the man in charge here. The power behind the throne.

They were standing at the top of a short flight of steps, preparing to leave the building, when Zahir suddenly stopped short, unexpectedly moving his arm around Anna's waist to pull her to his side. Looking outside, Anna could see a small crowd of people had gathered, leaning up against the ornate railings, peering up at the building expectantly.

Pulling out his phone, Zahir barked orders into it and from nowhere several security guards appeared. Dispatching a couple of them into the crowd, he waited impatiently, his grip around her waist tightening with every passing second. Anna could see a vein pulsing in his neck as his eyes darted over the crowd, missing nothing, a sudden stillness setting his features in stone. He reminded her of a dog on a leash, waiting to be set free to chase its quarry.

'What is it? What's the matter?'

'That's what I'd like to find out.'

The security guards returned and there was a brief

conversation, during which she saw Zahir scowl, then look back at her with obvious contempt.

'It would seem that the crowd are here to see you.'

'Oh.' Anna stood a little straighter, smoothing the creases of her dress. 'That's nice.'

'Nice?' He repeated the word as if it was poison in his mouth. 'I fail to see what's nice about it.'

'Well, it's not surprising that people want to meet me. They are bound to be curious about your fiancée. I suggest we go out there, shake some hands and say hello.'

'We will do no such thing.'

'Why ever not?'

'Because there is a time and a place for such things. I have no intention of doing an impromptu meet-and-greet on the steps of the Assembly House.'

'These things don't always have to be formal, Zahir. It doesn't work like that.'

'In Nabatean things work the way I say they will work.'

Anna bit down hard on her lip. There really was no answer to that.

'And, quite apart from anything else, there is the security issue.'

'Well, they don't look dangerous to me.' Staring out at the swelling crowd, Anna stood her ground. 'And besides...' she glanced at the security guards around them '... I'm sure these guys are more than capable of dealing with any potential trouble.'

'There will be no trouble. We walk out of here and get straight into the limousine without speaking to anyone— without even looking at anyone. Do I make myself clear?'

'Crystal clear.' Anna shot him an icy glare. Not that she intended to follow his dictate. If she wanted to smile at the crowd, maybe offer a little wave, she jolly well would. Who did he think he was with his stupid rules?

But before she had the chance to do anything she found herself being bundled down the steps, pressed so closely to Zahir's side that she could barely breathe, let alone acknowledge the crowd. She could just about hear their cheers, hear them calling her name, before Zahir, with his hand on the back of her head, pushed her into the car, following behind her with the weight of his body and instructing the driver to move off before the car door was even shut.

'For heaven's sake.' Anna turned to look at him, eyes flashing. 'What was all that about?'

Adjusting the sleeves of his jacket, Zahir sat back, staring straight ahead.

'Anyone would think you were ashamed of me, bundling me into the car like a criminal.'

'Not ashamed of you, Annalina. It was simply a question of getting you into the car as fast as possible and with the minimum of harassment.'

'The only person harassing me was you. That was a few people—*your* people, I might add—who wanted to greet us. If you want real harassment, you should try having thirty or forty paparazzi swarming around you, baying for your blood.'

Zahir shot her a sharp glance. 'And this has happened to you?'

'Yes.' Anna shifted in her seat, suddenly uncomfortable with this subject, especially as Zahir's eyes were now trained on her face, waiting for an explanation. 'When my engagement to Prince Henrik ended.' She lowered her voice. 'And other times too. Though, that was the worst.'

'Well, you will never have to endure such indignity again. I will make sure of that.'

Anna turned to look out of the window, her hands clasped in her lap. He spoke with such authority, such confidence, she had to admit it was comforting. All her life she'd felt as if she was on her own, fighting her own battles, facing up to the trials and traumas, of which she'd suffered more than her fair share, without anyone there to help her, to be on her side. Now, it seemed, she had a protector.

Suddenly she knew she could put her trust in Zahir, that she would put her life in his hands without a second thought, for that matter. Whether it was the paparazzi, a marauding army or a herd of stampeding elephants, come to that, he would deal with it. Such was his presence, the sheer overwhelming power of him. But the flip side was that he was also an arrogant, cold-blooded control freak. And one, Anna was shocked to realise, who was starting to dominate her every thought.

The rest of the journey back was conducted in silence, apart from the sound of Zahir's fingers jabbing at his mobile phone. Only when they were nearing the palace gates did he look up, letting out a curse under his breath. For there was a crowd here too, gathered around the palace gates, including some photographers who had climbed up onto the railings to get a better view.

'Dear God.' Zahir growled under his breath. 'Is this what I have to expect now, every time I leave the palace, every time I go anywhere with you?'

'I don't see your problem with it.' Anna twitched haughtily. 'You should be pleased that the people of Nabatean are interested in us. That they have gone to the trouble of coming to see us. Don't you want to be popular, for people to like you?'

'I don't care a damn whether people like me or not.'

'Well, maybe it's time you started to care.'

There—that had told him. Even so she averted her gaze, having no wish to witness the thunder she knew she would see there. Sitting up straighter, she arranged her hair over her shoulders. The palace gates had opened now and as the crowd parted to let their car through she turned to look out of the window and smiled brightly at everyone, giving a regal wave, the way she had been taught to do as a child. The crowd cheered in response, waving back and calling her name. Small children were held aloft to get a glimpse of her. Cameras flashed. Everybody loved it.

Well, not exactly everybody. A quick glance at her fiancé revealed a scowl that would make a tiger turn tail and run. But Anna refused to be cowed. She had done nothing wrong. Zahir Zahani was the one who needed to lighten up, respect his people by acknowledging their presence. Maybe even look as if he was a tiny bit proud of her. Though there was precious little chance of that.

Once inside, Zahir started to stride away, presumably intending to abandon her once again. But Anna had had enough of this. Taking several quick steps to catch up with him, she reached out, the touch of her hand on his arm stopping him in his tracks.

'I was just wondering...' She hesitated, pulling away her hand. 'Whether we would be having dinner together tonight.'

Zahir scowled, as if the possibility had hitherto never entered his mind. 'Dinner?'

'Yes.' She was tempted to point out that it was the meal at the end of the day that civilised people tended to share together. Self-preservation made her hold her tongue.

'That's not something I had planned.'

Picking up a length of hair, Anna curled it around her finger, suddenly hesitant. 'When you invite someone to your home, it's generally expected that you make some effort to entertain them. That is the role of a host. It's not much fun being left to rattle around here on my own.'

Deep brown eyes caught hers. 'I can see there are a couple of things I need to remind you of, Princess Annalina.' His sensuous mouth flattened into a grim line. 'Firstly, whilst it is true that you are a guest at the palace, I am most certainly not responsible for entertaining you. And, secondly, you should think yourself grateful that you have the freedom to *rattle around* on your own. The alternative would be to secure you in one room, have you watched over day and night. Something I did consider.'

'Don't be ridiculous.' Anna stared at him in horror.

Zahir gave an infuriating shrug. 'So perhaps you should see your freedom for what it is—a chance to prove yourself trustworthy—rather than complain about being neglected.'

Well, that was her put firmly in her place. Cheeks burning, she turned away, wishing she had never mentioned having wretched dinner with this wretched man.

'However, if it would please you, I can find time for us to dine together tonight. Shall we say in one hour's time?'

Anna swung round to face him again, the words *don't bother* tingling on her lips. But there was something about the narrowed gaze of those hooded eyes that made her stop.

It was surprise, she realised. Zahir was surprised that she wanted to any spend time with him. She was surprised too, come to that. It was like he had some sort of power over her, drawing her to the edge of the cliff when all her instincts were telling her to keep away. That blatant, raw masculinity made her keep coming back for more punishment. Anna had never thought of herself as a masochist. Now she was beginning to wonder.

Nervously licking her lips with the tip of her tongue, she saw his eyes flash in response, tightening the tendrils inside her. 'Very well.' Pushing back her shoulders, she tossed her hair over them. 'I will see you later.'

CHAPTER FIVE

ZAHIR STARED AT the young woman at the far end of the table—the European princess who was soon to be his bride. Something he was still desperately struggling to come to terms with. He had no idea who she was, not really. Earlier, when she'd talked about the press attention she'd received over the years, his blood had run cold in his veins. But fear about her morals had swiftly changed to the urge to protect her, his whole person affronted that she should ever have been subjected to such assaults. Because deep down some instinct told him that Princess Annalina was vulnerable and certainly not a woman who would give away her favours easily. Which was odd, when you thought about the way they had met.

She was certainly regal. From the fine bones of her face to the dainty set of her shoulders and the elegant, refined posture. Her hands, he noticed, were particularly delicate, long, slender fingers and pink nails devoid of nail varnish. They looked as if they had never done a day's work in their life. They probably hadn't.

He looked down at his own hands. A warrior's hands. No longer calloused from combat—he hadn't gripped a dagger or curled his finger around the trigger of a gun for over two years now—they were nevertheless stained with the blood of war and always would be. They had

been around the throat of too many of his enemies ever
to be washed clean—had been used to pull lifeless bodies
out caves that had become subterranean battlegrounds,
or recover corpses shrivelling in the scorching heat of
the desert with the vultures circling overhead.

His hands had closed the eyelids of far too many
young men.

And now… Could such hands ever expect to run over
the fair skin of the woman before him? Would that be
right? Permissible? They wanted to, that was for certain.
They itched, burned even, with longing to feel the softness of her pale flesh beneath their fingertips, to be able
to trace the contours of her slender body, to travel over
the hollow of her waist, the swell of her breasts. They
longed to explore every part of her body.

Feeling his eyes on her, Annalina looked up and
smiled at him from her end of the table.

'This is delicious.' She indicated the half-eaten plate
of food before her with the fork in her hand. 'Lovely and
spicy. What's the meat, do you suppose?'

Zahir glanced down at his plate, already scraped clean,
as if seeing it for the first time. Food was just fuel to him,
something to be grateful for but to be consumed as fast
as possible, before it was covered in flies or snatched
away by a hungry hound. It was certainly not a subject
he ever discussed, nor wanted to.

'Goat, I believe.' He levelled dark eyes at her.

'Oh.' That perfect pink mouth puckered in surprise
then pursed shut, her fork left to rest on her plate.

He stifled a smile. Obviously goat was not something
she was accustomed to eating. No doubt Annalina was
more used to seeing them grazing prettily in wildflower
meadows than having them stewed and presented before
her in a bowl of couscous. She knew nothing of the ways

of this country, he realised, and the smile was immediately replaced with the more familiar scowl.

Had he been wrong to insist that she marry him, to bring her to this foreign land and expect her to be able to fit in, play the role of his wife? It was a huge undertaking to ask of anyone, let alone someone as fragile-looking as her. And yet he already knew that there was more to Annalina than her flawless beauty might suggest. She was strong-willed and she was brave. It had taken real guts to refuse to marry his brother, to stand on that bridge and do whatever she thought it took to get her out of that marriage. To kiss a total stranger. A kiss that still burned on his lips.

It had all backfired, of course. She had leapt straight from the frying pan into the fire, finding herself shackled to him instead. He was nothing like his brother, it was true. But, in terms of a husband, had Annalina made the right choice? Would she have been better sticking with the relative calm of Rashid, his particular demons regulated by carefully prescribed medication?

Or Zahir, whose demons still swirled inside him, drove him on, made him the man he was. Power, control and the overwhelming desire to do the best for his country was the only therapy he could tolerate.

He didn't know, but either way it was too late now. The choice had been made. They were both going to have to live with it.

'I hope I haven't spoiled your appetite?' The food, he noticed, had now been abandoned, Annalina's slender hand gripping the stem of her glass as she took a sip of wine, then another.

'No, it's not that.' She gave an unconvincing smile. 'It's actually quite filling.'

'Then, if you have finished, perhaps you would like to be served coffee somewhere more comfortable.'

'Um, yes, that sounds a good idea.' She touched a napkin to her lips. 'Where were you thinking of?'

'I will take mine in my quarters, but there are any number of seating areas in the palace that are suitable for relaxation. The courtyards are very pleasant too, though they will be chilly at this time of night.'

'I'm sure.' She fiddled with a tendril of hair that had escaped the swept-up style. 'Actually, I think I will join you.' There was determination in her voice, but vulnerability too, as if she might easily crack or splinter if challenged. 'I would like to see your quarters.'

Zahir stilled, something akin to panic creeping over him. He hadn't intended to invite her to his rooms. Far from it. By suggesting that they took their coffee elsewhere, he had been trying to escape from her. Which begged the question, why? Why would he, a man who would take on a band of armed insurgents with the bravery of a thousand warriors combined, be frightened by the thought of sharing a cup of coffee with this young woman? It was ridiculous.

Because he didn't know how to behave around her, that was why. This relationship had been thrust upon him so suddenly that he hadn't had time to figure out how to make it work, how to control it. And being around Annalina only seemed to make the task more difficult. Rather than clarifying the situation, she seemed to mess with his judgement. He found himself torn two ways—one side warning that he must be on his guard, and watch over this wayward princess like a hawk to make sure she didn't try to abscond, while the other side was instructing him to take her to his bed and make her his, officially.

The latter was a tempting prospect for sure. And the way she was looking at him now, eyes shining brightly as she held his gaze, her hands steepled under her chin, fingertips grazing her lips, it would take all his self-control not to give in to it. But control it he would, because control was something he prided himself on. More than that, something he ruled his life by, using it both to drive himself on and deny himself pleasure. Because pleasure was nothing but an indulgence, a form of weakness, a slippery slope that led down to the bowels of hell. That he had discovered to his cost with the most tragic of results: the murder of his parents.

On the eve of his country's independence he had been in a rowdy bar, watching, if not actually participating, as his brave comrades had celebrated their tremendous victory with flowing alcohol and loose women. He had been relaxed, enjoying himself, accepting the accolades, full of pride for what he had achieved. And all the time, a few hundred miles away, his parents were being murdered, a knife being drawn across their throats. A tragedy that he would never, *ever* begin to forgive himself for.

But that didn't stop the weight of lust in his groin grow heavier by the second, spreading its traitorous warmth through his body as he stared back at Annalina's open, inviting face. He had no idea why she was looking at him in that way. The workings of a woman's mind were a complete mystery to him, and not something he had ever thought he would care to concern himself with. But now he found he longed to know what was going on behind those eyes that were glazed perhaps a little too brightly— found that he would pay good money to find out what was going through that clever, complicated mind of hers.

'I doubt you will find anything remotely interesting about my quarters.'

'You will be in them. That's interesting enough for me.'

There she went again, throwing him a curveball, mess-

ing with his head. Was she flirting with him? Was that
what this was? Zahir had experienced flirting before. His
position of power, not to mention his dark good looks,
meant he had had his fair share of female attention over
the years. Most, but not all, of which he had totally ignored. He was a red-blooded male, after all. Occasionally
he would allow himself to slake his thirst. But that was all
it had ever been. No emotion, no attachment and certainly
no second-guessing what the object of his attentions might
be thinking. The way he found himself puzzling now.

'Very well. If you insist.' Summoning one of the hov-
ering waiting staff with a wave of his hand, he gave his
orders then, walking round to the back of Annalina's
chair, he waited as she rose to her feet. 'If you would
like to follow me.'

Setting off at a rapid pace, he found he had to moder-
ate his step in order for Annalina to keep up. She trot-
ted along beside him, her heels clicking on the marble
floors, looking around her as if trying to memorise the
route back in case she should need to escape. Zahir found
himself regretting his decision to allow her into his rooms
more and more with every forceful footstep. No woman,
other than the palace staff, had ever been in his chambers. There had been no need for it. There was no need
for it now. Why had he ever agreed to let this woman invade his personal space?

By the time they had negotiated the labyrinth of corridors and he was inserting the key into the lock of his
door, Zahir's mood had blackened still further.

'You lock your door?' Waiting beside him, Annalina
looked up in surprise.

'Of course. Security is of paramount importance.'

'Even in your own palace? There are guards everywhere. Do you not trust them to protect your property?'

'Trust no one and you will not be disappointed.' Zahir pushed hard on the heavy door with the palm of his hand.

'Oh, Zahir, that's such a depressing ideology!' Annalina attempted a throwaway laugh but it fell, uncaught, to the ground.

'Depressing it may be.' He stood back to let her enter. 'But I know it to be true.'

Taking in a deep breath, Anna stepped over the threshold. This was not going well. Maybe it had been a mistake to ask to accompany Zahir to his quarters. It had certainly done nothing to improve his mood. The resolve she had had at the start of the evening, to sit down and talk, try to get to know him a bit, discuss their future, had been severely tested during the course of the torturous meal. Every topic of conversation she had tried to initiate had either been met with cool disregard or monosyllabic answers.

All except one. When she had mentioned his parents, tried to tell him how sorry she was to hear of their tragic death, the look on Zahir's face had been terrifying to behold, startling her with its volcanic ferocity. It was clear that subject was most definitely off-limits.

But, where their future was concerned, she had to persevere. She needed to find out what was expected of her, what her role would be. And, more importantly, she needed to tell Zahir about herself, her shameful secret. Before it was too late. Which was why at the end of the meal she had fought against every instinct to turn tail and run to the safety of her bed and had persuaded him to bring her here. And why she found herself being welcomed into his spartan quarters with the all the enthusiasm that would have been given to a jester at a funeral.

For spartan it certainly was. In stark contrast to the rest of the palace, the room she was ushered into was small and dimly lit, with bare floorboards and a low ceiling. There was very little furniture, just a low wooden table and a makeshift seating area covered with tribal rugs.

'As I said.' Briefly following her gaze, Zahir moved to put the key in the lock on this side. He didn't turn it, Anna noticed with relief. 'There is nothing to see here.'

'Something doesn't have to be all glitz and glamour for it to be interesting, you know.' She purposefully took several steps into the room and, placing her hands on her hips, looked around her, displaying what she hoped was a suitably interested expression. 'How many rooms do you have here?'

'Three. This room, an office and a bedroom. Plus a bathroom, of course. I find that to be perfectly adequate.'

'Is this the bedroom?' Nervous energy saw her stride over to an open door in the corner of the room and peer in. In the near darkness she could just about make out the shape of a small bed, low to the ground, rugs scattered on the bare boards of the floor.

So this was where he slept. Anna pictured him, gloriously naked beneath the simple covers of this bed. He was so vital, so very much alive, that it was hard to imagine him doing anything as normal as sleeping. But she wouldn't allow herself to imagine him doing anything else. At least, not with anyone else.

'You obviously don't go in for luxuries here.'

'I do not. The basics are all I need. I find anything else is just an unwanted distraction.'

As was she, no doubt. Anna tamped down the depressing thought. 'So why build a palace like this, then? What's the point?'

'Medira Palace is for the people, a symbol of the power and wealth of Nabatean, something that they can look upon with pride. I may not choose to indulge in its luxuries, but it's not about me. The palace will be here for many generations after I have gone. And, besides, it's not just my home. My brother lives here too, as of course will you.'

'Yes.' Anna swallowed.

'You have no need to worry.' Zahir gave a harsh laugh. 'I don't expect you to share these chambers. You may have the pick of the rooms of the palace, as many and as grand as you wish.'

'And what about you? Will you be giving up these chambers and coming to live in splendour with me?'

'I will not.' Zahir's reply was as bleak as it was damning. What did that mean—that they would inhabit different parts of the palace? That they would live totally separate lives, be man and wife in name only? A knock on the door meant that Anna had to keep this deeply depressing thought to herself for the time being, as a servant bearing a tray of coffee saved Zahir from further questioning. Bending down, she settled herself as best she could on the low seating area, tucking her legs under her before reaching to accept her cup of coffee from the silent servant. It was impossible to get comfortable in her high-heeled shoes so, with her coffee cup balanced in one hand, she took them off with the other, pairing them neatly on the floor beside her. For some reason they suddenly looked ridiculously out of place, like twin sirens in the stark masculinity of this room.

Raising her eyes, Anna saw that Zahir was staring at them too, as if thinking the same thing. She was relieved when he roughly pulled off his own soft leather shoes and sat down beside her.

'So your brother.' She decided to opt for what she hoped was a slightly safer topic of conversation, but as she felt Zahir stiffen beside her she began to wonder.

'You say he lives here in the palace and yet I haven't seen any sign of him.'

'There is no reason for you to have seen him, as he occupies the east wing. Given the circumstances, I doubt that either of you are going to deliberately seek each other out.'

'Well, no.' Annalina pouted slightly. 'Having said that, I don't believe he wished to marry me any more than I did him.'

She waited, pride almost wishing that Zahir would contradict her, tell her that of course Rashid had wanted to marry her, 'what man wouldn't?'.

Instead there was only a telling silence as Zahir drank the contents of his coffee cup in one gulp then reached for the brass pot to refill it.

'There is some truth in that.' Avoiding her gaze, he eventually spoke.

Being right had never felt less rewarding. Drawing in a breath, Anna decided to ask the question that had been niggling her ever since she had first set eyes on Rashid Zahani. 'Can I ask...about Rashid... Is there some sort of medical problem?'

That spun Zahir's head in her direction, the dark eyes flashing dangerously beneath the thick, untidy eyebrows. So close now, Anna could see the amber flecks that radiated from the black pupils, glowing as if they were just about to burst into flames.

'So what are you saying? That anyone who doesn't want to marry you must have some sort of mental deficiency?' Scorn singed the edges of his words.

'No, I just...'

'Because if so you have a very high, not to say misguided, opinion of yourself.'

'That's not fair!' Colour rushed to flush Anna's cheeks,

heating her core as indignation and embarrassment took hold. 'That's not what I meant and you know it.'

'Well, that's what it sounded like.' He looked away and she was left staring at his harsh profile, at the muscle that twitched ominously beneath the stubble of his cheek. There was silence as she battled to control the mixed emotions rioting inside her, as she waited for her skin to cool down.

'My brother has some personal issues to overcome.' Finally Zahir spoke again, leaning forward to replace his cup on the table. 'He suffers from anxiety due to a trauma he suffered and this can affect his mood. He just needs time, that's all. When the right person is found, he will marry and produce a family. Of that I am certain.'

'Of course.' Anna was not going to make the mistake of questioning that statement, even if secretly she had her doubts. There was something about Rashid that she found very unnerving. On the plane journey here she had looked up to see him staring at her in a very peculiar way, almost as if he was looking right through her. 'But does Rashid not get to choose his own wife? You make it sound as if he has no say in the matter.'

'Like me, you mean?' The eyes swung back, lingering this time, tracing a trail over her sensitised skin, across her cheekbones and down her nose, until they rested on her lips. Anna felt their burn as vividly as if she had been touched by a flame.

'And me too.' She just about managed to croak out the words of defiance, even though her heart had gone off like a grenade inside her.

'Indeed.' Something approaching empathy softened his voice. 'We are all victims of circumstance to a greater or lesser extent.'

Greater—definitely greater in her case. To marry this

man, tie herself for ever to this wild, untamed, warrior, had meant taking the biggest leap of faith in her life. But Anna didn't regret it. In the same way as some inner sense had told her that she could never have married Rashid Zahani, it now filled her with nervous excitement at the thought of marrying his brother. Excitement, exhilaration and terror all rolled into one breathtaking surge of adrenaline. But there was worry too—worry that maybe once Zahir knew all the facts he might no longer want to marry her. She was beginning to realise just how devastating that would be. Because she wanted Zahir. In every sense of the word. Drawing in a shaky breath, she decided she was going to have to just plunge in.

'About our marriage, Zahir.' She watched the play of his muscles across his back as he leant forward to refill his coffee cup again. 'There are things we need to discuss.'

'I've told you. I will leave all the arrangements to you. I have neither the time nor the interest to get involved.'

'I'm not talking about the arrangements.'

'What, then?' He settled back against the cushions, his eyes holding hers with a piercing intensity that made her feel like a specimen butterfly being pinned to a board.

She shifted nervously to make sure she still could. 'We need to talk about what sort of marriage it will be.'

'The usual, I imagine.'

'And what exactly does that mean?' Irritation and helplessness spiked her voice. 'There is nothing usual about this marriage, Zahir. From the fact that I have been swapped from one brother to another, to your disclosure just now that we won't be sharing the same rooms. None of it fits the term *usual*.'

Zahir gave that infuriating shrug, as if none of it was of any consequence to him.

'Will you expect us to have full marital relations, for example?' She blurted out the question before she had time to phrase it properly, using language that sounded far more clinical than she felt. But maybe that was a good thing.

'Of course.' His straightforward answer, delivered in that raw, commanding voice and coupled with the burn of amber in those hooded eyes, had the peculiar effect of melting something inside of Anna, fusing her internal organs until she was aware of nothing but a deep pulse somewhere low down in her abdomen. It was a feeling so extraordinary, so remarkable, that she found she wanted to hold on to it, capture it, before it slipped away for ever.

Zahir intended that they should have sex. That in itself was hardly surprising, considering that they were going to be man and wife. Why had it sent her body into a clenching spasm?

'Nabatean is a young country. It is our duty to procreate, to provide a workforce for the future, to build upon the foundations we have established.' Ah, yes: *duty*. They were back to that again. 'But I don't intend to make constant demands on you.' He paused, thick lashes lowering to partly obscure his eyes. 'If that is what you're worrying about.'

Did she look worried? Anna had no idea what expression her face was pulling—she was too busy trying to control her body. And the thought of him making constant demands on her was only intensifying the peculiar feeling inside her. She needed to get a grip, and fast.

'In that case…there is something that you need to know. Before we get married, I mean.'

'Go on.'

Suddenly her whole body was painfully alive to him, every pore of her skin prickling with agonising awareness. The hairs on her arms, on the back of her neck, stood on end with craving, desire and the tortured anxiety of what she had to tell him.

'I'm not sure.' She reached for the security of a tendril of hair, twisting it round and round her finger. 'But it's quite possible that I am not able to…'

'Not able to what?'

'Not able to actually have sexual intercourse.'

CHAPTER SIX

ZAHIR'S DARK BROWS LOWERED, narrowing his hooded gaze until it was little more than twin slits of glinting stone. He twisted slightly so that his knee now touched hers, moving one arm behind them and placing it palm down on the cushions so that it anchored him in place. Anna could sense it, like a rod of muscled strength, inert yet still exuding power. Even seated he was so much taller than her, so much bigger, that she felt dwarfed by him, shaded, as if weakened by his strength.

'I don't understand.' He stared at her full in the face, with no trace of embarrassment or sensitivity for her predicament. She had presented him with a problem, that much was clear from the brooding intensity of his gaze, but it was a determination to get to the facts that had set his face in stone. 'What do you mean, you can't have sexual intercourse? Do you have some sort of physical abnormality?'

'No!' Anna pulled at the neckline of her dress, hoping it would dislodge the lump in her throat as well as cool herself down. The temperature in the small room seemed to have ramped up enormously. 'At least, it wouldn't appear so.'

'Have you been examined by a physician?'

'Yes, I have, actually.'

'And what were the findings?'

'They could find no physical reason for the...problem.'

'So what, then? What are you trying to tell me?'

'I'm trying to tell you that, when it actually comes to... you know...I can't actually...I fear I'm not able to accommodate a man.' Anna finished the sentence all in a rush, lowering her eyes against the shame that was sweeping over her that she should have to confess such a thing to the most virile, the most sexually charged, man she had ever met. A man who was now no doubt about to break off their short engagement.

There was a brief silence punctuated by Zahir's shallow breathing.

'Can I ask what has led you to this conclusion?'

Oh, God. Anna just wanted to make this hell go away. To make Zahir and the problem and the whole miserable issue of having sex at all just disappear. Why couldn't she just forget men, and getting married, and go and live in spinster isolation with nothing but a couple of undemanding cats for company? But beside her Zahir was waiting, the small amount of space between them shimmering with his impatient quest for information. There was nothing for it. She was going to have to tell him.

'Prince Henrik and I...' She paused, cringing inside. 'We never consummated our betrothal. You might as well know, that was why he broke off our engagement.'

'I wasn't aware that that was a prerequisite of a fiancée.' His eyes scoured her face. 'A wife, yes, but surely before marriage a woman is at liberty to withhold her favours?'

'That's just it, I didn't deliberately withhold them. It turned out that I was completely...unsatisfactory.'

'So let me get this straight.' *Oh, dear Lord*, still Zahir persisted with his questions. Couldn't he let it drop now?

In a minute he would be asking her to draw him a diagram. 'You wanted to have sex with your fiancé but for some reason you weren't able?'

'Yes, well, sort of.' Since he had posed the question so baldly, Anna was forced to accept that she hadn't actually wanted to have sex with Henrik at all. In fact, the thought of his pallid, sweaty hands fumbling around her most intimate areas still made her feel a bit sick. But the point was it had been expected of her. And she had failed.

'It was more Henrik's idea. He said it was important that we consummated our relationship before the wedding. "Try before you buy", I believe was his expression.'

Zahir's lip curled with distaste.

'And, as it turned out, it was just as well he did.'

This produced a low growl, like the rumble of a hungry lion, then a silence that Anna felt compelled to fill.

'I just thought you ought to know. Before we marry, I mean. In case it might prove to be a problem for us.'

'And do you think it will, Annalina?' Leaning forward, Zahir stretched out a hand to tuck a stray lock of hair behind her ear, his touch surprisingly gentle. Then, holding her chin between his finger and thumb, he tilted her face so that she had no alternative but to gaze into those bitter-chocolate eyes. 'Do you think it will be a problem for us?'

With her whole body going into paralysis, including the beat of her heart and pump of her lungs, it was quite possible that staying alive might prove to be a problem. She stared at the sweep of his jawline—the one facial feature that probably defined him more than any other. As if hewn from granite, it was as uncompromising and as harshly beautiful as him. There was an indentation in the squared-off chin, she noted—not a dimple. A man like

Zahir Zahani would never be in possession of a dimple. A strong dusting of stubble shaded its planes.

On the bridge in Paris, when she had so recklessly decided to kiss him, she had been dimly aware that his skin had felt smooth, freshly shaved. But how would it would feel tonight, now, with that tempting shadow of dark beard? Suddenly she longed to find out, to feel it rasp against her cheek like the lick of a cat's tongue. He was so very close…so very difficult to resist.

'I don't know.' Finally finding her voice, Anna blinked against the erotic temptation. That was the truth: she didn't. Right now she didn't know anything at all. Except that she wanted Zahir to kiss her more than anything, more than she cared about her next breath. She found herself unconsciously squirming on the makeshift sofa, the rough weave of the tribal rugs scratching the exposed bare skin of her thigh as her dress rode up.

What was she doing? This had not been her plan at all. When she had summoned up her courage, faced Zahir with her guilty, frankly embarrassing, secret, it had been with the intention of letting him know what he was taking on here. That his fiancée was frigid. Anna still felt the pain of the word, hurled at her by Henrik as he had levered his body off her, before pulling on his clothes and storming off into the night. *Frigid.*

His accusation had torn into her, flaying her skin, leaving her staring up at the ceiling in horrified confusion. Not to be able to perform the most basic, natural function of a woman was devastating. She was inadequate, useless. Not a proper woman at all, in fact. The doctor's diagnosis hadn't helped. Being told there was nothing physically wrong with her, that there was no quick fix—no medical fix at all, in fact—had only added to her lack of self-worth. Neither had time softened the blow, her deficiency seeping into her pride and her confidence, leaving her feeling empty, like a hollow shell.

So what on earth was she doing now? Why was she writhing about like some sort of temptress, trying to get Zahir's attention, setting herself up for what was bound to be a painful and embarrassing fall? Because she wanted him, that was why. She wanted his lips against hers, touching, tasting, crushing her mouth, sucking the breath out of her until she was gasping for air. She wanted him to make her feel. The way no one ever had before. The way she now knew with a dizzying certainty that he could.

Zahir stared into Annalina's flushed face that he still held tilted up towards him. At the eyes that were heavy with a drugging sense of what appeared to be arousal. And once again he found himself wondering what the hell was going on in her head. If she had been flirting with him earlier on, this felt more like full-on seduction. And this after she had just told him she was incapable of sexual intercourse. It didn't make any sense. But neither did the drag of lust that was weighing down his bones, making it impossible to move away from her, or the prickle of heat that had swept through his body, like he'd been plugged into the national grid. He could feel it now, right down to his finger tips that were tingling against the soft skin of her chin.

And there was something else bothering him too. It had been building ever since Annalina had started to talk about this ex-fiancé of hers, Prince Henrik, or whatever his wretched name was. Just the thought of him touching Annalina, *his* Annalina, had sent his blood pressure rocketing. By the time she'd got to the bit about them not being able to consummate their relationship, he had been ready to tear the man limb from limb, happy to chuck the remains of his mutilated body to the vultures without a backward glance. And this aggression for a man he had never met—nor ever would, if he wanted to avoid a life sentence for homicide. He could still feel the hatred seething inside him now: that such a man had dared to try and violate this beautiful creature, then discard her like a piece of trash. It had taken all of his self-control not to let Annalina see his revulsion.

Now Zahir spread his hand possessively under her jaw, his eyes still holding hers, neither of them able to break contact.

'There's one sure way to find out.' He heard his words through the roar of blood in his ears, the throb of it pulsing in his veins. Not that he was in any doubt. He knew he could take this beautiful princess and erase the memory of that spineless creep of a creature, take her to his bed and show her what a real man could do. Just the thought of it made his hands tremble and he pressed the pads of his thumbs against her skin to steady them, rhythmically stroking up and down. He watched her eyelashes flutter against his touch and the roar inside him grew louder.

He might not be able to read Anna's mind, but he could read her body, and that was all the encouragement he needed. The angle of her head, the slight arching of her back that pushed her breasts towards him, the soft rasp of her breath, all told him that she was his for the taking. That she wanted him every bit as much as he wanted her. Well, so be it. But this time the kiss would be on *his* terms.

He lowered his head until their mouths were only a fraction apart. *Now*, a voice inside his head commanded. And Zahir obeyed. Planting his lips firmly on Annalina's upturned pout, he felt its warm softness pucker beneath him and the resulting kick of lust in his gut momentarily halted him right there. He inhaled deeply through his nose. This was not going to be a gentle, persuasive kiss. This was going to be hot and heavy and hardcore. This was about possession, domination, a man's need for a woman. His need for her right now.

He angled his head to be able to plunder more deeply, the soft groan as her lips parted to allow him access only fuelling the fire that was raging through him. His tongue delved into the sensual cavern of her mouth, seeking her own with a brutal feverishness that saw it twist around its target, touching, tasting, taking total control, until Anna reciprocated, the lick of her tongue against his taking him to new fervid heights. Releasing her chin, Zahir moved his fingers to the back of her head, pushing them forcefully up through her hair, feeling the combs and grips that held the tresses in their swept-up style dislodge satisfyingly beneath his touch until the thick locks of blonde hair fell free, tumbling down through his fingers and over her shoulders.

Grabbing a handful of this glorious, silken wonder, Zahir used it to anchor her in place, to hold her exactly where he wanted her, so that he could increase the pressure on her mouth still further, increase the intensity of the kiss, heighten the pleasure that was riotously coursing through him. And, when Anna snaked her hands behind his neck, pressing herself against him, her breasts so soft, so feminine against the muscled wall of his chest, it was all he could do to stop himself from taking her right there and then. No questions asked, no thoughts, no deliberation, no cross-examination. Nothing but a blind desire to possess her in the most carnal way possible. To make her his.

Which would be totally wrong. Releasing her lips, Zahir pulled back, the breath heaving in his chest, the tightening in his groin almost unbearably painful. A kiss was one thing, but to take her virginity—for surely that was what they were talking about here?—was quite another. This wasn't the time or the place. And to do it merely to prove himself more of a man than Henrik would be morally reprehensible. Somehow, from somewhere, he was going to have to find some control.

The look of dazed desire in Annalina's eyes was almost enough to make him claim her again, blow his newfound resolve to smithereens. But within a split second her expression had changed and now he saw a wariness, a fear almost, and that was enough to bring him forcibly to his senses. Realising that he was still clutching a handful of her hair, he let it drop and pushed himself away until he found himself on his feet, staring down at her from a position of towering authority that he felt far more comfortable with.

'I apologise.' His voice sounded raw, unfamiliar, as alien to him as the wild sensations that were coursing through the rest of his body. Sensations that he realised would be all too evident if Annalina raised her eyes to his groin. He shifted his position, adjusting the fit of his trousers.

But Annalina wasn't looking at him. She was busy with her hair, combing her fingers through the blonde tresses, arranging it so that it fell over her shoulders. Then she leant forward to retrieve the clips that had fallen to the floor.

'What is there to be sorry for?' Now her eyes met his, cold, controlled, defiant. 'We are engaged, after all.' She held the largest clip in her hand, a hinged, tortoiseshell affair which now squeaked as she opened and closed its teeth, as if it was ready to take a bite out of him. 'You are perfectly at liberty to kiss me. To do whatever you like with me, in fact. At least, that's been the impression you have given me so far.'

There was rebellion in her voice now, matched by the arched posture, the arrogant, feline grace. But her lips, Zahir noticed, were still swollen from the force of their kiss, the delicate skin of her jaw flushed pink where his stubbled chin had scraped against her. And for some reason this gave him a twisted sense of achievement—as if he had marked his territory, claimed her. Especially as, now, everything about Annalina was trying to deny it.

'Perhaps you would do well to remember that this is all your doing, Annalina. You have brought about this situation and you only have yourself to blame. I am merely trying to find a workable solution.'

A solution that should not involve ripping the clothes off her the moment they were alone.

'I know, I know.' Rising to her feet, Annalina planted herself squarely in front of him, sticking out her bottom lip like a sulky teenager. Barefoot, she seemed ridiculously tiny, delicate, her temper making her brittle, as if she would snap in two were he to reach forward and grasp her with his warrior's hands.

'And, whilst we're on the subject of workable solutions, perhaps you would like to tell me how long I am expected to stay in Nabatean. I have duties in my own country, you know, matters that require my attention.'

'I'm sure.' Zahir gritted his jaw against the desire to close the small gap between them and punish her impertinence with another bruising kiss. 'In that case, no doubt you will be relieved to know that you'll be returning to Dorrada the day after tomorrow.'

'Oh, right.' Annalina shifted her weight lightly from one foot to the other, placing her hand provocatively on her hip. 'Well, that's good.'

'I have a number of meetings scheduled for tomorrow but have cleared my diary for the following couple of days.'

He watched, not without some satisfaction, as her frown of incomprehension turned to a scowl of realisation. Her toes, he noticed, were curling against the bare boards.

'You mean…?'

'Yes, Annalina. I will be accompanying you. I very much look forward to visiting your country.'

CHAPTER SEVEN

OPENING THE SHUTTERS, Anna shielded her eyes against the glare of the sun. Not the sun glinting off the towering glass edifices of Medira this time, or shimmering above the distant desert, but bouncing off the freshly fallen snow that blanketed the ground, weighing down the fir trees and covering the roofs of the town of Valduz that nestled in the valley in the distance.

She was back at Valduz Castle, the only home she had ever known. Perched on a craggy outcrop at the foothills of the Pyrenees mountain range, the castle was like something out of a fairy tale, or a Dracula movie, depending on your point of view. Built in the fourteenth century, it was all stone walls, turrets and battlements, fully prepared for any marauding invaders. It was not, however, prepared for the twenty-first century. Cold, damp and in desperate need of repair, its occupants—including Anna, her father and the bare minimum of staff—only inhabited a very small portion of it, living in a kind of squalid grandeur: priceless antique furniture had been pushed aside to make room for buckets to catch the drips, steel joists propping up ceilings decorated with stunning fifteenth-century frescoes.

But all this was about to change. Turning around, Anna surveyed her childhood bedroom in all its forlorn glory. Once she married Zahir, money would no longer be a problem for this impoverished nation. Valduz Castle would be restored, and limitless funds would be pumped into the Dorradian economy to improve its infrastructure, houses, hospitals and schools. Dorrada's problems would soon be over. *And hers would be just beginning.*

But she could feel no sense of achievement for her part in turning around Dorrada's fortunes. Instead there was just a hollow dread where maybe pride should have sat—a deep sense of unease that she had sold her soul to the devil. Or at least as close to a devil as she had ever come across. And that very devil was right here, under the leaking roofs of this ancient castle.

They had arrived in Dorrada the previous evening, her father greeting Zahir like an honoured guest, clearly having no concerns that his daughter was marrying the wrong brother. The two of them had retired immediately to her father's study and that had been the last Anna had seen of them. Presumably the financial talks had been the top priority and had gone on long into the night. Anna was obviously of significantly less importance to either of them. Zahir, professional but detached, appeared to be treating this like just another business trip, all traces of the man who had been on the brink of ravishing her banished behind that formidable, impenetrable facade.

Anna closed her eyes against the memory of that kiss—hot, wild, and so forceful it had felt as if he was branding her with his lips, claiming her in the most carnal way. It still did. The memory refused to leave her, still curling her toes, clenching her stomach and heating her very core.

And Zahir had felt it too, no matter how much his subsequent demeanour might be trying to deny it. His arousal had been all too evident—electrifying, empowering. Trapped in his embrace, she had felt alive, confident, sexy. And ready. More than ready, in fact. Desperate for Zahir to take things further, to throw her to the floor and make love to her there and then, any way he wanted. To possess her, make her feel whole, complete, a real woman.

But what had happened? Nothing, that was what. Having taken her to the point of no return, he had stopped, leaving her a quivering, gasping, flushed-faced mess, unable to do anything other than stare up at him as he bit out between gritted teeth that he was sorry. *Sorry?* Anna didn't want sorry. It had taken every ounce of effort to come back from that, to hide the crushing disappointment and act as if she didn't give a damn.

But today was a new day. She was on her own home turf, the sun was shining and the stunning scenery outside was calling her. Pulling on jeans and a thick rollneck sweater, she released the curtain of hair trapped down her back and quickly fashioned two loose plaits. Grabbing a woolly hat, she was good to go.

The virgin snow crunched beneath her boots as she trudged around the wall of the castle, the white puff of her breath going before her. She didn't know exactly where she was headed, except that she wanted to enjoy this moment alone, commit it to memory. She loved mornings like this, bright and still, unchanged down the centuries. But how many more would she experience? No doubt once she was married she would be expected to spend all her time in Nabatean, to swap the sparkling cold of the mountains for the sweltering heat of the desert, the stark loneliness of her life here for the scary unknown that was her future with Zahir.

It was time to leave the child behind—Anna knew that. Time to grow up and do something meaningful with her life. And being born a princess meant making an advantageous marriage. She should have accepted the idea by now. After all, she'd had twenty-five years to get used to it. But even so, now it was actually happening, the thought of leaving everything she knew and marching off into the desert sun with this dark and mysterious stranger was completely terrifying.

The lingering child in her made her bend down and scoop up a large handful of snow, compacting it into a hard ball and then smoothing it between her icy hands. Her eyes scanned the scene for a target. A robin eyed her nervously before swooping off to the branches of a nearby tree. An urn at the top of the crenulated wall that wound its way down the stone steps had no such escape, though, and, taking aim, Anna held the icy missile aloft and prepared to fire.

'You'll never get any power behind it like that.' A strong, startlingly warm hand gripped her wrist, bringing her arm down by her side. 'Throwing is all about the velocity. You need to stand with your feet apart and then turn at the waist, like this.' The hands now spanned her midriff, twisting her body in readiness for the perfect aim. Anna tensed, staring at the snowball in her hand, frankly surprised to see it still there. The heat coursing through her body felt powerful enough to melt an iceberg. 'Now bring back your arm, like this...' he bent her elbow, holding her arm behind her '...and you are ready to go. Don't forget to follow through.'

The snowball arced above them before disappearing with a soft thud into a deep snowdrift.

'Hmm...' Turning to face her, Zahir quirked a thick brow. 'I can see more practice is needed.'

Anna stared back at him, drinking in the sight. He looked very foreign, exotic, in the bright, snowy whiteness of these surroundings. Wearing a long charcoal cashmere coat, the collar turned up, his skin appeared darker somehow, his close-cropped hair blacker, his broad body too warm—too hot, even—for these sub-zero temperatures. It was almost as if he could defy nature by appearing so unaffected by the cold. That you could remove the man from the desert, but not the desert from the man. Anna adjusted her hat, regretting her choice of headgear as she felt the silly bobble on top do a wobble. 'It's too late for me, I fear. After all, I won't be here for much longer.'

'Will you miss your country?' The question came out of nowhere with its usual directness. But his eyes showed his seriousness as he waited for her answer.

'Yes, of course.' Anna bit down on her lip, determined that the bobble on her hat was the only thing that was going to wobble. She would be strong now. Show Zahir that she was a capable, independent woman. That she would be an asset to him, not a burden. 'But I am looking forward to the challenges of a new life, with you. I am one hundred percent committed to making this union work, for the sake of both of our countries.'

'That's good to hear.' Still his gaze raked across her like a heat-seeking missile. 'And what about on a more personal level, Annalina? You and me. Are you one hundred percent committed to making that union work too?'

'Yes, of course.' Anna fought against the heat of his stare. What was he trying to do to her? She was struggling to put on a convincing performance here. She didn't need him messing with the script. 'I will try to be a good wife to you, to fulfil my duty to the best of my abilities.'

'*Duty*, Annalina. Is that what this is all about?'

'Well, yes. As it is with you.' Dark eyebrows raised and then fell again, taking Anna's stomach with them. 'But that doesn't mean we can't be happy.'

'Then you might want to tell your face.' Raising a hand, he cupped her jaw, his hand so large that it covered her chin and lower cheeks, seductively grazing her bottom lip. Anna trembled, his touch halting her cold breath painfully in her throat. 'What is it that you fear, Annalina? Is it the thought of tying yourself to a man such as myself? A man ignorant of the manners of Western culture, more at home in a desert sandstorm, or riding bareback on an Arab stallion, than making polite conversation in a grand salon or waltzing you around a palace ballroom?'

'No…it's not that.'

'I am not the cultured European prince you were hoping for?' Suddenly bitterness crept into his voice.

'No, it's not that, Zahir. Really.'

'What, then? I need to know.' The searing intensity in his eyes left her in no doubt about that. 'Do you fear that I am such a difficult man to please?' His voice dropped.

Yes. 'Impossible' might be a better word. Anna stared back at him, tracing the map of his face with her eyes: the grooves between eyebrows that were so used to being pulled into a scowl, the lines scored across a forehead that frowned all too easily. Had she ever even seen him smile? She wasn't sure. How did she have any hope of pleasing such a man?

'I fear I may need time to learn the ways to make you happy.' She chose her words carefully, trying to avoid snagging herself on the barbed wire all around her. Trying to conceal the inbuilt dread that she might not be able to satisfy him. Her abortive night of shame with Henrik still haunted her, plagued her with worry and self-doubt. And the way Zahir had dismissed it had done nothing to allay her fears either, merely demonstrated that he no idea of the scale of the problem. That he didn't understand.

'All being well, time is something we have plenty of, my princess.' The very masculine gleam in his eye only made Anna feel a hundred times worse. 'A lifetime together, in fact.'

'Yes, indeed. A lifetime…' Her voice tailed off.

'And learning to please one another need not be such an arduous task.' His thumb stroked over her lower lip.

'No, of course not.' Anna's heart took up a thumping beat. His gentle touch, the depth of his dark stare, spelled out exactly the sort of pleasure he was talking about: intimate, sexual pleasure. It shone in his eyes and it clenched deep down in Anna's belly.

She had spent so long worrying about how to satisfy Zahir that it hadn't even occurred to her that sex was a reciprocal thing. That he might be thinking of ways to pleasure her. Now hot bolts of desire ricocheted through her at the thought of it. Of Zahir's large rough-skinned hands travelling over her naked body, moving between her thighs, pushing them apart, spanning the mound of her sex before exploring within. A shiver of longing rippled through her and she had to squeeze her muscles tight to halt its progress.

'I must go.' Releasing her chin, Zahir let his thumb rest against her lip for a second, gently dragging it down. Then he took a step away. 'Your father has meetings arranged for me all morning. However, I have set aside this afternoon for us to spend some time together.'

'You have?' Anna couldn't keep the surprise from her voice, nor cover up the leap of excitement that coloured her cheeks.

'After your little lecture about the role of a host, I assume you will be willing to show me around Dorrada?'

'Yes, of course.'

'Time is limited—I leave for Nabatean first thing

tomorrow—but I should like to take in some of the sights before I go.'

'You're going back to Nabatean tomorrow?' This was news to her.

'Correct.'

'Alone?'

'I take it that won't be a problem?'

'Not for me, I can assure you.' Anna fiddled with one of her plaits. 'So does this mean you finally trust me or am I to be surrounded by your minders?'

'No minders.' Zahir narrowed his eyes as he contemplated her question. 'But trust is not something I find easy to give. Once you have suffered the sort of betrayal I have, it is hard to ever completely trust anyone again.'

'I'm sure.' Anna lowered her eyes. At first she had thought he was talking about her, what she had done on the bridge in Paris. But the pain in his eyes ran deeper than that, far deeper. She wanted to ask more but Zahir was already pulling down the shutters, aware that he had said too much.

'However, I'm prepared to give you the freedom to prove yourself.' He levelled dark eyes at her. 'Just make sure you don't let me down.'

'I suppose we should be getting back to the castle.' Night was starting to close in, the first stars appearing in the sky, and reluctantly Anna felt in her pocket for the car keys. Their whistle-stop tour of Dorrada was nearly over, something that disappointed Anna more than she would ever have imagined.

Zahir hadn't bothered to hide his surprise when she had pulled up in front of the castle in the battered old four-by-four vehicle and gestured to him to get in beside her. Warily easing himself into the passenger seat, he had shot her one of his now familiar hooded stares, leaving her in no doubt that this was a situation he did *not* feel comfortable with—whether that was being driven by a woman, or her in particular, she didn't know. And didn't care. She was a good driver, she knew the roads around here like the back of her hand, and the challenging conditions of this wintry climate posed no problems for her. And even if he'd looked as though he was coming perilously close to grabbing the wheel off her a couple of times—especially on some of the spectacular hairpin bends that snaked up through the mountains—he had just about managed to restrain himself, travelling every inch of the road with his eyes instead.

Deciding where to take her guest had been difficult. Dorrada was only a small country but the scenery was spectacular and there were so many places Anna would have liked to show him. But time was short so she had limited herself to a trip up into the mountains, with several stops to admire the views, including the place where an ancient cable car still vertiginously cranked tourists down to the valley below. Then she had given him a rapid tour of the town of Valduz, unable to stop because she'd known they would attract too much attention. People turned to stare at them as they passed anyway, rapidly pulling out their phones to take a photo, or just waving excitedly as their princess and her exotic fiancé drove by.

The last stop on Anna's tour had brought them to this mountain lakeside, one of her favourite places. Originally she hadn't intended to bring Zahir here but somehow it had happened and now she was glad of that. Because as they had crunched their way along the shoreline, stopped to take in the stunning sunset rippling across the crystal-clear water, she knew that Zahir was feeling the beauty

of the place every bit as much as her. Not that he said so.
Zahir was a man of few words, using communication as
a mere necessity to have his wishes understood or his orders obeyed. But there had been a stillness as he'd gazed
across the water to the snow-capped mountains beyond,
an alertness in the way he'd held his body, that had told
Anna how much he was feeling the magic of this place.
They hadn't needed any words.

'There's no rush, is there?' Zahir turned to look at
her, his face all sharp-angled lines and shadows in the
dim light.

'Well, no, but it's getting dark. There's not much point
in me taking you sightseeing if you can't see the sights.'

'I like the dark.' Zahir laid the statement baldly before
her, as if it was all that was needed to be said. Anna didn't
doubt it. She already thought of him a man of the night, a
shadowed, stealthy predator that would stalk his prey—
would curl his hands around the throat of an enemy before they even knew of his existence. 'Is that some sort
of cabin over there between those trees?'

Anna followed his finger, which was pointing to the
other side of the lake. 'Yes, it's an old hunter's cabin.'

'Shall we take a look?'

Anna hesitated. She didn't need to take a look, she
was all too familiar with the modest cabin. She should
be. She'd been escaping here for years, to her own little bolthole, whenever the bleak reality of her life in the
castle got too much for her.

It was to here that she had fled all those years ago, on
being told that her mother had died. That she would never
see her again. Here, too, much more recently, she'd sat
staring at the rustic walls, trying to come to terms with
the fact that a marriage had been arranged for her. That
she was to be shipped off to a place called Nabatean to

marry the newly crowned king. And look how that had turned out.

The cabin was her secret place. Taking Zahir there would feel strange. But somehow exciting too.

'Sure, if you like.' Affecting a casual tone, she started walking. 'D'you want to follow me?'

They set off, Anna leading the way around the lake and into the fringes of the forest of pine trees. It was too dark to see much but she knew the way by heart. Zahir was right behind her every step, so close that they moved as almost one being, their feet crunching on snow that had crystallised to ice. She could sense the heat from his body, feel the power of it all around her. It made her feel both safe and jumpy at the same time, butterflies leaping about in her tummy.

Finally they came to a small clearing and there was the log cabin before them, looking like a life-size gingerbread house. The door was wedged shut by a drift of snow but with a few swift kicks Zahir had cleared it and soon they were both standing inside.

'There should be some matches here somewhere.' Running her hands over the table next to her, Anna opened the drawer, relieved to feel the box beneath her fingertips. 'I'll just light the paraffin lamp.'

'Here, let me.' Taking the matches from her Zahir reached up and, removing the glass funnel from the lamp, touched a flame to the wick. 'Hmm...' With a grunt of approval, he looked around him in the flickering light. 'Basic but perfectly functional. You say it was a hunter's cabin?'

'Yes, hence the trophies.' Anna pointed to the mounted deer heads that gazed down on them with glassy-eyed stares. 'But it hasn't been used for years. Valduz Castle used to host hunting parties in the past, but, thankfully for the local wildlife, those days have gone.'

'But you come here?'

'Well, yes, now and again.' Was it that obvious? His directness immediately put her on the defensive. 'I used to like it here as a kid. Other children had play houses and I had my own log cabin!' She attempted a light-hearted laugh but as the light played over Zahir's harsh features they showed no softening. He merely waited for her to elaborate. 'And now I sometimes come here when I want to think, you know? Get away from it all.'

'I understand.' The deep rumble of his voice, coupled with the hint of compassion in his dark eyes threatened to unravel something deep inside her.

'Shall we light a fire?' Hideously chirpy—she'd be asking him if he wanted to play mummies and daddies in a minute—Anna moved over to the open hearth. 'There should be plenty of logs.'

Immediately Zahir took charge, deftly getting the fire going with the efficiency of a man well used to such a task. Anna watched as he sat forward on his haunches, blowing onto the scraps of bark until the smoke turned to flames and the flames took hold. There was something primal about his movements. Hypnotic. Mission accomplished, he sat back on his heels.

'I think there's some brandy here somewhere if you'd like some?' Needing to break the spell, Anna moved over to a cupboard and pulled out a dusty bottle and a couple of tumblers.

'I never drink alcohol.'

'Oh.' Now she thought about it, she realised she had never seen him drink. 'Is that because of your religion or for some other reason?' She poured a modest amount into one glass.

'I don't believe in deliberately altering the state of my mind with toxic substances.'

Right. Anna glanced at the drink in her hand, sheer contrariness making her add another good measure before turning back to look around her. There was only one chair in the cabin, a rickety old wooden rocker, but the bare floor was scattered with animal skins and she moved to seat herself beside Zahir in front of the fire.

Zahir cast her a sideways glance, as if unsure how to deal with this situation, before finally settling his large frame beside her, sitting cross-legged and staring into the flames. For a moment there was silence, just the crackling of the logs. Anna took a gulp of brandy, screwing up her eyes against its burn.

'So.' She'd been tempted to remain quiet, to see how long it would be before Zahir instigated some sort of conversation, but she suspected that would be the wrong side of never. 'What do you think of Dorrada?'

'Its economy has been very badly handled. I fail to see how a country with such potential, such a noble history, can have got itself in such a mess.'

Anna pouted. If she'd been expecting a comment on the beauty of the scenery or the quality of the air, she should have known better. 'Well, we don't all have the benefit of gallons of crude oil gushing out of the ground. I'm sure it's easy to be a wealthy country when you have that as a natural resource.'

Spinning round, his jaw held rigid, Zahir's looked ready to take a bite out of her. 'If you think there has been anything remotely *easy* about reforming a nation like Nabatean then I would urge you to hastily reconsider. Nabatean has not been built on oil but on the spilt blood of its young men. Not on the value of its exports of but on the courage and strength of its people. You would do well to remember that.'

'I'm sorry.' Suitably chastened, Anna took another sip

of brandy. Perhaps that had been a stupid thing to say. He had turned back towards the fire now, his whole body radiating his disapproval. 'I didn't mean any disrespect. I still know so little of the ways of your country.'

'You will have ample opportunity to learn our ways, our language and our ethos once you are living there. And may I remind you that Nabatean will shortly be *your* country too?'

'Yes, I know that.' Anna swallowed. 'And I will do my best to embrace the culture and learn all I can. But it would help me if you told me more about it now.'

Zahir shrugged broad shoulders.

'You say the war that brought about the independence of Nabatean cost many lives?'

'Indeed.' He shifted his weight beside her.

'And you yourself were in the army, fighting alongside your fellow countrymen?'

'Yes. As the second son, I always knew that the army would be my calling. It was an honour to serve my country.'

'But you must have seen some terrible atrocities.'

'War is one long atrocity. But sometimes it is the only answer.'

'And your parents…' Anna knew she was straying into dangerous territory here. 'I understand that they…died?'

'They were murdered, Annalina, as I am sure you well know. Their throats cut as they slept.' He stared into the flames as if transfixed. 'Less than twenty-four hours after Uristan had capitulated and the end of the war declared, they were dead. I was celebrating our victory with the people of Nabatean when a rebel insurgent took advantage of the lapse in security and crept into my parents' bedchamber to slaughter them as a final act of barbarity.'

'Oh, Zahir.' Anna's hands fluttered to her throat. 'How terrible. I'm so sorry.'

'It is I who should be sorry. It was my job to protect them and I failed. I will carry that responsibility with me to my grave.'

'But you can't torture yourself with that for ever, Zahir. You can't carry all that burden on your shoulders.'

'Oh, but I can. And I will.' His jaw tightened. 'It was supposed to have been a safe house. I had only moved them out of exile a week before, along with my brother. I was convinced no one knew of their whereabouts. But I was betrayed by a guard I thought I could trust.'

'And your brother, Rashid? He obviously escaped the assassin?'

'He awoke to hear my mother screaming his name. Even with a knife at her throat, seconds from death and with her husband already slaughtered beside her, my mother managed to find enough strength to warn her son. To save him. But, had I been there, I could have saved them all. I *would* have saved them all.'

Anna didn't doubt it for one moment. There wasn't an armed assassin in the world that would stand a chance against someone like Zahir.

'Your mother sounds like an amazing woman.'

'She was.'

'And I'm sure she and your father would be very proud of what you have achieved. You and Rashid.'

'Rashid, as I am sure you are aware, has not yet fully recovered from his ordeal.' His held his profile steady, stark and uncompromising.

Anna hesitated, choosing her words with care. She had no desire to get her head bitten off again. 'And that's the reason you're governing the kingdom, rather than him?'

'My brother is happy to let me run the country as I see

fit. His role is more that of a figurehead. He is temporarily unsuited to the rigours of leadership.'

So it was just as she thought. Zahir Zahani was the power and brains behind the success of Nabatean. She sat up a little straighter. 'I hope that you will allow me to assist you?' Determined that he should see some worth in her, she almost implored him. 'I'm a hard worker and a quick learner. I'm sure I have skills that you can utilise.'

'I'm sure you have.' Zahir turned towards her, his eyelids heavy, thick, dark lashes lowered. 'And I look forward to utilising them.'

The rasp of his words sent a tremor of anticipation through her. With the flames licking the shadows of his face, shining blue-black on his hair and gleaming in his eyes, she felt her heart pound, her body melt with the power of his raw sexual energy. There had been no mistaking the meaning behind his words. It pulsed from him, throbbed in the air between them, weakening her limbs with its promise.

Impulse made her reach for his cheek and gently run the back of her hand against it, feel the scratch of his stubble, the burn of the heat from the fire. Immediately he grasped her wrist, twisting her hand so that her fingers brushed his mouth and then, taking her index finger between his lips, holding it between his teeth, clenching down so that it was trapped, warm and damp from his breath, his bite hard but controlled. It was an action so unexpected, so intimate, and so deeply sexy that for a moment Anna could do nothing but stare at him, her whole body going into heart-stopping free fall.

She wanted more. She knew that with a certainty that thundered in her head, roared the blood in her ears and pulsed down low in her abdomen. She wanted him the way she had never wanted any other man in her life. She had no idea what would happen when it came to it, to the point where she had failed so pitifully before, but she knew she wanted to try. Right now.

CHAPTER EIGHT

THEIR GAZES CLASHED and Anna watched, spellbound, as the firelight danced across the surface of Zahir's black eyes. Slowly, seductively, his tongue licked the tip of her finger, sending a wave of pure lust crashing over her. She waited, desperate for him to suck it into his mouth, and when he released his teeth and did just that she closed her eyes and moaned with pleasure, revelling in the rasp of his tongue, the powerful suck of his mouth, the graze of his teeth against her knuckles.

She craved more, the thought of the suck of that mouth against other parts of her body…against her nipples, her inner thighs, her most intimate place…building inside her like a fleeting promise that she had to grab on to before it was taken away from her, before it vanished into thin air. Opening her eyes, she saw him staring at her, solemn and unsmiling, but exuding enough sexual chemistry to decimate an entire country.

'You leave tomorrow, Zahir.' Leaning towards him, she placed her hands on his shoulders, running them over the rough wool of the thick army jumper he was wearing. She loved the feel of him, the strength of the muscles, the way the thick column of his corded neck carried the pulse of his veins. 'I won't see you again before the wedding.'

'No.' His voice rumbled, deep and low, between them.

'If you wanted to make love to me...' she hesitated, trying very hard to control herself '...beforehand—now, even, I mean—I wouldn't object.'

'Of course you wouldn't.

Anna gasped at his chauvinistic attitude. But challenging it was going to be difficult when her body was still leaning in to him, inviting him, betraying her in the most obvious way.

'Are you so sure of yourself that you think you can have any woman of your choosing?'

'We are not talking about any woman. We are talking about my fiancée. You.' He lowered his mouth, his breath fanning across her face.

Anna swallowed. 'And that makes your conceit acceptable, does it?'

'Acceptable, inevitable, call it whatever you like.' His hand strayed to her neck, pushing aside the curtain of hair. 'And as for having no say in the matter...' Now his mouth was on her skin, the drag of his lips following the graceful sweep of her neck down to the hollow between her collarbone, muffling his words. 'You and I both know that you're desperate for me to make love to you.'

'That is very...' With her head thrown back to allow him more access to her throat, to make sure he had no excuse to stop lavishing this glorious attention on her neck, words were surprisingly hard to formulate. 'Ungallant.'

This produced a harsh laugh. 'I have never claimed to be gallant. Nor would you expect me to be. And, right now, I suspect gallantry is the last thing on your mind.' He raised his head his eyes drilling into her soul. 'Tell me, Annalina, which would you rather—a polite request to allow me access to your breasts, or an order that you remove your jumper?'

Anna gasped, the thrill of his audacious demand immediately shrivelling her nipples, producing a heavy ache in her breasts that rapidly spread throughout her body. It was outrageous, preposterous, that he should order her to strip.

'I thought as much.' Her second of silence was met with a growl of approval. 'Do it now, Annalina. Take off your jumper.'

She stared back at him, dumbfounded by the way this had suddenly turned around. How her tentative attempt to initiate lovemaking had resulted in an order to obey.

But still her fingers strayed to the bottom of her woollen jumper and she found herself pulling it up over her head, taking the tee-shirt underneath with it, until she was stripped down to her bra, her naked skin gleaming in the firelight.

'Very good.' Zahir's eyes travelled over her, his eyelids heavy, dark lashes flickering. Anna heard him swallow. 'Now, stay still.'

Raising both hands, he held them in front of her, their span so large, their skin so dark, as they hovered over the lacy white material of her bra. They were shaking, Anna realised. She was making the hands of this warrior man shake. Slowly they closed over her breasts, the heat of them searing into her, roaring through every part of her, right down to her fingertips that prickled by her side. And when his fingers traced where the swell of one of her breasts met the lacy fabric, dipping into the hollow of her cleavage before moving to explore the other, she thought she would combust with the agony and the ecstasy of it.

'Remove your bra.'

Reaching behind her, Anna did as she was told, any pretence of denying him or regaining control vanishing on the tidal wave of lust. As the bra fell to the floor, she

kept her eyes fixed on Zahir's face, determined that she
should see, as well as feel, his every reaction. He let out
a guttural growl that arched her back, pushing her breasts
towards him, inviting him to take her.

And take her he did. Cupping her naked breasts, one
in each hand, he touched her hardened nipples with the
pads of his thumbs, starting a rhythmic circular movement that had her writhing in front of him. Then, lowering his head, he took one nipple in his mouth, his breath
scorching against her as he slathered her with hot, wet
saliva before moving to the puckered peak, teasing his
tongue against it with a slow, drugging forcefulness.

Anna groaned, her body on fire, dampness pooling
between her legs, her skinny jeans suddenly unbearably
tight, horribly uncomfortable. She wanted to take them
off—bizarrely she wanted Zahir to tell her to take them
off. But first she needed him to attend to her other breast
before she died of longing.

A ragged sigh escaped her when he did just that, his
attention to her second breast no more hurried, no less
glorious. Anna plunged her fingers into his hair, pulling
him closer to increase the pressure, to hold herself steady.
She stared down, her eyes glazed, trance-like, as she
watched his head rock against her, his mouth still working its incredible magic. And when he stopped, pulling
away, ordering her to remove her jeans, she had no hesi-
tation, falling over herself to stand up, undo the buttons
and tug them down, cursing as they clung to her ankles
and standing, first on one wobbly leg and then the other,
as she pulled them inside out to get them off, ending up
all but falling into Zahir's lap.

Strong arms encircled her, adjusting her position
so that he held her, straddled across him, taking a second simply to look at her, his eyes raking over her like

hot coals. She was acutely aware that she was virtually
naked, whereas he was still fully dressed in rugged out-
door clothes, but for some reason this only increased her
rabid desire. The scratch of his rough woollen jumper
against her bare skin, the graze of the zips on the pockets of his cargo pants beneath her thighs, was something
else, something so thrillingly erotic, that Anna couldn't
hold back a squeak of surprise.

Zahir's erection, the enormous, rock-hard length of it,
was like a rod of steel positioned between her buttocks,
pulsing against her from behind. She tried to turn, to lift
herself off so that she could find the zipper of his fly,
her trembling fingers longing to yank it down, to release
him so that she could see for herself, *feel* for herself, this
extraordinary phenomenon. But Zahir held her firm, his
hands around her waist gripping her so tightly that she
could only move where he positioned her, which was
squarely down on his lap again. She squirmed provocatively against him, the only small movement she could
make. But even that was not allowed, as with a low growl
Zahir lifted her up, the small space between them suddenly feeling like a yawning cavern of rejection, before
he adjusted his position and sat her back down on him.

'Do not move.' The words roared softly into her ear
from behind and Anna could only nod her acceptance as
she felt one hand release her waist and move round to her
front, where it trailed down over her clenching stomach
muscles and slipped silently under the front of her skimpy
lace knickers. The shock halted her breath, setting up a
tremble that she couldn't tell whether was from inside
her, or out, or both. She found herself desperately hoping that this didn't count as moving because she couldn't
bear to disobey him now—not if it meant he was going to
stop what he was doing. Gingerly tipping back her head,

she rested it against the ridge of his collarbone, relieved when he seemed happy with this.

'That's right.'

His fingers brushed over her until they met the damp, throbbing centre of her core. Anna waited, poised on the brink of delirium, as one finger parted her sensitive folds, then slid into her with a slow but a deliberately controlled movement that shook her whole body from top to toe.

'Open your legs.'

The voice behind her commanded and Anna obeyed, parting her thighs, amazed that she had any control over any part of herself.

'Now, stop. Stay like that.'

It was like asking a jelly to stop wobbling, but Anna did the best she could, and with her head pressed hard back against his shoulder she screwed her eyes shut. Drawing in a breath, she waited, ready to give herself over to him completely, to do with her whatever he saw fit.

It was the most glorious, astonishing, explosion of mind-altering sensations. As his finger moved inside her, it rubbed against the swollen nub of her clitoris until he was just there, in that one spot, stroking it again and again with a pressure that could never be too much and never be enough. With the agonisingly pleasurable sensation swelling and swelling inside her, it felt as if her whole world had distilled into this moment, this momentous feeling. She would trade her entire life for the concentrated pleasure of this building ecstasy.

But trying to stay still was an impossibility. Even with the weight of Zahir's arm diagonally across her body she couldn't help writhing and bucking.

With his breath hot in her ear, the rock-hard swell of him beneath her buttocks, there was no way she could stop her legs from parting further, her back from arching against him, her bottom from pressing down into him. And as he continued his glorious attentions the pressure built more and more until what had seemed just tantalisingly out of reach was suddenly there upon her, crashing over her, carrying her with it. And, as that wave subsided and Zahir continued to touch her, another one followed, just as intense, then another and another, until Anna thought the moment might never end and that she had left the real world for ever.

But finally his hand stilled and slowly, slowly the feelings started to subside, sending sharp twitches through her body as reminders of what she had just experienced. Anna opened her eyes to see him staring down at her.

She looked so beautiful. Never had Zahir witnessed such beauty, such wild abandonment. Removing his arm, he released her body, moving her off his lap so that he could stand up, rip off his clothes and devour her in the way that he had been so desperate to do for the past hour…for the past twenty-four hours…ever since he had first clapped eyes on her. He had told himself that he would wait until after they were married, that that would be the right thing to do. But now waiting was an impossibility. Now the right thing, the *only* thing, he could think of was to claim this beautiful young woman for his own. To take her now, for himself, to satisfy his immense carnal need in the only way possible. By having her beneath him and making love to her in a way that neither of them would ever, ever forget.

With his breath coming in harsh pants, his chest heaving beneath the sweater that he tugged over his head, he was down to his boxer shorts in seconds, his powerful erection straining against the black cotton fabric, swollen and painful with need. He knew Anna was watching his every move from the floor, and that only increased his fervour, fuelled the frantic craving that was coursing through him.

'Lie down.' He barked the order without knowing why he felt the need to be so domineering.

Primal lust roared in his ears as he watched Annalina do as she was told, stretching out on the animal-skin rug, her body so pale in the flickering light of the fire, so delicate, so desirable. Bending down beside her, he pulled the scrap of fabric that was her panties down and over her legs, screwing them into a ball in his hand. Then he removed his boxers with a forceful tug and straddled her body with his own, holding his weight above her with locked elbows on either side of her head. She seemed so fragile compared to him, so impossibly perfect, that for a moment he could only gaze down at her, the corded muscles in his arms rigidly holding him in place, defying the tremor that was rippling through the rest of his body.

'You want this, Annalina?' He ground out the words, suddenly needing to hear her consent before he allowed himself to take her, this most precious creature.

'Yes.' It was the smallest word, spoken in little more than a whisper, but it was enough. And when her hand snaked between them, tentatively feeling for his member, he closed his eyes against the ecstasy, lowering his elbows enough to reach her lips and seal their coupling with a searing kiss.

Lifting himself off her, he unscrewed his eyes to look down at her again. Her hand was circling his shaft and it was taking all of his control not to position himself and plunge right into her. His need was so great, unlike anything he had ever felt before, that his body was screaming at him just to do it, to take her as fast and furiously as he liked, anything to satisfy this infernal craving. But he knew he had to find some restraint. If Annalina was a virgin, which it seemed she was, he had to try to take it slowly, make sure she was ready, control the barbarian in him. Though if she carried on the way she was right now, her fingers exploring the length of him, caressing the swollen tip, his body was going to have severe trouble obeying his commands.

'Is this right?' Slowly her hand moved up and down.

Zahir let out a moan of assent. Frankly she could have done it any damned way she liked, could have done anything she wanted. He was past the point of being able to judge.

'I don't want to disappoint you.'

Disappoint him? That was not going to happen. He was sure about that. He moved one arm to cover her hand with his own, to position himself over her, to the place he so desperately needed to be able to enter her. His fingers strayed to find her, to part her in readiness, but then something made him hesitate. The catch in her voice, the slight tremor, suddenly permeated the lust-ridden fog of his mind and now he rapidly scanned her face for clues.

'What is it? You have changed your mind?' It killed him to ask but he had to be sure.

'No, it's not that.'

'What, then?' So he had been right—there was something.

'Nothing, really.' She removed her hand, bringing her arms around his back. But, as they skittered over the play of his muscles, their touch was as unconvincing as her words.

'Tell me, Annalina.'

'Well, it's just...I'm a bit nervous.' Her throat moved beneath the pale skin of her throat. 'I hadn't realised that you would be so...large.'

'And that's a problem?'

'I don't know. I suppose it could be. I mean, there was a problem with me and Henrik, and he wasn't anything like as big...'

Henrik. The mention of his name on her lips had the effect of pouring an icy waterfall over Zahir, at the same time as stirring a roaring tiger in his chest. Henrik. He knew what he'd like to do if he ever got his hands on that slimy creep of an individual. He couldn't bear to think of him touching Annalina at any time, ever. But he particularly couldn't bear to think of him now.

'But I think we should try.' Still she was talking, seemingly oblivious to the cold rage sweeping through him, her voice nervous but determined in the now suffocating air of the cabin. 'Now—before we marry, I mean—to see if we can. I'm worried because of what happened with Henrik...'

'Henrik!' Zahir roared his name, making Annalina jump beneath him. 'Do you really think I want to hear about Henrik?' He moved his body off her, leaping to his feet, cursing the damned erection that refused to die, mocking him with its disobedient show of power. 'Do you really think I want to be compared to your failed lover?'

'Well, no, but...I just meant...' Annalina sat up, covering her chest with her arms, her blue eyes staring up at him, wide, frightened and beseeching.

'I know what you meant. You meant that I'm not the man that you were meant to marry, the man you wanted to marry. You meant that having sex with me was a chore that you were prepared to endure. Or maybe not.' Another thought tore through his tortured mind. 'Maybe you thought that if we weren't able to have sex, if you could prove that, you wouldn't have to marry me at all.'

'No, Zahir, you're wrong. You've got it all wrong.'

'Because, if so, you are going to be sorely disappointed. We will marry, as planned, and we will consummate our marriage on our wedding night. And believe me, Annalina, when we do, I will drive all thoughts of Henrik from your mind. Banish all thoughts of not being able, or not being ready, or whatever other pathetic excuses you seem to be toying with. For when we do make love, when it finally happens, you'll be thinking of nothing but me. Nothing but the way *I* am making you feel. And that, Annalina, is a promise.

CHAPTER NINE

FROM INSIDE THE chapel the organ music paused and Princess Annalina's grip on her bouquet tightened. As the strains of Wagner's *Wedding March* began she felt for her father's arm, slipping her own through the crook of it. This was it, then. There was no going back now.

Not that she had any choice. Beside her King Gustav stood rigidly to attention, his gaze fixed straight ahead. If he had any misgivings about handing over his only daughter to this warrior prince, then he wasn't letting it show. As far as he was concerned this wedding was a business deal, a means to an end, and his job was to deliver his daughter to her fate. And to make sure that this time nothing went wrong.

Sitting side by side in the vintage car taking them the short journey from the castle to the chapel on the Valduz estate, Anna had thought maybe this would be the moment her father would say something encouraging, comforting she didn't really know what. Instead he had simply checked his watch a dozen times, tugged on the sleeves of his morning coat and looked distractedly out of the window at the cheering crowds that lined the route as they passed. And when her hand had reached for his he had looked at it in surprise before awkwardly patting it a couple of times and handing it back.

More than anything in the world right now, Anna wished that her mother could be here to give her a hug, to make everything better. But sadly wishes didn't come true, even for princesses, so instead she ended up blinking back the tears as she stared out of the window, forcing herself to smile and wave at the crowds brandishing their paper flags. But inside she had never felt more lost. More alone.

The chapel doors opened to reveal the stage set for the ceremony. And it was beautiful. This was the first wedding the chapel had seen since her parents' nuptials and no expense had been spared, though it didn't take a genius to work out where the money had come from. With a green-and-white theme, the ancient pews were festooned with alpine flowers, their scent mingling with the incense in the air. Huge arrangements of ivy and ferns were positioned at the top of the aisle and behind the altar at the end—somewhere that Anna couldn't look at just yet. Because that was where Zahir would be standing. Waiting. That was where, in just a few short minutes from now, the ceremony would begin that would see her signing away her life, at least the only life she had ever known. Where she would hand herself over to this man, become his wife, move to his country, to all intents and purposes become his property to do with as he saw fit.

And Anna had been left in no doubt as to what that would entail, at least as far as the bedroom was concerned. It had been four weeks since that fateful evening in the log cabin, but the brutal memory of it would stay with her for ever—the way Zahir had taken her from wild ecstasy to the pit of misery before the aftershocks of delirium had even left her body. His rage when she had mentioned Henrik had been palpable, terrifying, a dark force that had shocked her with its vehemence, leaving her no chance to try and explain why she had said it, to justify herself. Instead she had hurried to pull on her clothes and followed him out into the night, the snow falling as he had unerringly led them back to where their vehicle was parked and sat beside her in stony silence as she had driven them back to the castle.

Zahir had returned to Nabatean the next morning and they hadn't seen each other since, any contact between them limited to perfunctory emails or the occasional phone call. But his parting words still clamoured in her head. *We will consummate our marriage on our wedding night.* It had sounded more like a threat than a promise, but that didn't stop it sending a thrill of tumult through Anna whenever she recalled it. Like now, for example. Because tonight was the night that Zahir would fulfil his prophecy.

But first she had a job to do. Glancing behind her, she forced a smile at her attendants, four little bridesmaids and two pageboys. The daughters and sons of foreign royalty she didn't even know, they were nevertheless taking their duties very seriously, meticulously arranging the train of Anna's beautiful lace wedding dress, the girls bossing the boys around, straightening their emerald-green sashes for them before clasping their posies to their chests, ready to begin.

The procession started, slowly making its way down the red carpet, the congregation turning to catch their first glimpse of the blushing bride, gasping at what they saw. Because Annalina looked stunning, every inch the fairy-tale princess about to marry her Prince Charming. She wore a white lace gown, the wide V neck leaving her collarbone bare to show off the diamond necklace that had belonged to her mother. With sheer lace sleeves and a nipped-in waist, it cascaded to the floor with metres of lace and tulle that rustled with every step. Every step that took her closer and closer to the towering, dark figure that stood with his back to her—rigid, unmoving, impossible to read.

Zahir Zahani. The man she knew so little of, but who was about to become her husband. The man whose hooded gaze burnt into her soul, whose harshly sculpted face haunted her very being. The man who somehow, terrifyingly, she seemed to have become totally obsessed with. Even during the weeks when they had been apart it had felt as if her every waking moment had been filled with the overpowering sense of him. And not just her waking moments. The force of his magnetism had invaded her dreams too, seeing her writhing around in her sleep, waking up gasping for air, her heart thumping in her chest as the erotic images slowly faded into the reality of the day.

Now she took her position beside Zahir, beside this immovable mountain of a man who still stared fixedly ahead. His immaculate tailored suit only accentuated the width of his back, the length of his legs, and when Anna risked a sideways glance she saw how stiffly he held his neck against the starched white collar of his dress shirt, how rigidly his jaw was clenched beneath the smooth, olive skin.

Next to him stood Rashid, who was to serve as best man. In contrast to Zahir's complete stillness he fidgeted, shifting his weight from foot to foot, smoothing his hands over the trousers of his suit. He shot Anna a cold glance and again she registered that same peculiar sense of unease.

And so the long ceremony began. The sonorous voice of the priest echoed around the vaulted ceiling of the chapel—a chapel full of honoured guests from around the world. But Anna was only aware of one man, so acutely aware that she thought she must shimmer with it, radiate an aura that was plain for all to see.

Somehow she managed to get through the service, the daze of hymns, prayers, readings and blessings, only seriously faltering once, when Zahir slipped the platinum wedding ring onto her finger. The sight of it there, looking so real, so *final*, sent her eyes flying to his face, searching for a crumb of comfort, some sort of affirmation that they were doing the right thing. But all she saw was the same closed, dark expression that refused to give anything away.

Finally the organ struck up for the last time and the bride and groom made their way back up the aisle as man and wife. As they stepped outside, they were met with a loud roar from the crowd and a barrage of flashing cameras. It seemed thousands of people had gathered to be a part of this special day, braving hours of standing in the cold to catch a glimpse of their princess and her new husband. A short distance away, the car was waiting to take them back to the castle for the wedding breakfast, but first Anna was going to spend a few minutes chatting to the crowd. They deserved that, at least. Walking over to the barrier, she bent down to accept a posy of flowers from a young child, smiling at the sight of his chubby little cheeks red from the cold. The crowd roared louder and suddenly arms were reaching out everywhere, bunches of flowers thrust at them, cameras and phones held out to capture the moment.

'We need to get into the car, Annalina.' Zahir was right behind her, whispering harshly into her ear.

'All in good time.' She politely accepted another bunch of flowers. 'First we need to acknowledge the kindness of these people who have been hanging around for hours waiting to congratulate us.' She could feel Zahir's displeasure radiating from him in waves but she didn't care. They weren't in Nabatean now. This was her country and she was going to set the rules. She continued to smile into the crowd, accepting armfuls of flowers that she then passed to a couple of burly men who had appeared behind them. She noticed they shot a startled glance at Zahir. 'Why don't you go and talk to the people over there?' She gestured to the barrier on the other side.

'Because this is not on the schedule, that's why.'

'So what? Life doesn't always have to run to a schedule.' She passed more flowers back to the minders, enjoying herself now, especially the sight of these burly men wreathed in blooms. 'You need to loosen up a bit, accept that this is the way things are done here.'

But Zahir showed no signs of loosening up. Instead he continued to move her forward by the sheer wall of his presence, so close behind her that his barely repressed ire bound them together. Anna turned her head, hissing the words past her smile: 'You might at least try and look as if you're happy.'

'This isn't about being happy.' No, of course it wasn't. How foolish of Anna to forget for a moment. 'Schedules are there for a reason. And impromptu *walkabouts* provide the ideal chance for a terrorist to strike.'

'This is Dorrada, Zahir.' Still she persisted. 'We don't have any terrorists.'

They had reached the car now, Zahir having to duck his head to get in to this ancient vehicle that had once been her father's pride and joy. He seemed far too big for it, caged in by it, as the doors closed behind them, muffling the cheers of the crowd.

'May I remind you that you are now married to me,

Annalina? To Prince Zahir of Nabatean?' He turned to
face her, his eyes as black as stone. 'And *we* do. From now
on, you will treat security with the respect it deserves.
Otherwise, you may not live to regret it.'

Zahir's eyes strayed across the crowded ballroom yet
again, searching out Annalina. She wasn't difficult to
find. Still wearing her wedding dress, she was by far the
most beautiful woman in the room without exception,
moving amongst the guests with practised ease, charming them with her grace and beauty, occasionally taking
to the floor to be whisked around by some daring young
buck or crusty old dignitary.

Zahir didn't dance. Never had he seen the need. But
tonight he found himself wishing that he did, that he
could have parted the crowd on the dance floor, firmly
tapped on the shoulder whichever interloper it was at
the time and removed Annalina from his clutches. Other
men touching his bride did not sit well with him. More
than that, it spread a hot tide of possessiveness through
him, the like of which he had never known before. It was
something he knew he had to keep in check.

At least until tonight, when he would have Annalina
in his bed. Then she would be all his, in every sense of
the word. It was that thought that had got him through
today: the long-drawn-out ceremony, the tedious wedding breakfast and now this irksome ball that it appeared
would never come to an end. His tolerance and patience
had been severely tested, neither being qualities that he
had in abundance. But the day was finally drawing to
a close, the waiting nearly over. And as the time approached when at last they would be together, alone, so
the thrum of awareness increased, spreading through

him, until it was no longer a thrum but a thudding, pounding urge that held his body taut, rang in his ears.

From across the other side of the room Annalina looked up, meeting his gaze, a gaze which he knew he had held for too long, that was in danger of betraying him with its intensity. She angled her head, something approaching a smile playing across her lips, her eyes deliberately holding his, refusing to look away.

God, she was beautiful. A fresh wave of lust washed over him, tightening the fit of his tailored trousers. She might be all demure decorum now but tonight he would have those restrained lips screaming his name in pleasure, those searching eyes screwed shut against the delirium of his touch, his heated thrust. Bringing her to orgasm that night in the log cabin had been the single most erotic experience of his life. But the experience had ended badly—seeing him consumed with rage, fighting to maintain his composure, dangerously close to losing it. This was what Annalina did to him. She stirred up emotions that were totally uncalled for. Awoke the warrior in him when the situation called for restraint and respect—not pumping testosterone and raging hormones.

As the supreme leader of the army of Nabatean, Zahir had seen some terrible things, had done some terrible things, that still had the power to haunt him when he closed his eyes against the night. But that was war, the most brutal savagery imaginable, man turning on his fellow man. It had been a hideous, necessary evil but he was vindicated by the fact that Nabatean was now a successful, independent country, free from the oppression and tyranny of its war-mongering neighbour. Many would say that Zahir should be extremely proud of his achievements. That he had accomplished what no man had ever thought possible. But, despite his pride in his country, Zahir would never be able to accept praise for his victory, let alone celebrate it. Not when his parents had paid for his success with their lives.

He had learned his lesson in the most painful way possible. Never again would he allow himself the luxury of such gratification, no matter for how brief a period of time. Self-indulgent pleasure was to be avoided at all costs. He just needed to remember that when he was around Annalina.

Not that his feelings for her were all about pleasure, far from it. Annalina stirred up extremes of emotions that were as threatening as they were mystifying.

For a slightly built young woman, weighing, he would estimate, little more than eight stone, this was extremely perplexing. Even if she'd been a trained assassin, armed to the teeth, he knew he would have no trouble overpowering her, throwing her to the ground, dispatching her if necessary. But she wasn't a trained assassin and she wasn't armed, at least, not with a recognisable weapon. She was no threat. So why did his body insist that she was, firing the blood through his veins as if he had stepped into an ambush, had a blade at his throat?

Because Annalina's weapons were of a different kind. Ice-blue eyes that flashed with a mystery all of their own. Plump lips, pert breasts, hair that tumbled over her shoulders…curves that begged to be stroked. These were her weapons. And Zahir was beginning to realise that they were more lethal than any he had come across before. They consumed his mind, invaded his consciousness, provoking feelings of anger, lust and a desperate need that had only increased in the weeks they had been apart. And there was another emotion, one he had never experienced before. *Jealousy*. The thought of Annalina with another man, past or present, innocent or not, gripped him hard enough to paralyse his whole body. It frightened him with its force, weakened him with its power.

Forcing himself to relax, he leant against a pillar festooned with winter foliage, flexing his fingers, half-closing his eyes. Eyes that still followed Annalina as she started talking to another guest—that narrowed further when he saw the man taking her hand in his, raising it to his lips, holding it there longer than was strictly necessary. He sucked in a breath. *Control yourself, Zahir. And find enough patience for another hour.* When they finally did come together, it would be all the sweeter for the wait.

He was glad now that they hadn't had sex that night in the cabin. At the time it had only been blind rage that had stopped him. But now he knew the timing hadn't been right. He had wanted her—God how he had wanted her! But deep down had he felt uneasy about despoiling such an exquisite creature? Felt unworthy, even? Now Annalina was his bride, his wife. Now he could legitimately claim her. And any unusually sensitive worries he might have had, any hesitancy about his rights or his responsibilities, had long since vanished in a sea of carnal craving.

Shouldering himself away from the pillar, he decided to go outside in search of some fresh air. He needed to cool himself down.

It was a beautiful night, crisp and clear, with a full moon shining on the virgin snow. Zahir paused to take in the view, the town of Valduz spread out in the valley below twinkling prettily, the mountains all around them soaring into the night sky. He set off around the side of the castle, his footprints sinking deep into the crunchy snow, breathing in deeply to relish the cold air that scoured his lungs. But then he stopped, his senses on high alert. Someone else was out here. He could hear the huff of their breath, a sort of shuffling noise, a mumbled voice.

Zahir moved stealthily forward, tracking the sound like the trained killer that he was. Now he could make out the shape of man leaning against the wall of the castle, see the glow of a cigarette burn more brightly as he took a deep drag before flicking it away into the snow. He watched as the figure raised a bottle to his lips—whisky, if Zahir had to guess— glugging from it greedily then wiping the back of his hand across his mouth before staggering a couple of steps sideways, then back again. The mumbling was him talking to himself. There was no one else was around. He was clearly very drunk.

Zahir stepped out of the shadows.

'I think you've had enough of this.' Removing the bottle from the man's grasp, Zahir flung it behind him.

'Hey!' Lunging forward, the man peered at him with glassy-eyed aggression. 'What the hell do you think you're doing?'

Zahir silently positioned himself in front of this creature, squaring his chest, towering over him. He wasn't looking for a fight, but neither was he going to let this guy drink himself into oblivion. Not here, at his wedding party.

'You have no right to...' Squinting up at Zahir, the man suddenly stopped. 'Well, look who it is. The mighty desert Prince.' A sneer twisted his thin lips. 'What brings you out here? Trying to escape already?'

Zahir's fists balled by his sides. This individual was seriously asking for a punch.

'You don't know who I am, do you?' Pushing himself unsteadily off the wall, he straightened up, holding Zahir's gaze, emboldened by the alcohol or stupidity, or both. 'Allow me to introduce myself. Prince Henrik of Ebsberg.' He extended a limp arm. 'Delighted to meet you.'

Blood roared in Zahir's ears, raging through his body, turning his muscles to stone. So this was the revolting individual who had once been engaged to Annalina. His fists by his sides flexed, then balled again, his nails digging into his palms.

'Ha.' With a dismissive laugh, Henrik withdrew his hand, folding his arms over his chest. 'So my name's familiar to you, then.' He put his head on one side, the sneer still curving his lips. 'You may not want to shake my hand, old chap, but perhaps you will accept my heartfelt commiserations instead. You have my deepest sympathies.'

A growl erupted from somewhere deep inside Zahir as he adjusted his stance, planting his feet further apart. 'And just what do you mean by that?'

'Oh, dear.' With a giggle, Henrik moved his hand to his mouth. 'Don't tell me you don't know. This is *so* much worse than I thought.'

'Don't know what?' Zahir ground out the question, more as a diversionary tactic to stop his hands from travelling to this man's throat rather than because he wanted an answer.

'About your new bride. I'm sorry to be the bearer of bad news, but Princess Annalina is not only as pure as the driven snow, she's as frozen as it.' Misinterpreting Zahir's thunderous silence, Henrik warmed to his theme. 'Yes, it's true. Beneath that pretty exterior there lies nothing but a block of ice.'

'Hold your tongue.' Zahir bent down, his face just inches away from his prey. 'You will not speak of my wife in such a way. Not if you know what's good for you.'

'Why not?' Henrik blithely carried on. 'I'm only tell-ing you the truth. Annalina is the original ice maiden. You will get no satisfaction from her. Take it from me. I should know. I've been there.'

Unbidden, Zahir's hands flew to Henrik's throat, grasping a handful of shirt and lifting his feet clean off the ground. The fury that engulfed him was so strong he could taste it, feel it rising up his throat, burning behind his eyes. The thought that this man had even touched Annalina was enough for Zahir to wish upon him the most slow and painful death. But to brag about it. To speak of her in that hideously insulting manner... Death would be too good for him.

He looked down at Henrik, now squirming in his grasp. Then, taking a deep breath, he let him go, watch-ing as he fell to his knees before scrabbling to stand up-right again.

'Tut, tut.' Brushing the snow from his hands, Henrik staggered a couple of steps away. 'It's not my fault that you've married a dud, Zahani. You should have taken a leaf out of my book and had the sense to try her out first. I had a lucky escape. But you, my friend, have been duped.'

'Why, you little...' Raging fury had all but closed Za-hir's throat, grinding his words to a low snarl. 'Get out of my sight while you can still walk.'

'Very well. But it won't change anything. The fact is, pretty Annalina is frigid. If it's any consolation, I had no idea either—not until she was in my bed, until she was under me, until it came to the actual point of—'

Crack. Zahir's fist connected with Henrik's nose, making a noise like the fall of a branch in the forest. With this vilest of creatures now splayed at his feet, his first thought was of satisfaction, that he had finally silenced his revolting words. But rampant fury was still pumping through his body, the temptation to finish what he had started holding him taut, tensing his muscles, grinding his jaw. He looked down at Henrik, who was whimpering pathetically, blood pouring from his nose.

'Get up.' He realised he wasn't done with him yet. He wanted him on his feet again, wanted him to fight back, to give him the opportunity to have another swipe at him. But Henrik only moaned. 'I said, get up.' Bending down, Zahir lifted him by the scruff of the neck again, holding him before him like a rag doll. 'Now put your fists up. Fight like a man.'

'Please, no.' Henrik raised a hand, but only to touch his damaged nose, recoiling in horror when it came away covered in blood. 'Let me go. I don't want to fight.'

'I bet you don't.' Zahir set him down again, watching Henrik's knees buckle in the struggle to keep him upright. 'Call yourself a man, *Prince Henrik of Ebsberg*?' He spat out the name with utter revulsion. 'You are nothing more than a pathetic piece of scum, a vile and despicable low life. And if I ever hear you so much as utter Princess Annalina's name, let alone defile her character as you have just done, you will not live to tell the tale. Is that understood?'

Henrik nodded and Zahir turned away, taking several steps, inhaling deeply as he did so, trying to purge himself of this man. He was ten or twelve feet away when Henrik called after him.

'So it's true what they say about you.'

Zahir froze, then slowly turned around.

'You really *are* an animal. The Beast of Nabatean.' His words slurred into one another. 'You do know that's what they call you, don't you?' He started to giggle idiotically. 'Despite your marriage, Europe will never accept you. So you see, you and Annalina, it's all been for nothing. Beauty and the Beast—you deserve each other.'

The space between them was closed in an instant, even though Henrik was backing away as fast as his collapsing legs would let him.

Zahir's fist connected with Henrik's face again—this time it was his jaw. And, when he fell to the snow again, this time there was no getting up.

CHAPTER TEN

CLOSING THE DOOR, Anna leant back against it and looked around. The room was empty. She was the first to arrive. Swallowing down the jittery disappointment, she drew in a deep breath. It was fine. She would have time to prepare herself before Zahir came to her. And when he did she would be ready. They would make love and everything would be wonderful. This was the night that finally, please God, she would lose not only her virginity but the terrible stigma that had haunted her for so long.

The room assigned to the newlyweds had been dressed for the occasion. Rugs were scattered over the polished wooden floor, heavy curtains pulled against the freezing night, an enormous tapestry adorning one stone wall. A fire roared in the grate and that, along with the guttering candles in the iron chandelier overhead, provided the only light.

Anna moved over to the bed. Centuries old, the oak construction was raised off the floor by a stepped platform, with four columns to support the heavy square-panelled canopy. Drapes were tied back to reveal the sumptuous bedding, piles of pillows and embroidered silk throws. She sat on the edge, sinking down into the soft mattress, then ran her fingers over the coverlet, her eyes immediately drawn to the wedding ring on her finger. So it was true—she really had married her dashing Arabian prince. There was her evidence.

Being reunited with Zahir today, seeing him again in all his gorgeously taut, olive-skinned flesh, had been both wonderful and agonising. Because it had confirmed what she already knew in her heart. That Zahir was like a drug to her, a dangerous addiction that had invaded her cells to the point where she found she craved him, ached for him. But, just like an addiction, she knew she had to face up to it in order to be able to control it.

Because giving in to her weakness, letting it take over, control her, would be her undoing. Over the years she had learnt how protect herself, to hide her emotional vulnerability. She had had to. Because there had been precious little love in her life since her mother had died. She didn't blame her father for his coldness. It wasn't his fault that he couldn't love her the way she wanted him to. It was hers. And when she'd tried to please him—agreeing to marry Henrik, for example—she'd ended up just making things worse. The broken engagement, the dreadful shame, the *crippling humiliation* only served to compound her feelings of lack of self-worth. She feared she wasn't capable of being loved, in any sense of the word. And for that reason she had to protect her own heart. She had to be very, very careful.

She thought back over the day she and Zahir had just shared, their wedding day. She had been so aware of his presence—every second of every hour—that it had felt almost like a physical pain. Standing rigidly beside her during the ceremony, silently consuming his meal next to her at the wedding breakfast or scowling across at her during the ball, her skin had prickled from the sense of him, the hairs on the back of her neck standing on end, her nerve endings tingling.

But then towards the end of the evening something had happened, something telling—thrilling. Their eyes had met across the ballroom and they had shared a look, an understanding. Zahir's gaze had scorched a path between them, his hooded, mesmerising eyes spelling out exactly what was on his mind. *Hunger and desire.* It had been a look of such unconscious seduction, such inevitability, that it had weakened her knees, caught the breath in her throat. Zahir wanted her. She was sure of that. And she wanted him too, more than she could ever have imagined wanting any man, *ever.* That didn't mean she could let down her guard—in fact now she would need to protect herself more than ever. But it did mean that the time was right. They were both ready.

So when Zahir had turned and left the ballroom Anna had prepared to leave too. Heart thumping, she had made her excuses to her guests, hurrying her goodbyes in her rush to follow him, to be with him. Because tonight was the night that Zahir would make love to her. And this time she was determined that everything would be all right.

Now she smoothed her hands over the folds of her wedding dress. All day long she had had visions of Zahir undressing her, his fingers impatiently tugging at the fiddly buttons, pulling the fine lace over her shoulders, watching the dress fall to the ground.

Well, maybe she would save him the bother. Standing up, she twisted behind her and undid the top buttons as best she could then wriggled out of the dress and placed it carefully over the back of a chair. Next she pulled out the clips that held up her hair, undoing the braids and threading her fingers through to release them until her hair tumbled over her shoulders. She looked down at herself. At the white lace bra and panties, the white silk stockings that revealed several inches of bare skin at the top of her thighs. Goosebumps skittered over her. Away from the fire, the room felt cold. But inside Anna already burned for Zahir's touch, her body clenching at the thought of it. She wanted him so badly.

On impulse she pulled back the covers and got into bed, squirming into the sheets. Would it please Zahir to come across her like this—still in her underwear? She had no idea. She had no sexual experiences to draw on. All she knew was that, lying here semi-naked like this, she felt as sexy as hell, and that had to be a good place to start. Her hand strayed to her panties, to the soft mound of hair beneath. Tentatively her fingers slipped under the skimpy fabric, finding their way to her intimate folds. She was damp, already very aroused. Slowly, slowly, she started to gently rub herself, prepare herself for Zahir, for what was to come. Letting out a sigh, she rested her head back against the pillow and closed her eyes.

A sudden noise snapped them open again—the wail of an ambulance siren. Pushing herself up to sitting, Anna rubbed her eyes. She hoped a guest hadn't been taken ill. What time was it? And where was Zahir? She noticed that the fire was burning low in the grate—she must have fallen asleep. Checking her watch, she realised that nearly an hour had passed since she had come to the bridal suite. More than enough time for Zahir to have joined her.

A terrible fear gripped her heart. Pulling back the covers, she tugged a throw off the bed and wrapped it around her, her body already starting to shake. She moved over to the fireplace, bending to pick up a log and throw it onto the glowing embers, watching the shower of sparks. Then, settling into a low chair, she drew up her knees and pulled the throw around her, her mind racing in all directions.

Maybe he had been waylaid. Perhaps one of the guests,

one of the many foreign dignitaries that he had been conversing with all day, had suggested they talked business before he retired to bed.

Maybe he hadn't been able to find the right room. Maybe he was wandering around the castle right now, opening doors, calling her name. Although it was pushing it to think that a man who could navigate the vastness of the desert by the stars alone would have trouble finding his way to the marital bed.

Or maybe he had been taken ill. The ambulance she had heard just now might be coming to whisk him to hospital because he'd been struck down with some mystery ailment. But that seemed equally unlikely. It was impossible to believe that Zahir Zahani had ever had a day's sickness in his life.

Which only left one more possibility—the most painful one of all. *He wasn't coming.* She must have misinterpreted the look he had given her in the ballroom—or, worse, she had imagined it completely. Like a starving dog, she had gobbled up the scrap being thrown to her, convinced that it was the start of a feast, that her hunger would finally be satisfied. But she had been wrong. And now, like a useless cur, she had been abandoned.

As she stared into the flames that were starting to leap into life, she felt the tears blocking her throat. Now the real reason Zahir wasn't here was all too obvious.

He didn't want her. Now he knew the truth, that she was frigid, incapable of ever being able to satisfy him, he had no use for her. *Somehow this time, without even having got Zahir to her bed, she had managed to fail yet again.*

Zahir stared at the man sprawled at his feet. Anger was still coursing through him, clenching his fists and his teeth, holding every muscle rigid in his body.

Bending down, he grabbed hold of Henrik's shoulder and roughly turned him over, hearing him moan as he did so. Blood stained the snow where his face had been, seeping into the icy imprint. His face was a mess with blood flowing from his nose and mouth, his lip split and swelling. Judging from the angle of his jaw, it was definitely dislocated.

Zahir let out a long, slow breath, releasing the last of his rage into the darkness of the night. *The Beast of Nabatean.* So that was how he was known in the West. And now he had just lived up to his name.

Well, so be it. He didn't give a damn. If European society wanted to look over their monocles, hide behind their simpering manners and call him a beast, then he would accept the title. Accept it with pride, in fact. For it was his strength, his fearlessness—and, yes, at times the brutality of his decisions—that had won his country their independence. He would value that over their delicate Western sensibilities a thousand times.

But Annalina...that was a different matter. Was that how she thought of him? Like some sort of beast or barbarian that fate had cruelly delivered to her door? To her bed? The thought struck him like a savage blow. Certainly he had done nothing to dispel the myth. He had never shown her the slightest care or consideration. Because he didn't know how. He was a military man, comfortable only with logic and detachment, proud of his nerves of steel. He could cope with any situation, no matter how horrific. Hadn't he demonstrated that with the way he had handled the slaughter of his parents? A situation that would have tested the strongest man. That had ripped his brother apart, both mentally and physically. But he had taken charge, dealt with the carnage the only way he knew how. By banishing his emotions, refusing to give in to any weakness and concentrating on finding the perpetrators. Then trying to minimise the repercussions for all concerned. He had never even let himself grieve. He couldn't afford to.

But the war was over now, and the military training that had held him in such good stead no longer applied. Now he found he didn't know how to behave. Now he was left wondering who the hell he was.

He looked down at his battered victim again. Beneath the anger he could feel another emotion pushing through—disgust. And not just for the man at his feet, although that was a palpable force. But disgust at himself too. Raising his hand, he saw the blood that stained his knuckles, knuckles that were swelling from the force of his punch.

He could have walked away. He *should* have walked away. But he couldn't do it, could he? He couldn't control himself. He was deserving of his title. A beast.

What he didn't deserve was the beautiful young woman he had married today. Who was expecting him in her bed tonight. Who no doubt was bracing herself, preparing to accept the fate that he had spelt out that night in the cabin. Not because she wanted to, but because she had no alternative other than to do as she was told. Zahir wanted her so badly, he had tried to justify his arrogant, dictatorial behaviour by telling himself it was her duty, not least because she was now his wife. But this wasn't about duty, no matter how much he tried to dress it up. It was about his carnal cravings. And there was no way he would allow himself to indulge them tonight. He had another man's blood on his hands. How could he even consider using these same hands to touch Annalina, to claim her for himself? He couldn't. It would be an insult to her beauty and to her innocence. Denying himself that pleasure would be his penance.

Henrik groaned again. He needed medical attention—that much was obvious. Pulling his mobile phone out of his pocket, Zahir called for an ambulance, ending the conversation before the operator could ask him any more questions. They knew enough to come and patch him up, restore his pretty-boy good looks.

Throwing his victim one last look of revulsion, he turned away. Then, jamming his hands down into his pockets, he hunched his shoulders against the cold and began to walk. He didn't know where to and he didn't know how far. All he did know was that he had to get away from here, from this creature, from the castle, and from the desperate temptation to slide into bed next to the luscious body of his new bride.

CHAPTER ELEVEN

A SMALL RECEPTION party had lined up to welcome Prince Zahir and his new wife when they arrived back at Medira Palace. As Zahir swept them through the massive doors, Anna forced herself to smile at everyone, especially when she saw Lana and Layla, standing on tiptoes trying to get a better look at them. They looked so excited it made her want to cry.

Little more than twenty-four hours had passed since their marriage ceremony, since they had stood side by side in the chapel in Dorrada and made their vows. But it had been long enough to spell out just what sort of a marriage it would be. Hollow and empty and desperately lonely. Long enough to firmly dash any hopes she might have foolishly fostered that they could ever be a real couple, come together as husband and wife, as lovers.

It was also a marriage where she was going to have to be constantly on her guard, hide her true feelings from Zahir. Because to show him even a glimmer of what was in her heart would be emotional suicide. She could hardly bring herself to examine the insanity of her own feelings, let alone expose them to the cold and cruel claws of her husband.

Her wedding night had been miserably sad, plagued by fitful dreams and long periods of wakefulness in a bed that had seemed increasingly empty as the hours of darkness had dragged by. Forcing herself to go down to breakfast this morning had taken all the will power she possessed but she'd known she had to face Zahir sometime. Somehow she had to cover up her broken heart. But as it turned out she'd been met, not by her husband, but with a note presented on a silver salver and written in Zahir's bold hand, stating that she was to meet him at the airport in two hours' time. That they would be flying back to Nabatean without delay. And that was it. No explanation as to where he had been all night, where he was now. No apology or excuses of any kind.

Because, as far as Zahir was concerned, she didn't deserve any explanations. She was now his property—by dint of their marriage, he had effectively bought her, no matter how it had been dressed up with fancy ceremonies and profuse congratulations. Now she belonged to him, in the same way as a herd of camel or an Arabian stallion. Except she was of considerably less use. If she couldn't satisfy him in bed, couldn't give him an heir, then, other than the connection with Europe that came with her position, what purpose did she actually serve?

No doubt Zahir was wondering the same thing. No doubt that was the reason he hadn't come to her bed last night and the reason he had totally ignored her on the flight to Nabatean, preferring the company of his laptop instead. The reason why his mood was as black as thunder as he briskly moved past the reception party and headed straight down the maze of corridors that lead to his private quarters.

Anna stood in the echoing reception chamber and looked around her, breathing in the foreign air of this gilded cage. Here she was in her new role, her new life. And she had no idea what she was supposed to do with it.

Declining the offer of refreshments, she allowed herself to be shown to the suite of rooms that had been assigned to her and Zahir. The grand marital bedroom had a raised bed centre-stage, like some sort of mocking altar, and the only slightly less grand bedroom, which she was solemnly informed was her personal room, just served to increase her sense of isolation, filled her with misery. What sort of marriage needed separate bedrooms right from the off? Sadly, she already knew the answer to that.

Wandering downstairs again, she found herself in one of the many empty salons and sat down on a window seat that overlooked a verdant courtyard. Darkness had fallen, the night having arrived with indecent haste in this part of the world, and the courtyard was floodlit, the palm trees and the fountain illuminated with a ghostly orange glow.

Anna felt for her phone in her handbag. She needed a distraction to stop herself from bursting into tears or running screaming into the wilderness of the desert, or both. Clicking on the site of a national newspaper in Dorrada, she scrolled through the headlines until she found what she was looking for. Just as she had expected, there was extensive coverage of the wedding of Princess Annalina to Prince Zahir of Nabatean, gushing descriptions of the beautiful ceremony, the sumptuous banquet and the glittering ball that had followed. Other European papers hadn't stinted either, all showing the official photographs accompanied by the obligatory text describing the couple's happy day.

Anna studied the images. She and Zahir, standing side by side, her arm linked through his. She could see the tension in her face, that the smile was in danger of cracking. And Zahir, tall, commanding, looking impossibly handsome with his shoulders back and his head held high. But his expression was masked, closed, impossible to fathom, no matter how much Anna stared at it. She was left wondering just who this man was that she had married.

She was about to put her phone away when a headline on one of the sidebars caught her eye. The shot of a battered face, captured by a zoom lens, by the look of it, was accompanied by the headline: *Prince Henrik arrives at hospital with facial injuries.*

A cold dread swept over her. With a shaky hand, she clicked on the link.

Prince Henrik of Ebsberg was seen arriving at a Valduz hospital on the night of his ex-fiancée's wedding, sporting what appeared to be significant facial injuries. One can only speculate as to how he acquired them.

Prince Henrik is known to have attended the grand ball thrown to celebrate the marriage of Princess Annalina of Dorrada to Prince Zahir of Nabatean. Could it be that the two men came to blows over the beautiful blonde princess? If so, it would appear that Prince Zahir's reputation as a formidable opponent is fully justified. Neither Prince Henrik nor Prince Zahir was available for comment.

No! Anna's heart plummeted inside her. Had Zahir done this to Henrik? She didn't want to believe it but her gut was telling her it had to be him. Head spinning, she desperately tried to think up some other explanation, figure out what could possibly have happened.

As European royals, the King and Queen of Ebsberg had been present at the wedding but Anna had been thankful, at that point, to see that their son, Henrik, hadn't joined them. She had completely forgotten about him until much later at the ball when out of the corner of her eye she had seen him arrive, looking unsteady on his feet, as if he had already been drinking. Having absolutely no desire to speak to him, she had deliberately kept out of his way, relieved that the relatively late hour meant she could legitimately slip away before he could corner her. But had Zahir spoken to him? Deliberately sought him out? Had it always been his intention to beat up her ex-fiancé?

The barbaric thought made Anna feel physically sick. But there was only one way to find out if it was true.

Leaping to her feet, she set off to find Zahir, pausing only briefly to try and get her bearings, to remember the way to his private quarters. With her pace quickening along with her temper, she flew along the echoing corridors, finally arriving at his door breathless and panting with anger. Rapping loudly on the panelling, she hurtled in without waiting for a reply.

'What is the meaning of this?' She advanced towards him, brandishing her phone before her like a weapon.

Rising from where he had been seated at a computer, Zahir met her head-on, towering before her. 'I could ask the same of you.' Deep-set eyes flashed dangerously black. 'I don't take kindly to being ambushed in my own study.'

'And I don't suppose Prince Henrik takes kindly to being beaten up by some vicious thug.' Trembling with animosity, Anna thrust the phone in his face. Taking it from her, Zahir gave it a cursory glance before tossing it back. Anna fumbled to catch it. 'Well? What do you have to say?' She could feel the hysteria rising in the face of his silence and the mounting realisation that she was right—Zahir had assaulted Henrik. 'Do you know about this? Did you *do* this?'

'I fail to see that this is any of your concern.'

'Not my concern?' Her voice screeched with incredulity. 'How can you say that? It's obvious that you attacked Henrik because of his association with me!'

'Trust me, there are any number of reasons I could have hit that creature.'

'So you admit it, then? You did assault Henrik?'

Zahir shrugged and his dismissive gesture only served to pour more fuel onto Anna's fury.

'And that's it? That's all you have to say on the matter?' She threw back her head so he couldn't escape her livid gaze. 'Aren't you at least going to offer some explanation, show some concern for what you've done?'

'I think you're showing enough concern for both of us.'

The air crackled between them, stirring the shadows of this cave-like room.

'What do you mean by that?'

'Some might say that you are unduly concerned about someone you should no longer have any attachment to.'

'Don't be ridiculous.'

'That you are displaying the behaviour of someone who still has feelings for this man.'

'No...'

'Are you regretting the past? Is that what it is? Do you wish you were married to him instead of me?'

'No, no, it's not that at all.'

'Isn't it, Annalina? Are you sure? You've told me yourself that it was Henrik who broke off your engagement. You still want him, don't you? That's the reason you are displaying such irrational behaviour.'

Irrational behaviour? Anna's eyes glittered back at him like shards of glass. She knew what he was doing:

he was trying to make out that she was overreacting—
that, even though he was the one who had committed
the crime, she was the one who should be examining her
motives. Well, she wasn't having it. Positioning herself
squarely in front of him, she clenched her teeth, ready
to fire at him with both barrels.

'Has it ever occurred to you, Zahir...' she swallowed
audibly '...that I may be displaying the behaviour of someone who's worried that they have married a monster?'

A terrible silence fell between them. For a moment
neither of them moved, their eyes locked in a lethal clash
that Anna couldn't break but that tore into her soul. She
could hear the roar of blood in her ears, feel the heavy
thud of her heartbeat, but she was paralysed, Zahir's painfully piercing black stare holding her captive as surely
as if she'd been nailed to the ground.

'And that's what you think, is it?' His voice was lethally low, barely more than a murmur. But it carried
the weight of the loudest scream. 'You think that I am
a monster?'

'I didn't actually say that.'

'Well, you are not alone. The Beast of Nabatean—isn't
that what they call me?'

'No, I mean...'

'Don't bother to try and deny it. I know full well how
the European bourgeoisie perceive me.'

'But not me, Zahir. I would never call you such a
thing.' Anna had heard the insulting title—of course she
had—but a loathing of prejudice and bigotry, and maybe
a smattering of fear, had made her dismiss it. Until now.
'This isn't about what other people call you. And it's
nothing to do with how I feel about Henrik. It's about
you going around beating people up.'

'And you think that's what I do?'

'Well, what am I supposed to think?'

'I'd like you to leave now.' He turned away and she was suddenly presented with the impenetrable wall of his back.

'What? No!' Horrified, she reached forward, her fingers clawing at the fabric of his shirt. 'I'm not going until we have discussed this, until you have heard me out.'

'I *said* I want you to leave.'

'And if I refuse?'

'Who knows what might happen, Annalina? How I might react.' Swinging round, he closed the space between them with a single step, then towered over her, his fixed gaze as black as a raven's wing. 'Are you prepared to take that risk? Are you prepared to incur the wrath of such a monster as me?' His words were clearly designed to intimidate her and it was working, at least to start with, Anna's throat drying, her hands shaking from the sheer force of his might.

But as she continued to stare at him a different reaction started to seep in. Suddenly her breasts felt heavy, her nipples contracting, her belly clenching with a fierceness that rippled down to her core, holding it tight in its grip. Suddenly her whole body was alive to him. And it was nothing to do with fear.

She watched as his pupils dilated, her own doing the same in response. So he felt it too. Anger still pulsed between them but now it was laced with hunger, a carnal craving that was growing more powerful with each suspenseful second.

She forced herself to swallow. How could she want this man so badly? It didn't make any sense. How could she have given her heart to a man capable of such savagery? Capable of hurting her so badly? The wounds inflicted on their wedding night, still raw and bleeding, were a painful testament to that. But a monster? No. Arrogant, insufferable, formidable... Anna could reel off a list of his shortcomings. But loyal too and fiercely protective. She had seen the way he was with his brother, glimpsed the burden of pain and suffering caused by his parents' tragic deaths before he had pulled down the shutters and pushed her away. She had heard the pride in his voice whenever he spoke of his country. No, Zahir was no monster.

'Well?' He bit out the word but there was an edge to his voice that betrayed him, angered him. He extended his arm, roughly clasping the back of her head, threading his fingers through her hair to bring her closer to him. 'I'm still waiting for your answer.'

His breath was hot on her face and Anna's tongue darted to wet her lips. 'I'm still here, aren't I?'

'So it would seem.' He moved fractionally closer until their bodies were touching. Heat roared between them, the unmistakable stirring beneath Zahir's trousers making Anna tremble violently. 'But what does that tell me? That you don't think that I'm a monster? Or that right now you don't care?'

'I'm not frightened of you, Zahir, if that's what you mean.'

'Hmm. And yet you are shaking. Why is that, Annalina?'

'I d-don't know.'

'Maybe it's that you crave the beast in me.' He moved closer still, pressing the length of his body against her, all heat and flexed muscle, hard bones beneath tautly drawn flesh. And raw, potent, sexual energy.

'And if I do?'

'Then perhaps it is my duty to satisfy that craving.'

Finally his lips came down to claim hers with a punishing kiss that sucked the air from her lungs, pumped the blood wildly around her body. He plundered her mouth, his tongue seeking and taking, his breath feverishly hot as he panted into her. It was a kiss that left Anna reeling from its force, melting beneath its pressure. She gasped as he finally pulled away, feeling her lips engorging with blood before he was kissing her again, moving his hands to span the small of her back, pressing her firmly against his erection. Complete abandonment washed over her as the most gloriously erotic feeling took over, obliterating all thought. Other than that Zahir *had* to make love to her. *Now.*

When their lips finally pulled apart she worked her hands around his waist to the strip of bare skin between his shirt and the low-slung pants, feeling him buck satisfyingly beneath her touch. Easily sliding her hands beneath the waistband, she slipped them lower, letting out a guttural gasp of longing when she realised he was naked underneath. Her fingertips skittered over the bare skin of his buttocks, leaving a trail of goosebumps behind them, the muscles clenching tightly beneath her touch. He felt so good, so gloriously hard, tight and male that Anna realised she was panting with excitement, her breath coming in short gasps.

Sliding her hands down further, she traced the underside of his buttocks and when she firmly cupped both cheeks in her hands, squeezing them tightly with a strength born of pure need, she was rewarded with a sharp hiss of breath and a bucking movement that thrust the shape of his mighty erection against her stomach.

Anna let out a low moan. Reaching up on tiptoe, she tried to make herself as tall as possible so she could feel his erection where she so desperately wanted it—against her groin. But Zahir went one better, lifting her off her feet as if she were weightless, one ankle boot dropping to the ground with a thud. Wrapping her legs around his waist, the glorious feel of him was now pressing against her sex and she closed her eyes against the thrill as she clung dizzily to him, her arms around his neck, feeling him turn and move towards his bedroom.

She opened them again as he set her down, wobbling unsteadily on her feet as she watched him tear his shirt over his head, his breathing heavy with need. It was dark in this cave-like room, the shutters closed against the night, the bed no more than a low shape on the floor. Stripped to the waist, Zahir brought Anna towards him again, sweeping her hair over one shoulder, nuzzling her neck with his lips as his hands slid the zipper of her dress down her back.

'You want this, Anna?'

It was the same question he had asked her in the log cabin before it had all gone horribly wrong. But she wasn't going to mess it up this time. Want was too small a word to describe the fervour she felt for Zahir right now. It was an overpowering, all-consuming madness. Something she couldn't bring herself to examine. For now, a simple yes would have to suffice.

She groaned the word hotly against his shoulder as he tugged at her dress and it fell to the ground. Now he was undoing the clasp of her bra, releasing her breasts until they were caught, heavy and aching with need, by his caressing palms, his thumb stroking over nipples that had shrivelled into hard peaks. Anna's hands strayed down to his loose-fitting trousers again, tugging at them until they were low over his hips, finally falling to the ground. He was naked, the force of his erection escaping at last, throbbing between them.

'Say it again, Annalina.' He ground out the words,

one hand reaching for her panties, pulling them down her legs, taking the remaining boot with them.

'I want you.'

With a guttural growl he swept her off her feet again, laying her down on the bed and positioning himself over her, his eyes shining like jet in the darkness as they raked over her face. With his jaw held fast, the sharp angles of his cheeks hollowed and shadowed, he looked magnificent. And he looked like a man on the edge.

'You're going to have to control me, Annalina.' He lowered his body until it was held fractionally above her by the flexed columns of his arms, his mouth just a centimetre from her own. 'Take me at the speed you are comfortable with.'

Anna gulped. She had totally lost control of herself—what hope did she have of controlling him? And 'comfortable' was not a word she was interested in. She wanted mind-blowing, all-consuming sex. Speech had all but deserted her but she did manage to drag up something that she suddenly knew to be true.

'I trust you, Zahir.'

This produced a stab of surprise that had his eyes widen then narrow again. Zahir hesitated, as if about to say something, then he changed his mind, moving his hand between her legs instead, pushing her thighs apart so that he could slide his fingers inside her.

Anna shuddered with pleasure at his touch, his fingers working to intensify her arousal, increase the wetness that slicked her core. As her whole body began to shake, she reached behind his back to steady herself, to stop him from moving away, her hands desperately gripping on to him. Her legs splayed wider, her back arching into his touch.

'God, Annalina. You have no idea what you do to

me.' He growled deeply before he took her mouth again, his tongue licking and tasting at the same speed as his finger stroked and rubbed. 'You need to say now if you want this to stop.'

'Don't stop, Zahir. Do it—make love to me.'

'Uh-uh.' With another thickly uttered growl, Zahir withdrew his hand and, reaching for Anna's, guided it to his member, curling her fist around the silky, heated girth of him. 'You are in control, Anna. Remember that. Whatever happens now is down to you.'

Oh, dear Lord. Anna wasn't prepared for this. She had fantasised about this moment for so long, yearned, craved and ached for it almost since the first moment she had clapped eyes on Zahir. But she had stressed about it too, agonised over what might happen, the dreadful accusation that had been implanted in her mind by Henrik refusing to be totally banished. But in every imagined scenario it had been Zahir taking command, taking her any way he wanted to, dominating her the way he had when they'd been in the cabin. Not that that hadn't been indescribably, erotically mind-blowing. But it had held an element of fear too.

This was different. As she started to slide her hand up and down the thick length of him, felt him shudder beneath her touch, any traces of fear subsided. He was big, so astonishingly, eye-wateringly enormous, but she wasn't scared. Just mindlessly high with exhilaration, as if he was a drug she could never get enough of.

And she knew she was ready for him, ready in mind and body.

Shifting her bottom, she spread her legs wider, positioning the head of his shaft exactly where she wanted it. Zahir froze, not moving, not even breathing, his whole body rigid with unspoken, unleashed power. She started to make small, circling movements with him, pressing him against her most sensitive spot, small mews escaping her lips. She was so wet now, so aroused. She paused, seeking his eyes, eyes that were black with desire, as drugged and drowning as her own.

'Now, Zahir.' She whispered the command hoarsely.

He didn't need telling twice. With his arms braced on either side of her head, he lowered his hips, plunging the head of his member into Anna's wet, tight, sensitised core. Anna gasped, her muscles clenching around him, holding him firm as her legs drew up, her hands clawing at his back.

'Annalina?'

'More, Zahir. I want more.'

'Oh, God.' With a primal groan, Zahir obeyed, pushing more of his length into her with a slick, hot, juddering force. He paused again as Anna's legs clamped around him, her nails digging into his flesh.

'All of it, Zahir. I want to feel all of you.' She had no idea who this dominatrix was—who had taken over her body—just knew that the control was intoxicating, banishing her fears. To have a man like Zahir obeying her commands was wildly exhilarating. Mind-blowing. And the feel of him inside her was indescribably, gloriously wonderful.

With one final, punishing thrust he was there, fully inside her, firmly gripped by muscles that pulsed and contracted with ripples of ecstasy. With a whimper of abandonment, Anna lifted her head and flung her arms around his neck, pulling his mouth down to meet hers, plunging her fingers into the thick mass of his hair to keep him there. With their breath and saliva mingled, their bodies sealed with sweat and joined in the most carnal of ways, Zahir began to move. Slowly at first, easing his length out of her, almost to the tip, before thrusting in again. But, as Anna urged him on with rasped, pleading words of need, he took over, the control now firmly his, pumping harder and faster, his breathing heavy and harsh, as again and again he plundered her body, each thrust bringing her further and further towards the oblivion of orgasm.

'Zahir!' She gasped his name as the tremendous sensation built and built until she could take no more, until she was at the very brink, hanging on with an agonising ecstasy that couldn't last any longer. 'Please...please...'

'Say it, Anna. What do you want?'

'You, Zahir.' Anna let out a whimper that ended in a strangled scream. 'I want you to come, now, with me.'

Her body started to shudder, trembling violently as she surrendered to the tremendous surge of sensation that flooded her from head to toe. She heard Zahir's breathing grow hoarse, felt his muscles flex and jerk as he pounded into her with the final delirious thrusts, his beautiful face contorted with the concentration and effort. For a split second he stopped, holding himself rigid, and then he was there, his orgasm intensifying hers, taking them both to unknown realms of euphoria. Anna cried out, totally lost in the moment.

But it was Zahir's primal roar that echoed round the room.

CHAPTER TWELVE

ANNA AWOKE WITH a start. The room was pitch-black and for a moment she had no idea where she was. Then in a rush she remembered: she was in Zahir's bedroom, in his bed. They had had sex—more than that, they had made love. And it had been the single most wonderful experience of her life.

She let the memory flood over her, reliving the wonder of it, the incredible coupling they had shared. The intensity of feelings she had experienced had gone far beyond just sex, or losing her virginity, or proving that there wasn't actually anything wrong with her, that she was a proper woman after all. In fact, it had gone far beyond anything she ever could have possibly imagined. Something momentous had happened between them, something very special. The floodgates had opened without permission from either of them, washing away all the anger and pride, the fears, resentment and battle for control that had been so painfully consuming them up until now. All gone on a tidal wave of unadulterated passion.

But something else had been washed away too. *The pretence.* The notion that what she felt for Zahir was simply infatuation or a wild obsession or a silly crush that she could somehow control. Because now she knew the indisputable truth. She was in love with Zahir Zahani. Deeply, desperately, dangerously in love.

Anna closed her eyes against the sheer force of the truth, powerless to do anything except accept it. She thought back to lying in Zahir's arms, sated and exhausted, to the pure pleasure of being held by him, listening to him breathing, her euphoria keeping her awake long after he had surrendered to sleep. She couldn't worry about the consequences of her love for him—at least not now, not tonight. She refused to let anything spoil this one, remarkable night.

Except maybe it was already spoiled. Stretching an arm across the crumpled sheets, she already knew that Zahir had gone. The fact that bed was still warm beside her was no consolation.

Anna held herself very still, listening. There it was again, the noise that had woken her up, a series of dull thuds coming from somewhere far away in the palace. Sitting up in bed, she pulled the covers around her shoulders. What was it? It sounded almost like a wrecking ball, a tremendous weight hitting something solid over and over again. She could hear voices now, muffled shouting, as if the whole of the palace had woken up. And then she heard the most frightening sound of all. A howl, like a wild animal, echoing through the night, and again, louder and more desperate. But what made it all the more terrifying, what made Anna cower back into the mattress, was the fact that the sound definitely came from a human.

Cautiously she got up off the bed. Now her eyes had acclimatised to the gloom, she could make out their discarded clothes scattered on the floor. She found her knickers, hastily pulled them on and was holding Zahir's shirt in her hand when another howl cut through the air. It seemed even louder this time. Suddenly finding the right clothes didn't matter. Getting out of here definitely did.

Hastily tugging Zahir's shirt over her head, she stepped out into the unlit corridor. The sounds were coming from somewhere above, harsh voices, a thumping noise like furniture being turned over, and still that horrendous howling. She knew she had to find her way back to her suite of rooms which were somewhere on the first floor but fear made her hesitate. What on earth was going on? What sort of a mad house had she come to?

Out of the corner of her eye she noticed a flight of stairs leading off the corridor to her left. They were narrow and dark but right now they seemed a better alternative to wandering into the main atrium of the palace and exposing herself to whatever hell was happening out there.

Stealthily climbing the stairs, she lifted the latch of the heavy wooden door at the top and it creaked open. She was in another corridor, wider this time, and dimly lit by wall lights. Hurriedly following what seemed like miles of passageway, her bare feet soundless on the wooden floor, Anna tried to figure out where she was, how she could find her way back to somewhere she recognised. When the corridor ended with another, grander door, she hesitated, listening for sounds on the other side. Nothing.

The howling had stopped now, along with the crashing and banging. All seemed quiet. Spookily so. She noticed that there was a key in the lock on this side of the door but the door opened easily on her turning the handle. She stepped into the room just as a strangled scream pierced the air. It took a moment to realise it had come from her.

She was standing in her own bedroom. And it had been totally trashed. The furniture had been reduced to firewood, an enormous gilt-framed mirror smashed to smithereens, glass all over the floor. The bed was in ruins, the stuffing pulled out of the mattress, the pictures on the walls punched through or hanging crazily from their hooks. Anna gazed around in speechless horror. The wardrobe was lying on its back, all her clothes wrenched from it and violently ripped to pieces, shredded by some maniacal hand. Dresses had been slashed and hurled to the ground. Tops, trousers, even her underwear, hadn't escaped the vicious attack, bras and panties torn to bits and scattered in amongst the piles of debris. It was a terrifying scene.

And in the middle of it were the two brothers—Zahir and Rashid. Rashid was crouched down, his head in his hands, silently rocking. Zahir was standing over him, wearing nothing but the same loose trousers Anna had lowered from his body a short while ago. But, as he turned to look at her, Anna heard herself scream again. His chest was smeared with blood, deep, vertical lacerations that looked as if they'd been made by some sort of animal. There were scratches all over his arms too, on the hands that he held up to ward her off.

'Get out of here, Annalina!'

But Anna couldn't move, frozen by the horror of the sight, her brain unsure if this was real or if she'd stepped into some terrible nightmare.

'I said *go*.'

No, this was real, all right. Zahir was advancing towards her now, bearing down on her with the look of a man who would not be disobeyed. Anna felt herself back away until she could feel the wall behind her.

'Wh…what has happened?' She tried to peer around Zahir's advancing body to look at Rashid, who had wrapped his arms around his knees and was still rocking back and forth.

'I'm dealing with this, Annalina.'

Zahir was right in front of her now, trying to control her with eyes that shone wild and black. She could see the thick corded veins throbbing in his neck, smell the sweat on him, sense the fight in him that he was struggling to control.

'And I am telling you to go.' Grabbing hold of her upper arms, his forceful grip biting into her soft flesh, he started to turn her in the direction she had come from. 'You are to go back to my chambers and wait for me.' When she finally nodded, he let out a breath. 'And lock the door behind you.'

She nodded again, her knees starting to shake now as Zahir herded her towards the door. Looking over her shoulder, she took in the scene of devastation once more, the thought of the demons that must be possessing Rashid to bring about such violence, to cause such destruction, striking fear into her heart. Because Rashid had done this. She had no doubt about that.

Suddenly Rashid threw back his head. Their eyes met and there was that stare again, only this time it was far more chilling, far more deranged. She watched as he stealthily rose to his feet, hunching his shoulders and clenching his fists by his sides. Now he was starting to step silently towards them but, intent on getting Anna out of the room, Zahir hadn't seen him. With her brain refusing to process what she was seeing, it was a second before Anna let out the cry that spun him around. A second too late. Because Rashid had leapt between them, knocking her to the ground and clasping his hands around her throat. She caught the bulging madness in his eyes as the pressure increased, heard Zahir's roar echo round the room, and then the weight of a tangle of bodies on top of her followed by silence. And then nothing but darkness.

Zahir stared down at Anna's sleeping face, so pale in the glow of light from the single bedside lamp. Her hair was spread across the pillow like spun gold, like the stuff of fairy tales. *Beauty and the Beast.* Suddenly he remembered how that creature Henrik had referred to them and now he wondered if he had been right. Because Zahir had never felt more of a beast than he did now.

Seeing Rashid attack Anna had all but crucified him, the shock of it still firing through his veins. That he had let it happen, failed to protect someone dear to him *yet again*, filled him with such self-loathing that he thought he might vomit from the strength of it. And the fact that this terrible attack had made him face up to his feelings only added to his torment. Because Annalina was dear to him. Dangerously, alarmingly dear. And that meant he had to take drastic action.

Somehow he had managed to control the surge of violence towards Rashid. It had been strong enough to slay him on the spot, or at the very least punch him to the ground, the way he had with Henrik. Because that was his answer to everything, wasn't it? Violence. The only language he understood. But with Annalina still in danger he had driven that thought from his mind. Prising his brother's fingers from around her neck, he had shoved him to one side, taking the punishment of his increasingly feeble blows to his back and his head as he'd bent over Annalina, gathering her against his chest and shielding her with his body as he'd crossed the debris-strewn room and locked the door behind him. Leaving Rashid and his terrible madness inside.

Out in the corridor a doctor was already hurrying

towards them. Zahir had called him earlier to attend to Rashid, before foolishly trying to go and reason with him himself. But right now Rashid would have to wait. Right now nothing mattered except Annalina. Ordering the doctor to follow him, he pounded along the corridors with Annalina in his arms, bursting into the nearest bedroom and laying her down on the bed like the most precious thing in the world. Because suddenly he realised that she was.

Her eyes were already fluttering open when the doctor bent to examine her—his verdict that the marks on her neck were only superficial, that she had most probably fainted from the shock, a massive relief before it had given way to the feelings of utter disgust towards himself.

With the doctor insisting that the only treatment Annalina needed was rest, Zahir had reluctantly left her in the care of the servants to be put to bed for what was left of the night. Annalina was already insisting that she was fine, that she was sorry for having been such a drama queen, that he should go to Rashid to see how he was.

But Zahir returned to his chambers, having no desire to see any more of his brother tonight. He didn't trust himself—his emotions were still running far too high. And, besides, the doctor would have sedated Rashid by now. He would be blissfully unconscious. Zahir could only yearn for the same oblivion. There was no way he would sleep tonight.

So instead he took a shower, feeling a masochistic pleasure in the sting of the water as it pounded over the cuts and scratches inflicted by his brother, towelling himself dry with excessive roughness over the clawed wounds on his chest, staring at the blood on the towel, as if looking for absolution, before tossing it to the ground.

Because there was no absolution to be had. Quite the reverse.

The thought that Annalina could so easily have ended up married to Rashid tore at his soul. Because the betrothal had been all his idea, his appalling lack of judgement. He had convinced himself that marriage and a family would be beneficial for Rashid, then had bullied him into agreeing to his plan.

He had told himself that his brother was getting better, that his problems would soon be solved with a bit more time and the right medication. Not because it was the truth—dear God, this evening had shown how desperately far from the truth it was—but because that was what he had wanted to believe. And not even for Rashid's sake, but for his own. To ease the weight of guilt. If it hadn't been for Annalina's courage, her bravery that night on the bridge in Paris, she would have found herself married to a dangerously unstable man. A man who clearly meant to do her harm. And that was something else Zahir could add to the growing list of things he would never forgive himself for.

The confines of his rooms felt increasingly claustrophobic as he paced around, the silence he had thought he craved so badly resonating like a death knell in his ears. And coming across Annalina's dress lying on his bedroom floor only intensified his suffering. Picking it up, he laid it across the bed, the sight of the crumpled sheets sending a bolt of twisted torment through him.

For sex with Annalina had been unlike any sexual experience Zahir had ever had before—so powerful in its intensity that it had obliterated all reason, all doubts. And, even more astonishing, afterwards he had fallen asleep, drugged by a curious contentment totally unknown to him. For Zahir had never, *ever* slept in a woman's arms.

The only sex he had ever known had been perfunctory, used solely as a means of release, leaving him feeling vaguely soiled, as if debased by his own physical needs. In short, once the deed had been done, he had been out of there. But with Annalina it had been different. He had felt stronger for having made love to her, calmer, more complete. Somehow made whole. But then with Anna everything was different.

But his euphoric peace had been short-lived, shattered first by howls and then sounds of destruction that he instantly knew had to be his brother. In his haste to go to him he had abandoned Annalina, not thinking that she would follow him, that she was the one who was in danger. That she would end up being attacked.

A surge of impotent energy saw him retracing his steps back up to the bedroom where she was sleeping, startling the young servant, Lana, who for some reason had taken it upon herself to keep a bedside vigil. Curtly dismissing her, he had taken her place, the realisation of what he had to do growing with every minute that passed as he gazed down at Anna's peaceful face. He had been wrong to marry her, to bring her here. No good would ever come of it. If he wanted to protect her, he knew what he had to do. He had to set her free.

Anna opened her eyes, at first startled, then feeling her heart leap when she saw that Zahir was at her bedside, staring at her with silent intensity.

'What time is it?' She started to push herself up against the pillows. What day was it, come to that? Crossing time zones, the glorious wonder of sex with Zahir, the terror of Rashid's assault meant she had totally lost all sense of date and time. Her hand went to her throat as the dreadful memory came back. It felt slightly tender, nothing more.

'About four a.m.' Zahir shifted in his seat but his eyes never left her face.

Anna sat up further, brushing the hair away from her face. 'What are you doing here?' Something about Zahir's still demeanour, the dispassionate way he was observing her, was starting to alarm her. She moved her hand across the coverlet to find his but, instead of taking it, he folded his arms across his chest, sitting ramrod-straight in his chair. 'Is it Rashid? Has something happened to him?'

'Rashid has been sedated. He will give us no further trouble tonight.'

'Well, that's good, I suppose.'

'You should go back to sleep. The doctor said you must rest.' Zahir rose to his feet. For a moment Anna thought he was going to leave but instead he moved round to the end of the bed where he stood watching her like a dark angel. A couple of seconds of silence ticked by before he spoke again. 'Your neck.' His voice was gruff, as if he had been the one with the hands around his throat. 'Does it hurt?'

'No.' His obvious anguish made Anna want to lessen his burden. 'Honestly, I'm fine. But what about you? The marks on your chest, Zahir, they looked bad.'

'They are nothing.' He immediately closed her down. They were obviously to be covered up by more than the loose white shirt that now clad his chest.

'I'm sorry that I made the situation worse by swooning like a Victorian heroine.' She pulled an apologetic face. 'I don't know what came over me. I think it must have been the shock.'

'You have nothing to apologise for.' His hands gripped the end of the bed. 'It is I who should be sorry.'

'What happened, Zahir?' She lowered her voice. 'Why did Rashid go berserk like that?'

Zahir looked away into the darkness of the room. 'Apparently he failed to take his medication when he was in Dorrada.'

'And that...that fury was the result?' She bit down on her lip. 'But why did he target me, Zahir? Rip up *my* clothes, try to attack me? What does he have against me?'

'He had no idea what he was doing. He attacked me too, his own brother.'

'But only because you were trying to stop him from trashing my room.' She hadn't been sure until that moment, but now she saw that she was right.

'It seems he regards you as some sort of threat.' Zahir still couldn't meet her eye. 'In his deranged state, he's somehow confusing you with the person who killed our parents.'

'Oh, how awful.' Anna's heart lurched with compassion and maybe a tinge of fear. 'Poor Rashid. Maybe if I tried to speak to him—when he's calmed down, I mean.'

'No.' Now his black gaze bored into her.

'Well, is he having any other treatment, apart from medication? Counselling, for example? I'm sure there will be a doctor in Europe who could help him. I could make enquiries?' She looked earnestly across at his shadowed form.

'That won't be necessary. Rashid is my problem and I will deal with him.'

'Actually, I think he is my problem too, in view of what you've just told me... In view of what happened tonight.' Hurt at the way Zahir curtly dismissed her offer of help hardened her voice.

'That will never happen again.'

'How can you be so sure when we're both living under the same roof?'

'Because you won't be for much longer.'

'What do you mean? Are you going to send him away?'

'No, Annalina.'

The seed of a terrible truth started to germinate. She stared at him in frozen horror.

'You're not saying…?' She swallowed past her closing throat. 'You are not intending to send *me* away?'

'I've come to the conclusion that bringing you here was a mistake.'

'A mistake?' The dead look in Zahir's eyes sent panic to her heart. 'What do you mean, a mistake?'

'I've decided that you should return to Dorrada.'

'But how can I go back to Dorrada when you are here in Nabatean?' She spoke quickly, trying to drown out the scream in her head. 'I am your wife. I should be by your side.'

'That was a mistake too.' A terrible chill cloaked the room. 'The marriage will be annulled.'

'No!' She heard the word echo around them.

'I have made up my mind, Annalina.'

This wasn't possible…it couldn't be happening. Pulling back the covers, Anna scrambled across the bed until she landed in front of Zahir with a small thump. He took a step back but the desperation in her eyes halted his retreat. He didn't mean it. He couldn't be ending their marriage, casting her aside just like that. *Could he?* But one look at the determined set of his jaw, the terrible blackness of his eyes, told her that he could. And he was.

Anna clasped her hands on either side of her head as if to stop it exploding. Had she failed again so spectacularly that Zahir was prepared to end their marriage without even giving it a chance? And to do it now—when she had only just accepted how deeply she had fallen in love with him—felt like the cruellest, most heart-breaking twist of all. Seconds passed before one small question found its way through the choking fog.

'But what about last night?' She despised herself for the pitiful bleat in her voice as she searched his face for a flicker of compassion. 'Did that not mean anything to you?'

His jaw clenched in response, the shadowed planes of his handsome face hardening still further in the dim light. A twitching muscle in his cheek was the only sign of insubordination.

'Legally it will make the marriage more difficult to annul, that's true.' He raised his hand to his jaw, pressing his thumb against the rebellious muscle. 'But I'm sure it can be arranged for a price.'

Was she hearing right? Had the single most wonderful experience of her life meant nothing to Zahir? Or, worse still, had she got it so wrong, somehow been such a failure without realising it, that he would pay any price to be rid of her?

'I don't understand.' She tried again, her voice cracking as she reached forward, placing the palm on her hand on his chest, as if trying to find the heart in him, make it change Zahir's mind for her. *Make him love her.* But instead all she found was unyielding bone and taut muscle concealed beneath the cotton shirt. 'Why are you doing this?'

'I've told you. Our marriage should never have taken place. It was an error of judgement on my part. I accept full responsibility for that and am now taking steps to rectify the situation.'

'And what about me?' Her voice was little more than a whisper. 'Do I have no say in the matter?'

'No, Annalina. You do not.'

Anna turned away in a daze of unshed tears. So this was it, then. Once more she was at the mercy of a man's decisions. Once more she was being rejected, pushed away for being inadequate. Not by her father this time, with his frozen heart, or Henrik, with his selfish needs. But Zahir. Her Zahir. Her only love.

The pain ripping through her was so fierce that she thought she might fold from the strength of it. But seconds passed and she found she was still standing, still breathing. She forced herself to think.

Clearly Zahir wasn't going to change his mind. The whole mountain of his body was drawn taut with resolve, grim determination holding him stock-still in the gloom of the room. She could beg. The idea certainly crossed her mind, desperation all too ready to push aside any dignity, pride or self-respect. But ultimately she knew it would be pointless. Zahir would not be moved, emotionally or practically. She could see that the decision had already taken root in the bedrock of his resolve. So that left only one course of action. She would leave. And she would leave right now.

Turning away, she ran into the middle of the room, but then stopped short, suddenly realising she had no clothes to wear. Her entire wardrobe had been ripped to shreds, along with her heart and soul. She looked down at the nightdress she was wearing. Lana had found it for her. She remembered her tenderly removing Zahir's shirt, remembered seeing the blood smeared across it from where he had held her to his chest, before Lana had slipped this plain cotton gown over her shaking body and helped her into bed.

But she could hardly go out dressed like this. Covering her face with her hands, she tried to decide what to do. The clothes that she had travelled in what seemed like several centuries ago now were scattered somewhere in Zahir's chambers. Much as she dreaded going back there, she had no alternative.

Turning on her heel, she set off, fighting back the tears as she hurtled down the corridors, down the stairs, Zahir following right behind her.

'What do you think you're doing?'

Anna quickened her pace, grateful that for once her sense of direction wasn't letting her down. She recognised this corridor. She knew where she was.

'I'm going to collect my clothes from your rooms and then I'm leaving.'

'Not tonight, you're not.' He was right by her shoulder, effortlessly keeping pace with her.

'Yes, tonight.' She had reached his door now, flinging it open, relieved to find it wasn't locked. She marched into his bedroom, switching on the light, hardly able to bring herself to look at the room that such a short space of time ago had been the scene of such joy. There was her dress, laid out on the bed like a shed skin, a previous incarnation. She rushed over to it, struggling to pull the nightgown over her head, not caring that apart from a pair of panties she was naked—that Zahir, who was standing silently in the doorway, was watching her every move, branding her bare skin with his eyes.

What did it matter? What did any of it matter now?

Stepping into the dress, she tugged up the back zipper as far as she could then cast around looking for her boots. Finding one, she clutched it to her chest and headed for the door, desperate to get out of this hateful den of misery while she still had the strength and the breath to do it.

But Zahir stood in the doorway, blocking her way.

'There is no need for this, Annalina.' Anna felt the searing heat of his hand wrap around her upper arm.

'On the contrary, there is every need.' She jerked her arm but it only made his grip tighten still further. 'Do you seriously think I would stay here a moment longer? Now I know that I am nothing more than a *mistake*, an *error of judgement*?' The words fell from her mouth like shards of glass.

'You will stay here until the morning.' He looked down at her, eyes wild and black, his heavy breath, like that of an angry bull, fanning the top of her head. 'I am not letting you leave while you're in this hysterical state.'

Hysterical state? The sheer injustice of his words misted her eyes red. Didn't she have every right to be hysterical? Didn't she have the right to scream and rant and rave—join Rashid in his madness, in fact—after the way Zahir had treated her tonight?

Yanking herself free from his clutch, she ducked under his arm and into the outer room, seizing her other boot and hopping from foot to foot as she pulled them on.

'I'll tell you what's hysterical, Zahir.' She spoke over her back, refusing to look at him. 'Me thinking that we could ever make a go of this marriage.' She straightened up, flinging her hair over her shoulders as her eyes darted around, searching for her bag and her phone. 'That we could be a proper couple, partners, lovers. That I could be a good wife to you. That what we did last night…a few hours ago…whenever the hell it was…' she choked on a rising sob '…was actually something very special.'

She stopped, making herself drag in a ragged breath before she passed out completely, shaking with misery, rage and the miserable injustice of it all.

But suddenly, there in the darkest moment, she saw

the gleam of truth. Suddenly she realised she had nothing to lose any more. The barriers between them had all come down, were flattened, destroyed. There was no reason to keep the very worst agony to herself any longer.

'And do you want to know the most hysterical thing of all?' She spun around now, pinning him to the spot with the truth of her stare, letting the rush of abandonment take control of her.

'I'm in love with you, Zahir.' A harsh laugh caught in her throat, coming out as a strangled scream. 'How totally *hysterical* is that?'

CHAPTER THIRTEEN

ZAHIR FELT THE words drive through him like a knife in his guts. *She was in love with him?* How was that even possible?

He stared back in numbed silence at the flushed cheeks, the glazed eyes, the tousled blonde hair that fell down over her heaving breasts.

He longed to go to her, to break the spell, to pin her down, literally there on the floor where she stood blinking up at him. He wanted to make her say the words again, to feel them against his lips as he devoured her, made love to her again. But instead he hardened his heart. If it was true that she loved him, then that was all the more reason for him to do the right thing, the only thing, and set her free. Before he dragged her down, weakened her, destroyed her, the way he did anyone who was unfortunate enough to care for him. He simply couldn't bear that to happen to Anna.

'Well?' Finally she spoke, her voice sounding hollow, empty. 'Do you have nothing to say?'

Zahir wrestled with his conscience, with his heart, with every damned part of his body that yearned to go to her.

'It makes no difference to my decision, if that's what you mean.' His damning words were delivered with a cruel coldness born of bitter, desperate frustration. He watched as Annalina's lovely face twitched, then crumpled, her lip trembling, her eyes glittering with the sheen of tears. He deliberately made himself watch the torture, because that was what it was. He had to feel the punishment in order to keep strong.

'So…' She pushed her hair away from her face with a shaky hand. 'This is it, then?' She spoke quietly, almost as if she was asking the question of herself. But her eyes held his, the pupils dilated, like twin portals to her soul.

Zahir looked away. He couldn't witness this, not even in the name of punishment.

He sensed Annalina hesitate for a second, then heard a rustle and turned to see her slinging her bag over her shoulder and marching towards the door. A roar of frustration rang in his ears and he closed his eyes, digging his nails into the palms of his clenched fists. He would allow himself the indulgence of a couple of minutes of the agony before setting off after her.

She was at the main entrance when he caught up with her, tugging furiously at the handle of the door that was securely locked, becoming ever more desperate as she heard him approach.

'You are not leaving like this, Annalina.' He stood behind her, solid, implacable.

'No? Just try and stop me.'

'And where exactly do you think you're going, and how are you going to get there?'

'I don't know and I don't care.' She was banging her fists against the panelled door now. 'And don't pretend you care either. This is what you want, isn't it? To be rid of me as soon as possible? I'll find someone to take me to the airport and then you need never see me again.'

Reaching over her shoulder, Zahir covered her flailing fists with one hand, but Annalina pulled them away from under him.

'I mean it, Zahir. I can't stay here a minute longer. I'm leaving now.'

'Very well.' Pulling his phone from his pocket, he made a call, punching in the code of the wall safe to retrieve the keys to both the front door and his SUV as he waited for the reply. He opened a wall cupboard, taking out a coat and passing it to Anna without meeting her eye.

She was right. This was what he had told her he wanted: her gone, out of his life. The fact that it was tearing him apart only proved his point. Proved what a lethally dangerous combination they were. 'I will drive you to the airport myself.'

Anna listened as he ordered the jet to be put on standby, silently taking the coat from him before he unlocked the door and ushered her out into the cold night air. So it was really happening. She was to be banished. Cast aside like the worthless acquisition that he obviously thought she was.

Once inside the powerful SUV, she was grateful for the feeling of paralysis that had come over her, as if her body was protecting her the best it could by rendering her almost comatose. She couldn't look at Zahir, in the same way that he couldn't look at her. Instead he focussed with leaden concentration on manoeuvring the vehicle out of the electric gates that swung open for them.

They drove in total silence, Anna fighting to hold on to the merciful state of the numbness, frightened it could so easily thaw into a tidal wave of grief if she let it. She felt weighted down by the sense of him all around her, the invisible pressure bearing down on her shoulders, ringing in her ears. She stared through the windscreen, at the world that was still there, seemingly impervious to her heartbreak. Dawn was starting to break, a thread of orange lining the horizon in front of them.

The car sped silently towards it, the orange glow spreading rapidly as the peep of the sun appeared, tingeing the wispy clouds pink against the baby-blue of the sky, blackening the desert below it.

The headlights picked up the sign for the airport as they flashed past. Soon they would be there. Soon she would be leaving this country, presumably never to return. For some reason, that realisation felt like another body blow, as if someone had kicked her in the guts when she was already writhing on the ground.

She bit down on her lip, twisted her hands in her lap and fought madly to stop the tears from falling as she stared fixedly ahead at the unfolding drama of the dawn. Sunrise over the desert—one of nature's most spectacular displays.

Suddenly Anna wanted to experience it, to be a part of it. Not from here, from the agonising confines of the car, but out in the open with the cold air against her skin and the freedom to breathe it in, to be able look all around her, lean back and let the majesty unfold above her head. She needed to prove to herself that there was wonder and beauty to be had in this world, no matter how it might feel right now. If she was leaving this remarkable land for ever, she wanted one lasting memory that wasn't all about sorrow and heartbreak.

She turned her head, steeling herself to break the brittle silence, the sight of Zahir's harsh profile spawning a fresh onslaught of pain. His Adam's apple moved as he swallowed, the only visible sign that he was aware of her gaze.

'Stop the car.'

Zahir's hands tightened on the steering wheel as he shot her a wild-eyed glance.

'What?'

'I want you to stop the car. Please.'

'Why?' Alarm sounded in his voice as his eyes flashed from the road to her face and back again. 'Are you ill?'

'No, not ill.' Anna shifted in her seat. 'I want to watch the sunrise.' She tipped her chin, fighting to hold it steady, swallowing down the catch in her voice. 'Before I leave Nabatean for good, I would like to see the sunrise over the desert.'

She saw Zahir's flicker of surprise before the brows drew together, lowering to a scowl. There was a second's silence as the car continued to speed onward.

'Very well.' His jaw tightened. 'But not here. I will find a more advantageous view.'

Anna sat back, releasing a breath she didn't even know she'd been holding in. She had no doubt that Zahir would know exactly where to take them. It seemed to her that he knew every grain of sand of this desert, that it was a part of him, of who he was, wild and bleak.

Sure enough, a short while later he swung the vehicle off the main road, bumping it over the rough terrain, and almost immediately they appeared to have left civilisation completely and become part of the barren wilderness of the desert. Zahir pushed the SUV hard, bouncing it over the hard ridges of compacted sand at great speed, navigating along a dried-up riverbed before swinging off to the right and powering up the side of a dune the size of a small mountain.

Beside him Anna clung to her seat, grateful for the mad recklessness of the journey that temporarily obliterated all other thoughts. Finally they skidded to a halt with a spray of sand and she peered through the speckled windscreen, seeing nothing but the grey shadowed desert. Abruptly getting out of the car, Zahir came round and opened her door for her.

'We will need to do the last bit on foot.' He held out his hand but Anna ignored it, jumping down unaided and focussing on nothing but this one goal as she followed Zahir up the towering peak of the dune, her thighs aching as she tried to keep up with him, her boots sinking into the shifting sand. Ahead of her Zahir had stopped to hold out his hand again and this time Anna took it, feeling herself being pulled up onto the very top of the dune. And into another world.

If it was wondrous beauty that she wanted, here it was, spread out before her. The sky was on fire with oranges, reds and yellows, the horizon a vivid slash of violet, the colours so amazingly vibrant that they looked to have been splashed from a children's paint box. Before them the dunes rolled like waves of the sea, washed pink by the fast-rising sun that highlighted the thousands of rippled ridges with finely detailed shadows.

Anna dropped to her knees and just stared and stared, intent on blocking everything else out, storing this image so that it would be there for ever. She didn't even notice the tears that were starting to fall.

Zahir cast his eyes down to where Annalina knelt beside him, her profile glowing amber in the light of the sun. The sight of the tears rolling unchecked down her cheeks threatened to undo him so completely that he had to look away. Whatever had he been thinking, bringing her here? What madness had made him want to prolong the torture? He scowled, channelling his agony into determination. He had to be cruel to be kind.

Minutes passed with no sound except the occasional cry of a bird, the rustle of the wind as it danced across the sand, the beat of his pulse in his ears. He had never known Annalina to be so silent, so still. The soft breeze that lifted her hair went unnoticed. It almost felt as if she had left him already. He pushed the sharp pain of that thought away and, staring out at the barren landscape, sought to find some words to end this agony.

'This is for your own good, Annalina.' He forced the words past the jagged blades in his throat. 'After what happened with Rashid, it is clear that you can no longer stay here.'

He saw her twitch inside the coat that she had pulled tight around her body. But she remained infuriatingly silent.

'And besides.' Her refusal to agree with him only made him more coldly determined, crueller. 'This is no place for you. You don't belong here and you never will.'

'Is that so?' She spoke quietly into the cold, new day, still refusing to look at him.

'Yes. It is.'

'And now I will never be given the chance to prove otherwise.' She hunched her shoulders, still staring straight ahead. 'By banishing me, you're simply confirming your assumptions. You're shoring up your own prejudices.'

'I am doing no such thing.' He heard himself roar his reply. Raising a hand, he covered his eyes, squeezing his temples to take away the anger and the pain. Why did she persist in arguing like this, goading him? Or had he provoked the reaction—in which case, why? He was certainly regretting it now. 'That is not true.'

'No? Are you sure, Zahir?' He could hear her fighting to control the tremor in her voice. 'Because that's what it feels like to me. There is no reason for me to leave Nabatean. We could find some help for Rashid—intensive psychiatric counselling. We could focus on making our relationship work, on building a future together.' She turned to give him a look full of scorn but beneath the scorn was hurt, that terrible hurt. 'But, what you really mean is, you don't want me here.'

Zahir forced himself to watch as she turned back, roughly brushing away the tears and biting down on her lip to steady it. He wanted her to stay more than he had ever wanted anything in his life. But he could not let her see that. He could not let his lack of judgement jeopardise her safety any more than it had already. Let his own desires compromise her well-being. More than that, he could not let his *selfishness* crush the life out of this precious creature. Because that was what would happen if she put her happiness in his hands.

'Very well.' He hardened his heart until it felt like lump of stone inside him. 'Since you put it that way, you are right. I don't want you here.' It crucified him to say the words, but say them he had to. 'The sooner you leave, the better for all concerned.'

She flinched as if he had struck her, and Zahir experienced the same horror, as if he had done just that.

'Well, thank you for the truth.' Finally she spoke, her words floating softly into the air before the dreadful silence wrapped itself around them again.

Zahir looked over his shoulder. He couldn't take any more of this. 'We need to get going.' He paced several steps across the top of the dune, glancing back to where Annalina hadn't moved. 'The crew will have the jet ready for take-off.'

He didn't give a damn about the jet or the crew. He just knew he had get away from here, deliver Annalina to the airport and put an end to this agony.

'In a minute.' She spoke with icy clarity. 'First I would like a little time alone. You go back to the car.'

Curbing the desire to tell her that he was the one who gave the orders around here, and that furthermore he expected her to obey them, Zahir drew in a steadying breath. Certainly there was no way he was going to leave her up here on her own. 'Five minutes, then.' He looked around them, pointing his finger. 'I will wait for you over there.'

Anna watched as he strode away, the breeze billowing the loose fabric of his trousers as he climbed up onto the next dune and stood there with his hands on his hips, tall and dark against the skyline.

The shock of his rejection had hardened now, the misery solidifying inside her until it felt less like a bad dream and more like leaden reality. The way Zahir had so callously dismissed her declaration of love still threatened to flay her skin but now she saw that it had been inevitable. A man such as Zahir would never be able to graciously accept such a sentiment. He didn't know how. His own heart was too neglected. It was buried too deep.

She was staring into the crimson wash of the sky when a sudden thought came to her, dawning like the new day. It trickled slowly at first, but soon started to warm her, to heat her from within, until she began to throb with the idea of it—whether through hope, desperation or fear she didn't know. If Zahir's heart was so buried, so unreachable, perhaps it was up to her to try and change that.

Perhaps it was her duty to try and find it.

Zahir watched as Annalina got to her feet, expecting to see her start the descent back to the car. But instead she was heading towards him, scrambling over the sand that was shifting beneath her feet in her hurry to reach him. He saw her stumble and instinctively started to go to her but she was up on her feet again, using her hands now to propel herself forward until she had reached the top of the dune and pulled herself up beside him.

'I know you don't want to hear it but I'm going to say it again anyway.' Her words came out all of a rush as her breath rasped in her throat, her chest heaving beneath the padded coat. 'I love you, Zahir.' She gulped painfully. 'And nothing you can say or do will ever alter that.'

She was staring at him now, her hair blowing around her flushed cheeks, those beautiful blue eyes searching his face, beseeching him. Why? For what reason? He didn't even know.

'Love has no place here.' He struggled wildly to release himself from her gaze, from the grip of her declaration. But when that bleak statement didn't work, when she still refused to look away, he tried again, desperately searching for some sort of logic to make her see sense.

'Besides, I suspect it is no more than an aberration.' He tried to soften his voice, to sound reasonable, even though he had never felt less reasonable, more cut loose from sanity, in his life. 'When you return to your country, you will see that.'

'This is no aberration, Zahir.' Stubbornly she refused to back down. 'I will do as you say. I will get on that plane and fly back to Dorrada. But I guarantee it will change nothing, no matter how much you want it to. Neither time nor distance nor death itself will change how I feel. I love you, Zahir. And I always will.'

Zahir closed his eyes against the astonishingly punishing power of her words. He couldn't accept them. He refused to accept them. A beautiful creature such as Annalina could never truly love a brute like him. He struggled to try and find the words to explain that to her, cursing when they refused to come to him, as if his vocabulary was deliberately defying him.

'And what's more…' She held the moment in her hand, poised for the final thrust. 'I think that you love me too.'

CHAPTER FOURTEEN

ANNA SAW HIM FLINCH, felt the twist of it inside her. She had no idea if it was true. It was as deranged a notion as it was incredible. The tortured look on Zahir's face told her nothing either, except that her rash words had affected him deeply. But it was worth a try. What did she have to lose? Certainly not her pride—there was precious little of that left to worry about. And self-respect? If that was hanging by a thread too maybe it was time to stand up for herself, to challenge Zahir's decision. All her life she had been the victim of other people's schemes and machinations. Well enough. This time she was going to fight for what *she* wanted. She was going to fight for the man she loved.

'Zahir?' Gathering her courage around her, she broke the silence softly, like popping a bubble in the air. 'Do you have nothing to say?' She stretched out a hand to his face, turning him towards her. 'Look at me, Zahir. Tell me what you're feeling.'

'I see no purpose in that.' He turned against her hand, his stubbled jaw rough against her fingers as he presented her with his most harsh profile.

'Tell me why you flinch when I talk about love.' Still Anna persisted. 'What is it about the idea that frightens you so much?'

This spun his head back round, made her drop her hands from his cheeks. The notion of Zahir being frightened of anything was totally ridiculous and yet, as she searched his furious gaze, she could see that it was true.

'I have no idea what love is,' he fired back. 'It is beyond my reasoning.'

'No, Zahir. I don't believe you. I could hear the love in your voice when you spoke to me of your mother. I can see it in the patience you show to Rashid. You are capable of love, no matter how much you want to deny it.'

'And look what happened to them, to my parents, to Rashid.' He let out a cry that echoed around them. 'Look what happens to the people that you claim I love. They are either murdered or left mentally deranged. Is that what you want for yourself, Annalina?

'Stop this, Zahir!' She matched his cry. 'You can't go on blaming yourself for what happened for ever.'

'I can and I will.'

'Then so be it.' She knew there would be no changing his mind when it came to that terrible night. The guilt was too deep-rooted, too all-encompassing. 'But you have no right to punish me for it as well.'

'You!' His eyes flashed with fire. 'Can't you see I'm trying to protect you, not punish you? I'm trying to save you from the hideous consequences of falling in love with me.'

'It's too late for that. And, even if it weren't, I would be prepared to take the risk if there was any possibility that you might return my love.'

'Really? Then you are a fool. Because misery is the only reward you will get from such a return.'

'No, I am not a fool, Zahir. I love you.' She countered his temper with calm assertion, pressing down on the tightly coiled spring inside her to stop it from wreaking unimaginable havoc. 'I think I have always loved you, from the very first moment we met. It is an emotion out of my control. There is absolutely nothing I can do about it.'

She paused, her eyes trained on his, refusing even to blink. 'Up until the time we made love, only a few short hours ago, I would never have dared to think that you might love me too. But I felt the heat of your body as you touched me, heard your cry of release when you came, listened to the beat of your heart as you fell asleep with me in your arms. And that has given me hope.

'So, if there is any chance that you might love me too, then I'm going to drag it out of you. It doesn't have to make any difference to our relationship. I will still leave for Dorrada, if that's what you want. I will agree to the annulment of the marriage, sever all contact with you for ever, if you truly believe that's how it has to be. But, if you feel any love for me, I believe I have the right to be told.'

Zahir felt Anna's impassioned speech rock the very foundation of his being, dislodging the corner stone that kept him upright, made him the man he was. He could feel himself wobble, threatening to tumble like a pile of building blocks at her foot.

All his life he had been so sure of his focus. His beloved country had been what mattered. That was at the heart of everything he did, including the reason he had married Annalina and brought her here. But his judgement had been flawed, and not for the first time. Now she was challenging his decision to release her, pushing and pushing, messing with his head until he no longer knew right from wrong any more. Her declaration of love, delivered with such composure, had ripped him wide open. And now she seemed determined to make him stare into the very depths of his own heart.

He looked down at her beautiful, open face, so moved by her words that he couldn't think straight. He wanted to be able to formulate some sort of reply but nothing would come, his throat choked with something that felt alarmingly like tears. Turning his head away, he swallowed madly.

'Zahir?' She reached for him again, taking his face in her hands and holding it firmly in her cold grip, her gaze raking mercilessly over every tortured inch of it. Zahir tried to blink, to look away, but it was too late. She had already seen the sheen in his eyes. 'Oh, Zahir!'

Raising herself up, she touched his lips with her own, nudging them with the gentlest feather-light pressure. 'Say it. Say it to me now.'

'No!' Her breath was a soft whisper on his skin but still he fought off its assault. Anger was beginning to surge through him now at the way she was clawing at his masculinity, delving into his soul. That he, Zahir Zahani, the warrior prince, had been almost reduced to tears by this young woman was unthinkable. He would not stand for it. 'I will not say it. I cannot.'

'Why, Zahir? Because it isn't true? Or because you refuse to accept it?'

'Either, both, I don't know.' Screwing up his eyes, he wrenched her hands from his face and took a step back. 'This subject is now closed. We are going back to the car.'

'No, not yet.' Still she persisted, her feet firmly planted in front of him. 'I'm not going anywhere until I have seen you let yourself open up to the possibility of the truth.'

Zahir scowled at her through the slits of his eyes. 'And what the hell does that mean?'

'It means that I want you to promise that you will sit and let yourself feel. Just this once. Just for me. I want you to banish the pride, the fear or whatever else it is that's holding you back and let the truth come through. Set it free. Whatever that truth is, I will accept it and I will never ask you to speak it again. But you owe me this one thing, Zahir.'

Zahir hesitated. If this hippy nonsense meant that she would finally release him, end this terrible inquisition, then maybe he would do it. 'Very well.' He watched as Annalina moved away to give him some space, sitting herself down and hugging her knees, her focus straight ahead. Suddenly it was just him and the sparkling clarity of the new day. There was nowhere to hide.

He let his eyelids drop. Presumably this was what she expected of him so he would play along. He breathed in and out, letting his shoulders drop, the arms that were folded so tightly across his chest loosen. He felt himself relax.

Annalina. The spirit of her came out of nowhere, filling his head, his heart, his whole body. He tried to fight against it, against the witchcraft, black magic or whatever spell it was that she had cast over him, but it was hopeless. Suddenly he was exposed, laid bare, everything he had been denying, blocking out, pushing away, presented before him with bruising clarity. And, more than that, as if a tap was being turned on inside him he could feel the empty vessel that he had once been filling, gushing and gushing until he was almost drowning from the flood of it, gasping for air. And then it was too late, he had no control any more, and the wave crashed over him. And suddenly he recognised the phenomenon for what it was: the acceptance of love.

Beside her Anna felt Zahir move, closing the gap between them until he was in front of her, standing so tall that he blotted out the rising sun. She forced her eyes slowly to travel up the length of his body but they halted at his chest, the terrible fear of what she might see refusing to let them go to his face. She was wrong. He didn't love her. It was a crazy, stupid idea, born of desperation and the blindness of her own feelings.

'Anna?' He stretched out his hands to her and she took hold of them, letting herself be pulled to standing. It was the first time she had heard him shorten her name. 'Please forgive me.' She felt her heart stutter with panic as his eyes sought hers, the near-black intensity impossible to read.

'Just now I called you a fool, but now I see that I am the fool.' He spoke softly but with grim determination. 'Now I see that what I took for strength and responsibility was actually bullying and intimidation. Never once did I allow myself to stop and look at you for who you really are because that would have exposed my own weakness.' He looked down at their joined hands then back to her face.

'For not only are you beautiful, Annalina—the most remarkable, extraordinary woman that I have ever met—but you are also brave. So much braver than me. Somehow you found the courage to declare your feelings for me, even in the face of my callous hostility. Whereas I...' He paused, the effort of overthrowing a lifetime of crippling detachment evident from the glitter in the depths of his eyes. 'I was too scared to examine how I felt for fear of what I would find there. A man who was unworthy of you in every way, who could never hope to earn your affection, let alone your love. I thought your love was far beyond anything I could ever deserve and that is why I dismissed it so cruelly. And the reason why I beg your forgiveness.'

'There is nothing to forgive, really.' Suddenly Anna didn't want to hear any more. If this was Zahir letting her down gently it was even more unbearably painful than his cold-blooded disregard. 'You don't have to explain any further.'

'Oh, but I do.' He brought her hands to his chest, clasping them against his heart. 'I have been callous and I have been cruel. By sending you away I thought I was protecting you from my brother but in reality I was only protecting myself, my own heart. But your courage has stripped away that defence and made me see what was there all along. And that is this.' He paused, raking in a breath that came from deep, deep within his soul. 'I love you, Annalina. I think I always have and I know I always will.'

For a second Anna let the words sink in, feeling them spread through her body with a ripple of pleasure that grew and grew until she thought she might explode with the joy of it. Then, throwing herself forward, she fell against him, revelling in the glorious strength of his arms as they wrapped around her, holding her so tightly against him. For several precious heartbeats they stayed locked in this embrace until Zahir loosened his hold and pulled back so that he could take her face in his hands.

'My most precious Annalina. You have shone light into my darkness, filled a void that I didn't know was there, stirred a heart that didn't know how to beat. And you have even made me find the words to tell you that.' He smiled now, the most wonderful, tender smile, and Anna felt the warmth of it flood over her, filling her to the brim with love. 'If you will have me, I am yours for ever more.'

'Oh, yes, I will have you.' With his features blurred by tears, Anna let her fingers trace the familiar contours of his face. 'And what's more, Zahir, I will never, ever let you go.'

Zahir gave a primal groan, lowering his head until he found her lips and immediately the arousal leapt between them, just as it always did. Just as it had that very first time when Anna had forced him to kiss her on the bridge in Paris. As the kiss deepened their bodies melted, moulding into one another, becoming one.

And all around them the new day burst into life.

'I have something for you.' Coming up behind her, Zahir spoke softly into the ear exposed by the swept-up tresses of Anna's intricate hairstyle.

Anna turned to look up at him, catching her breath at the stunning sight of her husband in Eastern clothes. He was wearing a long cream *shirwani* with a stand-up collar and a single row of buttons down the front and loose dark-red trousers beneath. He looked more impossibly handsome than any man had a right to be. Because he was.

Lana and Layla, who had been tweaking the folds of Anna's splendid red-and-gold gown, respectfully stepped back into the shadows of the dressing room.

'I don't think you should be here.' Anna smiled into his serious eyes, her mild rebuke melting like a wafer on her tongue. 'Isn't it supposed to be unlucky to see me before the ceremony?'

'We make our own luck, *aziziti*. Besides, this is blessing, not a wedding. I don't believe the same rules apply.'

'And even if they did I doubt very much whether you would obey them.'

'It is true that I would never obey a rule that kept me away from you.' His solemn words, accompanied by the furrowed brow, threatened to turn Anna's bones to jelly once again. That would teach her for trying to be flippant.

These past few weeks had been the most wonderful, magical time imaginable. With Zahir permitting himself some rare free time, they had scarcely left each other's sides, travelling around Nabatean so that he could show off his country, finding secret hideaways that only he knew about—a shaded oasis in the desert or ancient caves with prehistoric paintings on the walls, where he would show off something rather more private, and definitely more thrilling.

She had watched him as he worked too, patiently explaining the procedures he was involved with or taking her to meetings where he made sure that her views were respected, his obvious respect for her opinions filling her with pride. But it was the nights that had been the most special. Exploring each other's bodies in the dark, finding new ways to bring each other to soaring heights of ecstasy, before finally falling asleep in a tangle of sweat-sealed limbs. Anna marvelled at how they could never seem to get enough of one another, rejoicing in the fact that they would never have to. Because this was just the start of their lifetime together.

'So what is it, then—this something you have for me?' Tamping down the curl of longing, she smiled up at him.

'Um… it's just this.'

She watched as he felt in his pocket, producing a blue velvet ring box. He was nervous, she realised, definitely out of his very masculine comfort zone. And that made her love him all the more. He opened the lid of the box and offered it to her, almost shyly.

'Zahir!' Anna gasped at the sight of the sapphire ring, the stunning stone set in platinum and surrounded by a circle of diamonds. 'It is absolutely beautiful. Thank you!'

'I'm glad you like it. I thought the colour would match your eyes.' He gave a small cough, clearly ill at ease. 'Consider it a late engagement ring. I've noticed that you never wear the other one.'

'No.' Now it was Anna's turn to feel uncomfortable. 'I'm sorry, but…'

'You don't need to apologise, or explain.' Zahir interrupted her, taking her hand and slipping the ring onto her finger where it sat so perfectly, felt so right, that Anna could only stare at it, brimming with happiness. 'The other ring was never meant for us. By rights it should be somewhere in the mud at the bottom of the Seine. In fact…' He flashed her a mischievous grin. 'If you like, I will take you back to Paris and you can finish what you started and chuck the thing in.'

'No!' Anna raised her eyes from admiring her ring and placed her hands gently on his shoulders. 'I've got a much better idea. We will keep it safe for Rashid until he finds someone to love, someone who will make him the perfect wife.'

'Do you think that will ever happen?'

'Of course. He has only being undergoing treatment with Dr Meyer for a week but I understand that he's already making tremendous progress.'

'And I have you to thank for that, *aziziti*. For forcing me to swallow my pride and accept proper help for him. For using your contacts in Europe to find the very best doctor for him. Thank you so much.'

'Think nothing of it. Seeing Rashid return from Germany having banished his demons is the only thanks I want. And it will happen. I am sure of it.'

'You know what? I'm sure of it too.' Zahir took her hands and pressed them to his lips. 'You are the most wonderful, remarkable woman, Princess Annalina Zahani. Have I ever told you that?'

'Once or twice, I think.' Anna put her head on one

side thoughtfully. 'But a girl can never receive too many compliments.'

'Hmm… Well, maybe I'll save them until after the ceremony. We don't want your head getting too big for that tiara thing, now, do we?'

He glanced across to where Lana was still patiently waiting with the jewelled headdress in her hands.

'I guess not.' Leaning forward, Anna kissed him on the lips then, turning her head, whispered in his ear. 'And I will save something for you until after the ceremony too.'

Pulling away, their eyes met, Anna's wicked twinkle dancing across Zahir's heated gaze. 'In that case, my princess, I suggest we start the ceremony without further ado. Suddenly I find I am rather impatient.'

'Suddenly I find that I agree with you.'

Sitting down just long enough for Lana to secure the headdress, Anna rose majestically to her feet and, linking her arm through Zahir's, the couple prepared to leave for the throne room.

'I love you, Annalina Zahani.' They started walking, perfectly in step, towards their future together.

'I love you too, Zahir Zahani.'

Somewhere behind them Lana and Layla sighed with delight.

* * * * *

MILLS & BOON®

MODERN™

POWER, PASSION AND IRRESISTIBLE TEMPTATION

MILLS & BOON®

EXCLUSIVE EXTRACT

Even unsentimental Alessandro Di Sione can't deny
his grandfather's dream of retrieving a scandalous
painting. Yet its return depends on outspoken Princess
Gabriella. Travelling together to locate the painting,
Gabby is drawn to this guilt-ridden man.
Could their passion be his salvation?

Read on for a sneak preview of
THE LAST DI SIONE CLAIMS HIS PRIZE

Alessandro was so different than she was. Gabby had
never truly fully appreciated just how different men and
women were. In a million ways, big and small.

Yes, there was the obvious, but it was more than that.
And it was those differences that suddenly caused her to
glory in who she was, what she was. To feel, if only for
a moment, that she completely understood herself both
body and soul, and that they were united in one desire.

"Kiss me, Princess," he said, his voice low, strained.

He was affected.

So she had won.

She had been the one to make him burn.

But she'd made a mistake if she'd thought this game
had one winner and one loser. She was right down there
with him. And she didn't care about winning anymore.

She couldn't deny him, not now. Not when he was
looking at her like she was a woman and not a girl, or
an owl. Not when he was looking at her like she was

the sun, moon and all the stars combined. Bright, brilliant and something that held the power to hold him transfixed.

Something more than what she was. Because Gabriella D'Oro had never transfixed anyone. Not her parents. Not a man.

But he was looking at her like she mattered. She didn't feel like shrinking into a wall, or melting into the scenery. She wanted him to keep looking.

She didn't want to hide from this. She wanted all of it.

Slowly, so slowly, so that she could savor the feel of him, relish the sensations of his body beneath her touch, she slid her hand up his throat, feeling the heat of his skin, the faint scratch of whiskers.

Then she moved to cup his jaw, his cheek.

"I've never touched a man like this before," she confessed.

And she wasn't even embarrassed by the confession, because he was still looking at her like he wanted her.

He moved closer, covering her hand with his. She could feel his heart pounding heavily, could sense the tension running through his frame. "I've touched a great many women," he said, his tone grave. "But at the moment it doesn't seem to matter."

That was when she kissed him.

Don't miss
THE LAST DI SIONE CLAIMS HIS PRIZE
By Maisey Yates

Available February 2017
www.millsandboon.co.uk

MILLS & BOON®

Why shop at millsandboon.co.uk?

Each year, thousands of romance readers find their perfect read at millsandboon.co.uk. That's because we're passionate about bringing you the very best romantic fiction. Here are some of the advantages of shopping at www.millsandboon.co.uk:

Get new books first—you'll be able to buy your favourite books one month before they hit the shops

Get exclusive discounts—you'll also be able to buy our specially created monthly collections, with up to 50% off the RRP

Find your favourite authors—latest news, interviews and new releases for all your favourite authors and series on our website, plus ideas for what to try next

Join in—once you've bought your favourite books, don't forget to register with us to rate, review and join in the discussions

Visit **www.millsandboon.co.uk** for all this and more today!